D0803182

Presented by *Colorado Country Life* magazine
and your local Electric Cooperative.

LOVE IN AN ENVELOPE

# LOVE IN AN ENVELOPE

*A Courtship in the American West*

*Edited by* DANIEL TYLER
*with* BETTY HENSHAW

UNIVERSITY OF NEW MEXICO PRESS

ALBUQUERQUE

13  12  11  10  09  08    1  2  3  4  5  6

Library of Congress Cataloging-in-Publication Data

Carpenter, Leroy S., 1843–1927.
Love in an envelope : a courtship in the American West /
edited by Daniel Tyler ; with Betty Henshaw.
p. cm.
Compilation of 54 letters exchanged between Leroy Carpenter
and Martha (Bennett) Carpenter.
Includes bibliographical references and index.
ISBN 978-0-8263-4534-9 (cloth : alk. paper)
1. Carpenter, Leroy S., 1843–1927—Correspondence.
2. Carpenter, Martha Bennett, 1854–1930—Correspondence.
3. Courtship—United States.
4. Man-woman relationships—United States.
5. Letter writing—United States. 6. Farm life—West (U.S.)
7. West (U.S.)—Rural conditions. 8. Sex role—West (U.S.)
I. Carpenter, Martha Bennett, 1854–1930. II. Tyler, Daniel.
III. Henshaw, Betty. IV. Title.
CT275.C3136A4 2008
973.5092—dc22
[B]
2008016950

Designed and typeset by Mina Yamashita.
Composed in Minion Pro, an Adobe Original typeface
designed by Robert Slimbach.
Printed by Thomson-Shore, Inc. on 55# Natures Natural.

*For all the descendants of*

*Martha and Leroy Carpenter*

*and*

*for everyone else who wishes to know*

*"how to write a good, sensible love letter"*

*(Leroy S. Carpenter)*

# Contents

# List of Figures

# Acknowledgments

I AM INDEBTED FIRST AND FOREMOST to Ward and Bill Carpenter, great-grandsons of Leroy Carpenter and Martha Bennett. They gave me permission to publish these courtship letters, and Ward reviewed one of the final manuscript drafts. His perceptive comments and expression of feelings about ancestors, regarding whom he had known very little, validates all the work that went into this book.

Other readers contributed enormously to my perspective. Peter Kafer, Robert McCown, Kate Alexander, Patty Rettig, Christy French, Florence Koplow, and Wayne Carpenter all read drafts and provided me with valuable suggestions. Jennifer Carrell Helenbolt, from whom I took instruction when attempting to write a fish story a few years ago, inspired me to rework the introduction with a more appealing "hook." And my esteemed Colorado State University colleague, Ruth Alexander, generously took time away from teaching and research to offer me the benefit of her experience as an expert on class and gender issues. I also wish to extend most sincere thanks to Virginius C. Hall, retired associate director of the Virginia Historical Society, whose commitment to improving the clarity of my grammar and syntax made this a better work. His generosity is enormously appreciated.

In our travels to various places in Colorado and Iowa, Betty Henshaw and I relied heavily on the magnanimous assistance of many people: Sandy Harmel in Tipton; Anne Soenksen in De Witt; Kathryn Hodson at the University of Iowa, who was unfailingly prompt and thoughtful in responding to questions; Ellen Jones and Sandy Keller at the University of Iowa Law Library; Jan Hansen, research volunteer at the Clinton Historical Society; Joe Piersen from the Chicago and North Western Historical Society; Janice Dunn, Greeley Methodist Church archivist; historian Louise Johnson of Greeley; and Peggy Ford, research coordinator for the City of Greeley Museums. Peggy read a draft of this manuscript. She saved me from making more than several mistakes, and her passion for the Carpenters produced a wealth of historical background, as well as photographic suggestions, that have been included in the final draft. I am truly indebted to her.

As with all authors, I am alone responsible for any errors that appear in this book. But I am hoping that the assistance, advice, and insight I received from Betty Henshaw have elevated this work to a level of gender sensitivity that would not have been possible had we not met serendipitously several years ago. At that time, I had just begun to think about this project and had made copies of the letters so I could do the transcription and editing at my home in Steamboat Springs, Colorado. I had also placed an ad in the *Harvard Magazine*, stating my interest in finding a "kind, optimistic, upbeat and generous woman" to share my intellectual and outdoor interests. Betty Henshaw responded from her home in Cincinnati. "I don't know exactly why I am writing," she said in an e-mail, "as I clipped out your 'personal' for a friend. As I reread it, I thought, why don't I write as I think of myself as optimistic and generous with outdoor interests?"

As they say, the rest is history. We corresponded by e-mail for three months before I made a visit to Cincinnati. We talked about politics, religion, our respective families, views of the future, and our value systems. And when I mentioned my interest in Leroy and Martha, it became obvious to us both that our experience via the Internet was in some ways a modern-day version of the courting that had consumed the imagination of Martha and Leroy in the 1870s. The passion we both feel for *Love in an Envelope* is intensified by feelings of discovery, by the privacy of their communication, and by our own parallel adventures. Consequently, the work on this love story has been enormously satisfying and pleasurable. We were both able to immerse ourselves in the evolving romance of Martha and Leroy with a fresh understanding of how good communication enriches a relationship. For her wisdom, common sense, patience, gentleness, and optimism, I am indebted most of all to Betty Henshaw. ❦

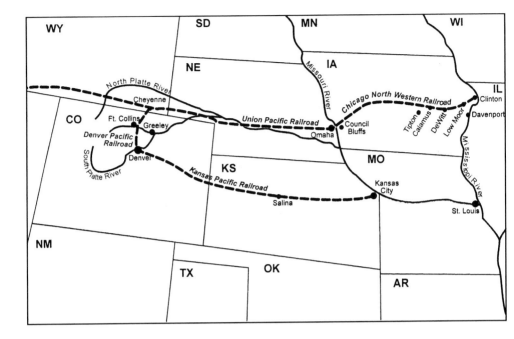

Rivers, Towns, and Railroads

# Introduction

AS HE BOARDED A WESTBOUND TRAIN near his Tipton, Iowa, home in April 1871, Leroy S. Carpenter eagerly looked ahead to a new future in the recently settled Union Colony of Greeley, Colorado. He had almost no regrets leaving the lands his father had broken out two decades earlier. At age twenty-seven, most of his life had been spent working on the family farm. He had tried a year of college in Iowa City during the Civil War, but found the course work difficult and the prolonged absence from family upsetting. He was ready for a new challenge, and so was his father. At seventy-five, Daniel Carpenter exuded the classic characteristics of a typical frontiersman. He decided to sell all the improved Iowa property, pocket the cash, and invest in undeveloped lands in the West. Leroy and three siblings accompanied their parents on this pioneer enterprise.

But Leroy's ties to Iowa were not destined to be completely severed. Although his principal thoughts on the train may have focused on potential adversities awaiting the family in Colorado, he carried in his heart the image of a young lady from De Witt, Iowa, whom he had met during the fall of 1870. Her name was Martha A. Bennett. She would turn seventeen a few days after the Carpenters arrived in Colorado. Martha and Leroy had been introduced by Methodist relatives, and because both families attended church regularly and farmed within thirty miles of each other, they had been able to visit on at least two occasions prior to Leroy's sudden departure.

The two began exchanging letters in December 1870 when both were still living in Iowa. They continued to write for the next sixteen months, Leroy posting most of his letters from Greeley, and Martha replying from several post offices in Iowa near the schools where she was teaching. In April 1872, with his first Colorado crops in the ground, Leroy returned by train to marry the woman with whom he had fallen in love through correspondence. They had been separated for over a year.

Fifty-four letters survive: thirty from Leroy, twenty-four from Martha. I found them in a rough-cut wooden box, buried in the bottom of a container filled with papers relating to Carpenter family history. At the time of discovery, I was working on a biography of Martha and Leroy's second son, Delphus. Being the first person to have access to the entire collection of Carpenter Papers, I had already come to expect surprises. The materials, now archived at Colorado State University in one hundred boxes, had been gathered and partially organized by Donald Carpenter, Leroy's grandson. When water invaded his home in 1993, the collection was hastily moved to a safe location at the Northern Colorado Water Conservancy District, where I commenced work on *The Silver Fox of the Rockies: Delphus E. Carpenter and Western Water Compacts* (Norman: University of Oklahoma Press, 2003).

I was not prepared for what I found in that small wooden box. As I began to liberate a few of the letters from their long imprisonment in tightly creased envelopes measuring five by two inches, I became aware of being one of the first, if not *the* first, to witness the private thoughts, questions, and intimacies of two people who gradually learned to love each other through long-distance correspondence. It was like finding unexpected and undeserved riches.[1] At first I felt I might be violating the confidentiality of Leroy and Martha's most private moments. Perhaps I was prying too deeply into someone else's life. But after I had read their own views of these letters, I realized how proud they were of their epistolary courtship, and I concluded there was considerable value in publishing their love story.

"I have every one of your letters," Martha wrote two months before they were married, "and my portfolio was so full I had to put some of them in a box for safekeeping. Your mind and mine are alike in keeping them, or each other's. It may be pleasant to look them over some day which will be a very pleasant way of refreshing our memories of former days."

Leroy concurred. "I want to put them [the letters] in a bundle," he wrote, "and lay them where they will be safe, as I expect to keep them through life. And if when I am gone, others wish to know how to write a good sensible love letter, they might do so by reading one of those from Miss M. A. Bennett to this boy."

More than "sensible," this aggregation of letters documents the sincere, authentic, and deliberate efforts of a man and woman in nine-teenth-century America to construct a relationship based on affection, understanding, and trust. Although some readers may be surprised that two writers with only a rural Iowa education were capable of such direct and guileless prose, the power of their correspondence is related pre-cisely to their innocence, candor, and lack of badinage. Many letters are filled with mundane ramblings about ordinary events. Metaphorical analogies and literary references are scarce. But readers who stick with the sometimes repetitive descriptions of life's amusements, daily tasks, and the spiritual infrastructure that sustained the writers' lives will be entering the private world of rural, middle-class Americans, about whom little is known.[2] Because these letters also provide a glimpse of the extent to which social reforms of the era had entered the thinking of midwestern farmers, they provide a measure of balance to the many studies of class and gender that have focused on the eastern, urban, and industrialized part of the country. More than anything, the exchanges between Martha and Leroy represent an unpretentious conversa-tion, illuminating what the principals were truly thinking and feeling. Although the letters vary in accuracy and interest, they are true to life, and in that sense, they have a value of their own.

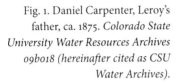

Fig. 1. Daniel Carpenter, Leroy's father, ca. 1875. *Colorado State University Water Resources Archives 09b018 (hereinafter cited as CSU Water Archives).*

Martha and Leroy began their writing formally, respectfully, tempting each other only indirectly with romantic suggestions. But as they gained confidence, they shared feelings in a rising crescendo of affection, culminating in their wedding at the Bennett homestead in Iowa. After reading what they wrote, one would have difficulty denying their feelings of romantic love when the letter writing ended.

In addition to being lovers, they were pioneers. They both knew that once betrothed, they would be raising a family in a frontier environment about which they knew little. As with most others who courted in the post–Civil War era, a decision to marry was based on their own feelings, on instincts and observations, not on parental recommendations. They realized and accepted that their knowledge of each other was grounded almost entirely on revelations they were willing to exchange in letters. While their love blossomed and flourished with each passing mail delivery, Martha and Leroy also recognized the need to discuss the more pragmatic challenges of homemaking in Colorado. Their

Fig. 2. Nancy Scott Carpenter, Leroy's mother, 1882. *CSU Water Archives 09b023.*

exchanges are a blend of the romantic and functional—an unusual juxtaposition, perhaps. But the effective conjunction of these themes makes their correspondence distinctive in the genre of nineteenth-century Victorian courtship.

Some of their letters are missing. I have noted these gaps where it is obvious. But those that remain clearly convey the gradual progression of intensified feelings between lovers. They wrote on the average of every week to ten days under cramped living conditions, with family and friends as constant distractions. They persisted, because they truly believed they had found love. As they asked and answered questions in an effort to become better acquainted, both took enormous pleasure in acknowledging that their Iowa values and upbringing were strengths that would ultimately form an indestructible marital bond.

Neither was a native-born Iowan. Both were from families who had come west in 1849 to take advantage of cheap lands and business opportunities. This pioneer restlessness, born of a desire to establish

a family farm where land was cheap, was accompanied by considerable risk. But the experiences of sharing in this enterprise influenced
the character of the Carpenter and Bennett children, whose proximity to parents and value as family workers forged resilient personal
qualities and intense loyalties. These qualities are evident in Martha
and Leroy's correspondence and in the life they made for themselves
after marriage.

Leroy was born in Newville, Ohio, on August 18, 1843.[3] At the time
of his birth, his father, Daniel, already had eight children by his first
wife, Sally Northway. Daniel originally came from New York where he
enlisted as a young man in the War of 1812. When the war ended, he
moved to Ohio with his bride, opening a general merchandise store,
tannery, distillery, and soap factory. He lost everything during the economic depression of the 1830s, including his first wife. But in 1840 he
married his second wife, Nancy Scott. Soon thereafter he became a temperance man, viscerally hostile to the manufacture and sale of alcoholic
beverages. Temperance was a secular reform movement, evolving in the
1840s as a protest against a primarily male behavior that was seen as
destructive to families. Although women dominated the temperance
ranks, some men also understood that the unrestrained use of alcohol was undermining civil society. They participated willingly in the
movement and helped energize it through much of the late nineteenth
century. For reasons that are not entirely clear, Daniel became a strong
proponent of temperance after running a distillery business in Ohio.

Nancy and Daniel had five children. The three youngest—Leroy
(age six), Mattie (age four), and Silas (age one)—along with Sarah (age
twelve) from Daniel's first marriage, accompanied their parents from
Ohio to Cedar County, Iowa, in 1849. Unbroken lands appealed to
Daniel. Though he was essentially bankrupt when he left Ohio, a new
beginning was made possible by his eligibility to file on a soldier's homestead near the town of Tipton. During the next twenty years the family
farm in Iowa increased significantly in size and productivity. As a result

Fig. 3. West Bethel Methodist Church, Tipton, Iowa. *CSU Water Archives 09f042*.

of his agricultural success, his leadership in construction of a nearby Methodist church, and development of a rural school, Daniel became one of the pillars of the Tipton community. At age seventy-five he might have retired quietly to his Iowa home, turning over the farming duties to Leroy and Silas. But another adventure awaited.

In 1871 the family decided to move west again. The lure of unbroken lands in Colorado was part of Daniel's motivation, but there were other reasons for him to sell his Iowa farm. He was attracted by the conditions of settlement in the Union Colony of Greeley, located at the junction of the South Platte and Cache la Poudre rivers. One of a handful of cooperative colonies established in Colorado in the 1870s, the Union Colony was the brainstorm of Nathan C. Meeker, agricultural editor of Horace Greeley's New York *Tribune*. With land purchased from the Denver Pacific Railroad, the incorporated Union Colony began offering

Fig. 4. Dr. Peter Carpenter, Leroy's stepbrother. *Courtesy Wayne Carpenter, Ft. Collins, Colo. Photo also published in Harold George Carpenter,* Some of Our Family History. *Alamosa, Colo.: Ye Olde Print Shop, 1960.*

memberships to prospective colonists who had cash, an identifiable skill, and an aversion to the consumption of alcoholic beverages. Daniel was committed to temperance, skilled as a farmer, and in possession of $16,000 in marketable assets.

Additionally, he wanted to keep some of his family around him in the waning years of his life. He had an especially close relationship with his son Peter, from his first marriage. Peter, now a doctor, had contracted consumption during the Civil War. In an effort to find a location where dry air would alleviate the pain in his lungs, Peter made a tour of eastern Colorado after the war. He homesteaded land in Colorado on the Cache la Poudre River in 1869 and returned to Ohio to gather his young family. On the way, he persuaded his father that the designated site for the Union Colony, not far from his own lands, would be an excellent location for farming and general good health. Concerned about daughter Mattie's unidentified physical debilities, and hoping to

Fig. 5. Mary Pierce Scarborough Carpenter, Leroy's sister-in-law. *Courtesy Wayne Carpenter, Ft. Collins, Colo. Also published in Harold George Carpenter,* Some of Our Family History. *Alamosa, Colo.: Ye Olde Print Shop, 1960.*

provide for his children by taking advantage of rising land prices in the Union Colony, Daniel sold his Iowa lands to neighbors and made plans to move to Colorado. Leroy, Silas, Mattie, and Sarah joined him and Nancy on the train headed west to Greeley in the spring of 1871. A six-year-old girl, Agnes Murray, who had been abandoned by her widowed father, accompanied them.

Six months prior to their departure, Nancy's sister and brother-in-law, Martha and Andrew Coleman, had introduced Martha Bennett to Leroy Carpenter. Coleman, a clergyman, had been assigned at different times to churches near the Carpenter farm in Tipton and the Bennett homestead near De Witt. It is clear from the courtship letters that Martha and Leroy paid reciprocal visits to each other's homes, but we do not know how many times they saw each other before the Carpenters left town. The extant correspondence suggests that Leroy and Martha were in the process of becoming friends as of April 1871.

Fig. 6. Reverend Andrew Coleman, Oskaloosa, Iowa. *CSU Water Archives 09e044.*

Fig. 7. Aunt Martha Coleman, Oskaloosa, Iowa. *CSU Water Archives 09e047.*

Martha Bennett was born in Brownsville, Pennsylvania, on April 19, 1854. Her father, William Henry Bennett, a Virginian, worked as a merchant and money lender on the Monongahela River not far from Pittsburgh. The year Martha was born, he had aggregate taxable property valued at one thousand dollars, and he was active in local politics and the Cumberland Presbyterian Church. When he came to Iowa Territory in 1849, he, too, was looking for cheap land. Clinton County records indicate he purchased two quarter-sections (totaling 320 acres) and returned to Brownsville. Six years later, he brought his wife, five daughters, and a son to settle these Iowa lands. Bennett lived out the rest of his life as a farmer. His wife, Mary Ann, survived him and eventually moved to Colorado where she died in Martha and Leroy's home in 1889.

Fig. 8. William Henry Bennett, Martha's father. *CSU Water Archives 09e010.*

Fig. 9. Mary Ann Wood Bennett, Martha's mother, with Martha. *CSU Water Archives 09e007.*

When she was introduced to Leroy in the fall of 1870, Martha was teaching at the Hatfield School near her home. She had been a determined student in religious studies at the Methodist Church and in the small De Witt Independent School. She graduated at the top of her class in December 1869, excelling in history, spelling, grammar, and algebra. Two months later, she sat for an examination with the Clinton County superintendent of schools, from whom she received a probationary second-class teaching certificate good for one year. A first-class certificate was issued to her a year later, distinguishing Martha as a marketable and accomplished teacher. Although she was a young teacher by today's standards, women were increasingly involved in teaching across the country as an answer to the nation's burgeoning educational needs. Many school boards hired women because they believed they could be paid considerably less than the salary demanded by men. The only other possibility for Martha to make money was to enter domestic service as a maid, housekeeper, cook, or nurse. Because capital was in short supply in frontier farming communities, these jobs, in addition to their obvious risks for single women, were scarce and undesirable.

William Bennett had difficulty providing for his family. When the daughters reached an age to marry, he made clear his inability to provide a dowry for them. Martha recognized the importance of salaried employment as a way to help her parents and to save for her own future, but as will be noted in the following letters, she also resented being taken advantage of by a school system that paid women less for the same work done by men.

Prior to receiving her first students at Hatfield, Martha underwent a phrenology exam. This cranial inspection, not uncommon in the late nineteenth century as a method of determining one's personality traits and potential for success in life, revealed Martha's strengths: sensitivity and love for others; feelings of justice, duty, honor, and truth; and a keen appreciation for written and vocal music. No matter how unscientific, the phrenology report seemed to endorse her career choice. It also underscored quite accurately certain aspects of her character and personality.[4]

When she began her correspondence with Leroy, Martha was in the process of relocating from Hatfield to the Brushville school four miles south of Calamus, Iowa. Although she felt comfortable in the home where she was quartered, the students who came to her at the log schoolhouse were unruly. When her contract expired, she transferred to a school at Low Moor where she enjoyed a loving Quaker home and a school of responsive children. She was a good teacher. The superintendent wanted her to continue, but his hopes were dashed by Martha's growing interest in Leroy.

Leroy was essentially a farmer. His early education took place at the Bethel School within a mile of his father's farm. The schoolhouse, adjacent to the West Bethel Methodist Church, was built by Daniel for the families in the area. Leroy acquired basic literacy at the school and made an effort to continue his education at the University of Iowa. In 1865, at the age of twenty-two, he enrolled as a "preparatory" student, hoping to gain full admission after a year of study. He took instruction in rhetoric, singing, algebra, elocution, penmanship, and reading. During the winter semester he noted in his diary that the "lessons [were] quite hard." He was also homesick. In the middle of March he asked to be excused from his classes so he could return home. He had expanded his horizons, sharpened his verbal and oral communication skills, and determined from experience that farming was the life for which he was best suited. When his father suggested a move to Colorado five years later, he was ready to test himself in a new environment. In all likelihood, he was also content to work for his parents, because he probably had no assets of his own, and the only way he might better himself would be to assist his aging mother and father on the farm in return for future land ownership. This was a typical father-son pattern of American farm families in most regions of the country where urbanization and industrialization had not begun to offer alternative employment opportunities.

But Leroy felt homesick for Iowa soon after the Carpenters arrived in the Union Colony. He missed his friends and familiar routines. Additionally, the arid climate with its sudden winds, radical temperature changes, and rock-hard soil caused him to wonder frequently if he would last long enough to be a successful pioneer in Colorado. The back-breaking work associated with irrigated agriculture, and the early failure of crops due to inadequate and unscientific water applications, discouraged him. But his father was both optimistic and determined. Leroy was twenty-eight years old and ready to raise a family of his own. If he could persuade Martha Bennett to marry him, perhaps they could conquer the frontier together. His only hope was to woo her by correspondence. His letters would have to show her that in addition to being a competent farmer, he was a cultivated man, worthy of her love.

They entered into correspondence formally, following conventions generally recognized by authorities on Victorian etiquette. Beginning letters at first with "Dear Friend," and closing with "Your friend," or "Your affectionate friend," they slowly graduated to "My Dearest," and ended with expressions of love and commitment. Although Emily Thornwell's 1856 booklet, *A Lady's Guide to Perfect Gentility*, urged correspondents to leave ample margins and to write legibly without using up the entire sheet of paper, Martha and Leroy found that four sides of two sheets were not enough for all their thoughts and questions. About the time they began to speak of a possible life together, the content of their letters expanded to eight pages and included additional postscripts in the margins. Although they occasionally complained about not knowing what to write, for the most part, they continued exchanging a full eight pages until their correspondence ended. Because the letters were carefully preserved in a wooden box, the writing is still legible, although the ink has faded somewhat over time.

As other scholars have noted, nineteenth-century courtship correspondence based on romantic love often proved to be the happiest and most fulfilling period for couples who planned to marry.[5] It was a time when individuals could abandon the sex role limitations assigned to them by Victorian culture. And for those who courted after the Civil War, when the concept of separate spheres for men and women was intertwined with egalitarian concepts of partnership in marriage, it was possible to engage in a degree of self-revelation that nurtured feelings of love and influenced the very character of the correspondents. Throughout post–Civil War America, women were beginning to leave home for work in nearby urban centers, thus expanding expectations that female virtue might have as positive an impact on society in general as it was expected to have on the home. But when Martha and Leroy exchanged their views on gender roles, they reflected the limitations and disparities inherent in the doctrine of separate spheres,[6] because they were located—geographically and culturally—in a part of the country where families still lived with some of society's older values. In fact, one could say that the Carpenter and Bennett families straddled both the modern and traditional worlds. The courting correspondence of Leroy and Martha contains a mixture of each.

The Carpenter and Bennett families were immersed in the old agrarian culture where urbanization or industrialization were distant realities. They came together with other farming families in church and town, forming the nucleus of a small, rural community. In this setting, males were still patriarchal in the sense that they wielded economic and political power in the home. But the old tradition of coverture (antedating the idea of separate spheres for men and women), in which a woman lost her identity and most legal rights the moment she married, was gradually being eclipsed by the passage of marital rights laws in many states. Martha seems to have known this. She also knew that women who wed in the second half of the nineteenth century still risked more than men, because marriage was considered a private institution into which the state should not intrude as a guardian of female prerogatives. As Elizabeth Cady Stanton and Susan B. Anthony discovered during their travels in the 1870s, the women to whom they spoke about the importance of political enfranchisement were often more interested in discussing how the laws could be amended to protect them from physical abuse in marriage. The legal concept of coverture, or marital unity, stipulating that man and woman were legally one, and that the "one" was the man, died slowly.

Rather than fearing a loss of identity in marriage, however, Martha expressed more concern that her future husband would maintain the same degree of religious steadfastness when they were married as he professed in his courtship letters. She had older sisters who had married successfully, and her parents had presented a model of spirituality, hard work, and unity that gave her confidence in the institution of marriage. While much of the nation was pursuing a secularization of life in which the individual was being glorified at the expense of a God-centered world view, Martha adhered tenaciously to her religion. God's will was what would determine the outcome of events in her life, and she made clear to Leroy that church worship, Sunday school, and prayer would govern her daily life after marriage. But as her letters clearly indicate, the romantic love she felt for Leroy gradually matured into another strong emotion that blended easily with her devotion to God. Fortunately, Leroy was of a like mind, although far less evangelical. The Methodist Church was an integral part of his self-identification, and his letters are filled with references to the importance of a family life in which religion played a dominant role. Such reassurances could only aid him in courting Martha.

As was typical of most nineteenth-century courtships based on romantic love, Leroy urged Martha to reveal her most personal thoughts. She responded in kind, insisting that she was far from perfect, that she was too young to know much about homemaking, and that her many faults might challenge his love. It was a form of testing that frequently appeared in courtship correspondence once a couple was engaged. It was meant as a warning to Leroy that he was expected to love her in spite of her imperfections. She reciprocated his appeal for sincere, open, and in-depth dialogue. His responses echoed similar feelings of inadequacy, along with a stated recognition that courting, which had brought them both so much pleasure, was by its very nature a far different association than the marriage they were both planning. What counted most for each was religious faith, their willingness to express true feelings, and the respect they would have for each other's equal role in their future family.

In a nutshell, Martha and Leroy's courtship correspondence was both atypical and analogous to extant collections of nineteenth-century courtship correspondence originating from urban communities. They observed the general form of courtesy and politeness typical of the period. They teased each other about their respective foibles; they expressed great concern about health issues, especially when letters were delayed by storms or irregular train service; and they described rapturously the feelings of joy that filled their hearts as the wedding day neared. What "love" meant to each of them is probably as mysterious now as it was then. But it appears they felt immense relief and satisfaction at finding another person of similar values and beliefs. This feeling opened doors to expressions of their innermost feelings—an act of love itself, especially when these feelings were reciprocated. Even though their married life began in close proximity to Leroy's parents, they rejoiced at the prospect of being able to live by themselves in their own home, beginning a new life together, and enjoying a companionate marriage of equal partnership. Their discussions of women's rights, division of labor in the household, and the need to share farm work mark these letters as singular examples of a courtship that looked beyond romance into the practical challenges of keeping a home. Their writings remained positive in tone, direct in meaning, considerate, humorous, and earthy. They apologized for lapses in style, unpolished prose, and problems with expression, but their letters are remarkably articulate. Once they recognized their betrothal, the affection they expressed was enriched by imagining how they would deal with the everyday exigencies of the life that awaited them in Colorado.

Other courtship letters of the nineteenth century tend to be more sophisticated, characterized by prose that inclined more to form than substance. References to classical literature, history, and the natural world were intended to convey double meanings, allowing the writer a means of escape if the relationship soured. In some communities and at social levels where wealth played a role in mate selection, courting was extremely complex, requiring misdirection and obfuscation. Wit and decorous prose were championed, and the elegance of letters often served as the primary basis for the feelings of love that overwhelmed the correspondents. For those who enjoyed such badinage, the gap between the fantasy of epistolary courtship and the reality of marriage remained. If the desired partnership failed to meet expectations after the wedding, couples found themselves disillusioned and bitter. The individualism encouraged in a courtship based on romantic love could easily disintegrate in a marriage where the doctrine of separate spheres was misapplied by men as an excuse to keep their wives at home in demeaning and inferior roles.

By contrast, Leroy and Martha courted with an honesty that served them well long after the wedding day. Like most who courted by mail in the Victorian era, their communications were conducted in an aura of secrecy. They searched, usually unsuccessfully, for privacy to write and to read the letters which occasionally took on anthropomorphic form; the more private their correspondence and engagement, the deeper their love. With friends, family, and acquaintances, they reveled in preserving the secret of their betrothal. It was the most intimate aspect of their lives to date, and they were reluctant to share it publicly for fear the experience of love would become less intense.

Betty Henshaw and I have wondered many times what Leroy and Martha felt the first time they saw each other after a separation of more than a year. The anticipation must have been nearly overwhelming. In today's electronic world, those who decide to meet face to face after extensive communication on the Internet have had the advantage of exchanging pictures, talking on the phone, and getting instantaneous responses to questions. First meetings are difficult under any circumstances, but when Leroy and Martha met at the Bennett home to take their vows, that moment had to be wondrous.

To get a better sense of who they were and the environment in which they matured, we traveled to Tipton, De Witt, Clinton, Davenport, Calamus, Low Moor, Iowa City, Greeley, and Fort Collins. We searched county archives, local newspapers, histories, assessors' records, land plats, church records, and other sources that might provide information on the Bennett and Carpenter families. We talked to senior citizens, visited cemeteries, and engaged the services of the University of Iowa and local historical societies. With a firmer sense of Iowa in the 1870s, Betty transcribed Martha's letters, while I took on

Leroy's. We both tried to be as faithful as possible to what was written, without revising sentences or changing spelling to accommodate modern readers. We have made some minor punctuation changes, and some paragraphing has been attempted to better set off the subjects each discussed. We eliminated duplicate words, indicated unreadable words and phrases with brackets around ellipses ([ . . . ]) and occasionally inserted words or letters within brackets to help the reader understand what was being said. What we offer as a product of our transcription, research, and editing is the narrative of an intensifying passion between two people who not only had a strong desire to present themselves and their ideas meaningfully and respectfully, but who thought deeply about who they were and what they wanted in the way of a marriage partner. The letters they wrote bear witness to the maturity and devotion of each correspondent.

I have added notes that I hope will assist the reader in two ways. First, I wanted to place the correspondence into some sort of regional and national context. Martha and Leroy wrote to each other during the Victorian era when rules pertaining to heterosexual interaction and social behavior were changing. Secondly, I wanted to flesh out some of the people, places, and ideas they mention. For those interested in Iowa and Colorado history, I tried to identify the social, political, religious, and economic landscape that affected their lives. Because this courtship correspondence seemed to offer a small window into life in rural, midwestern, middle-class America, I have also provided some background information, sometimes at length, on health issues, the Methodist Church, the women's rights movement, and temperance.

What readers will find herein are the honest hopes and fears of two young people who fell in love by mail. Their profession of faith in a just God, their determination to prepare for the "next life," and their commitment to doing God's will in an "unfriendly world" dominate an animated discourse that reflects their Methodist upbringing. The charm of their letters rests on the sincerity and decency of their communication.

Fig. 10. Leroy and Martha's golden wedding anniversary, 1922. *CSU Water Archives 09b133.*

There is nothing phony, contrived, or pretentious in what they wrote. Neither was trying to be someone he or she was not. They wanted their love to be based on friendship, mutual respect, trust, and an intelligent perception of the frontier life that awaited them.

Did it work? Martha and Leroy celebrated their fiftieth wedding anniversary in 1922 with their three children and a dozen grandchildren. Leroy died in 1927 at the age of eighty-four. All who knew him recognized his generosity and his belief in justice for rich and poor alike. Martha died of double pneumonia in 1930 at the age of seventy-six after protesting in the rain against movie going on Sundays. She believed it was her duty to protect the Sabbath as a day of reverence without the need for entertainment. The very qualities that Leroy and Martha had revealed in their courtship letters seem to have accompanied them through their married life. The love that had blossomed in small, white envelopes with three-cent stamps endured a lifetime. ❦

# Letters

Tipton, Iowa
December 19, '70
Miss Bennett
Dear Friend,

Your much welcomed and very interesting letter has been received. Was glad to learn of your enjoyment while on your visit. It is a pleasure that is given us to enjoy in this country blessed with liberty. We received a letter from our sister who lives in Oskaloosa[1] on last Saturday stating that Uncle and Aunt Coleman are enjoying their new home very well.[2] It has been some work to get ready for their new home, being about three weeks since they moved into their own house. Uncle preaches to the darkies as a portion of his charge. It would be a pleasure to drop in some time and hear the colored folks sing their songs which they so much delight to do. You asked if Mr. Taylor remembered where I have heard him. I believe he preached in our church, Bethel, in this neighborhood one time on a cold Sunday in winter on the subject of the Bible verse.[3] There was but few there so that it was rather an address. When Albert Coleman[4] and I were taking our pleasure trip four years ago, we stayed over Sunday at Davenport and Rockingham west of Davenport.[5] I attended services in one of the ME [Methodist Episcopal] churches of that city in the evening and heard Mr. Harding preach a good sermon. It has been some time since I have been in Davenport and have thought sometime of going down there again to see the improvements as a city.

This certainly is a curious winter for the State of Iowa, at least over here as yet not having [ . . . ] had but little snow or rain. Tis nice weather to get up the fire wood and prepare for the winter which may commence [*sic*] about the first of March or April. It is the intention of the Methodist people of Tipton to dedicate their new church about New Years Day if it can be made ready that soon. Do not know yet who will conduct the exercises. We of the Society of Bethel [ . . . ] want to offer to the people a Sunday School concert about the last of the holidays if things can be made ready for that time. There will be an admission fee of ten cents taken, for the purpose of getting S.S. books and other things much needed. As last winter it is the intention to keep our Sunday School in operation during the winter. It would seem lonesome to be without that privilege now. I am at home and expect to be this winter, doing such work and other things as may be found to do. I have sometimes thought of taking a trip out west to look at the country and if I could get sufficient means might get a piece of western land provided I liked the country and soil. No doubt the West will enjoy all the privileges that we do before ma[n]y years. The chances that are offered to settlers are such as to invite all foreigners to move from their own country to this as soon as possable. I [am] hoping that you enjoy going to school if you are doing so. I would continue to be your affectionate friend.

L. S. Carpenter

Calamus Station
January 12th, 1871
Dear friend Carpenter,
I received your letter about three weeks ago. I presume you see from the heading of my letter that I am a little farther *west* than I was when I last wrote to you. At that time I had thought I would not teach this winter as the schools seemed to be engaged, that is all I knew of. But about

five weeks ago, the county superintendent came to me and wanted to know if I would teach this school [Brushville School]. I started as soon as possible and have been here nearly four weeks. By here I mean five miles south of Calamus.[6] I have thirty-eight names registered in my register and an average attendance of thirty-three and of course, I have enough to keep me out of mischief. Three or four of the boys are old enough to be *called* young gentleman and that is all. One of them is a very disagreeable person, and has caused some trouble but he will not have chance to cause much more. The director is a very pleasant man, and told me if I had any trouble to let him know of it and he would see that the offender was duly attended to. I think the scholars are about as rude as any school I ever saw, but I have no doubts of my succeeding.

I am glad Mr. Coleman has a home of his own and something to do. He will be much happier. I should like very much to see his congregation and hear them sing.

I hope you had good success at your Sunday School Concert, and realized enough from it to fill your library with good books. You spoke of the Sabbath School being a privilege you would not like to be without. When I have been where there was no Sunday School, I have felt as if I [would] give any thing in my power to give, could I but go to Sunday School. There is a Sunday School here and preaching nearly every Sunday, and I of course feel more at home on that account.

You spoke in your letter of going out west to look at some land. I should think it would be quite a good purchase, for I expect the land that can be bought now for a small sum, will be worth considerable in a few years.

I have, since I came, joined the order of Good Templars in Calamus.[7] We meet every Saturday evening. There [are] about one hundred members. I have met a good many persons there that I have found to be very pleasant people, and I think very good associates. There are quite a number of the members that are pretty well advanced in years, and they keep the children in order. I attended the Christmas Tree at the good

Templars Hall, Christmas Eve. We had a very pleasant time. There were some essays read and some singing, before the presents were distributed. I received four very nice presents and I thought was doing very well for a stranger. I also had the pleasure of attending an entertainment at the Methodist Church, New Years Eve. The entertainment was for the benefit of the Sunday School. There was watch meeting afterward.[8] I staid untill the New Year was announced by the tolling of the bell. [We] had a very good meeting. Wishing you a very late, Happy New Years. I will close. Your Friend,

Please address Martha. A. Bennett,

Calamus, Station

Clinton Co.

leave of W. L. Hawkins. Iowa

[This letter was] Ans[wered by Martha] Feb 10th 1871

Tipton

Jan 31st 1871

Miss Bennett:

My dear friend,

I would express my thanks to you for your kind wish toward me for a Happy New year, by wishing that the present year would be one of enjoyment to you. No doubt you are busily engaged these days in your school room. In speaking of the bad conduct of some of your pupils, you have my entire sympathy while endeavoring to instruct them. There certainly cannot be anything more trying to ones patience than a bad scholar. I have sometimes wondered why it is that some persons are so much in want of any Principle. And cannot give any reason unless from the fact of the depravity of the human heart. Where we find bad conduct abroad I think we may generaly find a lack of government at home. Is not that your Belief? I am in hopes that you will succeed for nothing can

Fig. 11. First capitol building in Iowa before the state capital moved to Des Moines. This building was also the first edifice of the University of Iowa where Leroy attended classes, 1865–1866. *Kent Collection, Special Collections, University of Iowa Libraries.*

give me so much pleasure as that of learning of your prosperity and success. My expectations were not fulfilled in either the Dedication of the new church or our S.S. [Sunday School] concert. The factory in Chicago from which they expected to get the upper windows for the church was burned down last fall, and the other work not enough advanced are the principal reasons. Our S.S. having made an exchange with the Congregational S.S. in Tipton and getting the Bright [ . . . ] we have not yet fully learned the pieces of music some of which are a little difficult for us. Having had three S.S. concerts last year we were given [a] chance of this one about the time spoken of, but are in hopes to come before the public this winter if those pieces can be learned.

No doubt you have lively times in your lodge [Templars] when you meet. While I was going to school at Iowa City I became a Good

Templar. We had some amusement at times in the discussions and election of new officers. It is an order in whose sentiments I agree with one exception that is in regard to the drinking of cider. I have never thought it wrong to enjoy the reviving taste of good cider.[9] I know that there are good reasons for not using it, but I think others as good for its use. People will think differently in these things. What is your opinion? When I left the university[10] I received a letter of introduction that might have been used in the Tipton lodge but never have used it. We have been having an interesting time over last Sunday it being the time of our second quarterly meeting.[11] Mr. Brooksome the Tipton preacher [is] acting as Presiding elder. He is very much liked in town. There is preaching every evening and will be at least this week with the hope of doing some good.

You certainly were very much favored in the receiving of those presents that you spoke of. It has the pleasant influence of making a person feel at home. You are quite fortunate in having a good and kind school director to provide for your wants, etc. It is space [that] does not permit my writing any more at present but will feel much interested in hearing from you often.

Yours in true friendship,

L. S. Carpenter

Calamus

Feb 10th 1871

Mr. Carpenter,

Dear Friend,

I received yours of the thirty first, the first of *this* month. I cannot help but feel glad that this is the last of another week. I am not homesick, but I am glad of a few days rest. I have only four weeks to stay here and then I presume I shall return to spend a short time at home. I don't know whether I shall get home before my school is out or not. I have heard from home but twice, but mother has so much to attend to, I do not feel uneasy. You spoke of there being a lack of government at home when the scholars did not conduct themselves properly away from home. Indeed I know that to be the case in several families I have had to deal with. I am sorry you did not get ready to have your concert during the holidays, for if the people are similar [to] those around here, they will attend such an entertainment better at such times of the year, and consequently you would have better success.

We do not have such pleasant times in our lodge [Good Templars] as we might have. Some of the members seem to like to discuss upon subjects that incline to cause bad feeling. They have conferred charges that are of no consequence, and they bring all such business before [the] lodge and sometimes they hold their meetings untill twelve or after. We might have a very pleasant time but for that.[12]

You asked my opinion about drinking cider. It is this, there may not be any harm in taking now and than a drink of *new* cider, if a person can always judge when it *is* fresh. It is something like forming the habit of drinking tea or coffee. If the habit is once formed it is hard to break off from it and if the habit is *not* formed there will be no cause of after regrets and cider is something that will intoxicate, or *may* create an appetite for something stronger. As you asked my opinion, I have given it to you as nearly as I could.

You spoke of enjoying the quarterly meeting. I have not had the chance of attending many Methodist meetings since I came. There is preaching here every other Sunday, but they are of the Baptist persuasion. I have not any objections to offer to them, but I feel more at home in the Methodist Church. Mr. Rogers is the minister at Calamus. He appears like a very fine man. The M.E. church had a festival at Calamus for the benefit of the minister last week Wednesday. They invited me to assist in the singing, and other exercises of the evening and of course I was willing to do any thing in my power as there are but few members and I a member of the same denomination. I accepted of the company of a young gentleman a member of the church. As I was liable to be thrown in any one's company I counted it as a wise matter of etiquitte and accepted his company for the evening. I think I have sufficient proof of his character as a young man. I enjoyed the evening very much and always do an entertainment of the kind especially when I can make myself useful. We had tableaux and singing[13] and supper afterwards, and of course there is plenty for ladies to do at such a time. If it would not discommode you too much I would like to have you call and visit my school in Brushville. As ever

Your true friend

Martha A. Bennett

Greeley, Colorado

April 15th '71

Dear friend, Miss Bennett,

We have as you will notice succeeded in getting to our desired destination. As there was so much to do before starting, did not leave our old home until the Wednesday following the week you left us.[14] Arrived at Oskaloosa on Thursday at 3½ o'clock PM. Remained there until Monday morning. We found our folks[15] well and expecting us along sooner. Wednesday at 4 PM found us where we are.[16] It was one week from the time of starting to that of our arrival here. Our trip, although somewhat tiresome, was interesting being an entire new scenery on the whole route. Nerly the entire country after leaving Omaha is an extended plain with an occasional range of sand and stone combined. Near Chene [Cheyenne] is where may be seen the first view of a portion of the Rocky mountains called the Black Hills.[17] From here to the mountains it is about thirty miles, although appearing not more than five or six miles away. As they are of a dark color, it has the appearance of an approaching rain in mid summer. Greeley is improving rappidly. Although not one year since the first house was built, [the community] contains 12 hundred inhabitants with others coming on the cars every day. We do not yet know what our real oppinion is, but intend staying long enough to find out what it may be. When I left you in De Witt I felt somewhat lonesome. But there are times when we may meet and times when we must part, through the course of a lifetime, and it can not be avoided. I received that money from Smiths amounting interest and principal to $36.4½. I may have told you to that effect before. Our trip cost us each $59.70. Didn't have to pay any for Aggie the child.[18] Our friends here are very kind to us, indeed could not be more so. Father and mother felt a strong regret that they were not at home when you left to bid you good by. In fact they did not know your intention was to leave at that time as I had not told them so. But you have their entire kind wishes you may be sure. Most likely you soon will be if not already are again performing the duties of a school teache[r]. I wish you much enjoyment.

Hoping soon to learn from your heretofore interesting pen, I would remain your fine friend.

Roy Carpenter

P.S. These are the first lines that I have written since our arrival here.

Greeley

May 2nd 1871

Dearest friend,

Your welcome letter has been received on last Thursday. You speak of writing on [the] Sabbath as something not to be desired. It has always been my opinion that if possable we should use other das [*sic*] for that pleasant duty. To make a comparison of my own views it seems to me

A: Meeker School  B: Barnum hall  C: Hotel de Comfort  D: Burned Block  E: Exchange Hotel  F: Denver Pacific Station  G: Barrel Hoops

Fig. 12. Early Greeley: Distant view looking west. Hotel de Comfort labeled "C." *City of Greeley Museums, Permanent Collection.*

what we can talk on Sunday is not mean[t] to [be] written on that day.

We have just returned from a very interesting lecture on the subject of Temperance by Miss Emmery[19] of Illinois to a crowded hall they call the Tabernacle.[20] After which the initiating of new officers took place. It was very entertaining, indeed.

In speaking of your enjoying a good sermon at home, you call my mind to many reflections on the important subject of religion.[21] It certainly affords me the greatest pleasure to know that you do enjoy the blessing of God in the heart. Feeling the interest that I do for your good, I can but enjoy what you enjoy in know[ing] of the facts. I have always regarded the Christian's life as being one of the greatest of responsibilities to act out in life. This is, perhaps, the principal reason of my not being a professor of religion. As to familiarity upon any subject whatever it may be, you need not hesitate the least to express your oppinion at any time. And I can only hope for the time when our conversations may be fully enjoyed together without any hinderance. If at any time you notice that I have or may have repeated anything, please pass it by. As yet we are living in the small rented house with its shaking floor, but expect to move next week into one we have bought which is a little larger than this one. With the house and ½ acre lot we also get 80 acres of land which cost $1350. Writings are also drawn for 160 acres 18 miles northwest from town which cost $800. We are in hopes that all will prove for the best. Enclosed may be found a recipe for sore eyes which was highly recommended to us last summer by a young man. Write soon. Sincerely yours

L. S. Carpenter

Calamus Station

May 12th '71

Dearest friend,

I received your welcome letter a week ago tomorrow evening. I should have answered sooner but I prefer putting *your* letters in the office myself, and as that is Lodge night it is the only one in which I can go to town myself. Today completes another week of school, the second one. I have registered twenty two names, and have an average attendance of seventeen. I am working for my board at Mr. Algare[22] (you recollect that large white house near the school house) that is the one. I like the people quite well. There are six in the family including myself. I have enough employment to keep out of mischief. I have taken the infant class in the Sabbath School and have a very interesting one. There is nothing in the Sabbath School that suits me better than teaching the little ones. There is preaching here nearly every Sunday and all taken into consideration we expect to enjoy the summer quite pleasantly. I will now try to finish this letter. I wrote a little last night, but had not time to finish. You know I have to catch my chance. You were very kind to send that recipe to me, and I am very much obliged for it. I have not used it because my eyes were so much better, I thought it was not necessary, but I will keep it for future use. My eyes are always weak, and I think the cause of their being sore, was that I sewed very steadily for two weeks, and iritated them. They are as well as usual now. I am in hopes you will succeed in arranging every thing for the best and for your comfort. As for a home and getting land is concerned, you did not say whether you were all well pleased or not, but I suppose so or you would not have purchased. How is Mattie's health and indeed how are all your family? If it would not be too much trouble I would like you to give me a description of the place you have bought. I have an idea how the country appears, and I would like to know how nearly it is right. If you were an artist, I might demand a painting of the country, but I will not trouble you for that now, unless you send it of your own accord. If you should conclude to paint a picture of the country I should want your picture some place in full view, now don't forget that part.

You wrote of having attended a Temperance lecture. I presume it was quite interesting as most of lectures upon that subject are. Was the lady pretty well informed? It must be quite pleasant if you have the privilege of attending such lectures frequently. Last Saturday evening, I was given the place of left hand supporter [?] rather a conspicuous position for a *country schoolmarm*, don't you think so? I should think the W. C. [?] would feel highly honored, and I am appointed a critic for this evening.[23] I ought to study my Grammar a little while perhaps, but I don't believe I shall go to the trouble. The Lodge is expecting to have a picnic or fishing party the twentieth of this month. I suppose we will have a very jolly time, I hardly believe there will be many fish caught. There may be some hearts though; if I hear of any I will let you know.

You wrote in your last of your hopes for the time when our conversations should be enjoyed without any hinderance.[24] I think if it is God's will, that such will be the case. We [know] not what the future may bring but we may place all our affairs in God's hands and feel that they are safe. I will inclose a few lines to Mattie. Give my love to all your family (and, of course keep some for yourself).

Your true friend

Martha Bennett

Greeley, Colo.
May 28th '71
Dearest friend,

Your interesting letter of late has been received. It has always been my luck thus far when writing to *you*, that one little sheet of paper has not been enough space for me to express my scattered thoughts upon. I suppose the principal reason being that it requires many words from me to express a few thoughts. I have just returned from Baptist preaching at eleven o'clock A.M., there being no Methodist services today. We are well and enjoy a good appetite. It afforded me much pleasure to learn of your eyes being better and am in hopes such may continue to be the case until they become well. No doubt you folks enjoyed your fishing excursion very much. I hope so, and if any hearts were won, [I] hope they may prove true to each other. On that day I was hunting for a horse that had got loose two nights before, but found it about 2 o'clock P.M. where some other one had left [the horse] for me to get. So, it wasn't stolen. I am glad you are so highly honored in your occupying the position you do in the Lodge, for it is only another proof of the real worth of a country school marm. But I think you would be just the person to fill the office of W. M. (which means Worthy Martha). You ask whether Miss Emmery was well informed. She appeared to have good use of language as well as composure in speaking. I should [have] liked very much to have heard your speech to your S.S. at home that you spoke of in your first letter out here. We *sometimes* think that we like this country better than at others. As I am not an artist, I can't supply you with a sketch of this town and its surroundings, but wish I could. Mr. Johnson the artist here told me yesterday that the town laid to low from the bluffs to admit of a good picture. I have sent you a map of the colony and its surroundings. We moved into this house, one that was bought with the half acre in town on the 16th of this month.[25] [It] is a little larger than the other, but not such a one as we would build if we were to do so. The two plots of ground, the one near the river 6 miles southeast of Camp Collins, the other 1 mile northwest of town on the north side of the river containing 80 acres are both good ground, that is said to be. Of the two pieces, I think you and I could have our choice if we like the country well enough to stay here. I would want you to like the country in order to live here and that I can't tell untill after trying. As it is, we (our folks) think of remaining until we can determine more fully in the matter. If you and I should not like to stay here we might try some other place I suppose. I told you that we were well. I meant those of us here. Our brother Peter, who lives near the 160 acre piece of ground is quite feeble with his disease, the consumption which he came here in the hopes of affecting a cure.[26] But we fear [he] will not succeed. Please write a long letter soon.

Truly yours,

Leroy Carpenter

Calamus Station

June 2nd '71

Dearest friend,

I received your *very* welcome letter yesterday. I guess you will not think it intruding too much, if I answer it now? I guess not, and I think you will not care if I manage to write a wider sheet than I have envelope long, full to you. I can not get such paper as I like in Calamus as the stock of stationary is not very large, but will do the best I can, as I cannot do otherwise, and I *know* if it does not bother you any more than it does me to read a long letter, you will not get tired reading this. I am enjoying *very* good health, better than I have for several summers, and am succeeding quite well with my school. You wrote that you had just returned from Baptist meeting. It would be strange if we should both turn Babtist, as I attend every Sabbath and you may attend frequently but I hardly believe we will. I am afraid you would not have heard much of a speech if you had heard me in our S.S. [Sunday School] at home. I am not used to making speeches in public. I presume Miss Emmery would have smiled had she have heard it. Mr. Rogers (the Methodist minister) came down to see me last week and wanted me to go to the Maquoketa caves with him. They first intended having an excursion, but failing [that] he wished me to go, and we would visit my sister living near Maquoketa.[27] I should have enjoyed visiting my sister very much, but I did not think it prudent to go and therefore refused his invitation. He expressed a wish to become better acquainted with me. He is from the East and has a few friends here, and wishes to become acquainted with some there. I hope he may, but I cannot accept of his attentions conscientiously.[28]

You were *very* kind to send me a map of the vicinity of Greeley or location of Union Colony. I can imagine very much how the country appears. It must be beautiful. I expect the mountains look majestic at times. I hope you did not think I *really meant* you to send me a *picture* of Greeley. Of course I should feel it a very acceptable gift, but when I wrote I was jesting more than otherwise. I am inclined to do so, and if I write sometimes rather joyfull you must remember it is me. Mother says I am very mischievious, and I often write mischieviously.

I am glad you are living in your own house. It is so much more pleasant than to live where you may be throwing labor away if you attempt any improvment. You wrote about my liking the country. I wish you to feel at liberty to select a place or do anything for the best. I will be content where every you will be. You are a more competent judge of a place than I would be, and do whatever you think best. Our views are very much alike about such things. It is very kind in you to think so much of *my* comfort, as to wish me to be satisfied with the country and place, but I shall not be very hard to suit, and am willing you should decide the matter. If after trying the land it does not suit you, and you would like to try another tract, do not hesitate on my account, but do whatever you think proper. I received a few lines from Mattie and was very glad to hear from her. I will answer them some other time, as I have not the opportunity now.

I am sorry your brother's health still remains poor.[29] It must be a great affliction to all of you to think that he may be taken from you at any moment, but if he is *prepared* to go from this world to another, it will not be so hard for you to part with him. When I last heard from home our folks were well. How do your parents stand the change of climate, as well as the rest of you? Tell Silas he must not forget me, for I often think of him. Have you ever heard anything of Aggie's father since I was at your house? But I shall weary your patience and would close this letter by wishing you enjoyment and prosperity.

As ever, Yours,

Martha Bennett

Greeley

June 10th 1871

My Dearest friend,

Received your very interesting letter on Wednesday evening, this being Saturday P.M. at six o'clock. I am glad to know that your health is so good and hope you may continue thus prospered and enjoy yourself. We are well at home. Brother Peter continues about the same in health. Father and Mother were up there last Monday, it being 18 or 19 miles

Facing page: Fig. 13. Martha Bennett, "Sweet 16" in 1870. *CSU Water Archives 09e006.*

toward Camp Collins. We cannot get there as often as we would like to. He believes he will not live long but has good hopes of enjoying the Christians' hope of getting safely housed in Heaven. The weather is quite warm in day time, but cool and refreshing at night. So that after having done a hard day's work, one can enjoy a good night's sleep to prepare him for working on the ditches that we have been engaged at for irrigating the crops.[30] You need not have any fears of writing to often or too long letters as you spoke of in your last letter. But write two or three or more sheets if you please and it will interest me more than all else of my reading put together. I told Silas of your kind regards to him. He said that you was a lady that would bear easy maintenance. It affords me much knowledge [Leroy crossed out "pleasure" and replaced it with "knowledge"] to know that Mr. Rogers takes a fancy to you as by his actions he certainly does if I may be allowed to judge of a young man's actions. But our purposes being fully determined,[31] nothing shall sever our purpose unless it should be death and "God may choose our future enjoyment by being in each other's presence for many years."

We went on a pleasure excursion last week making two wagon loads of ribs [fence posts]. When our wagon was unloading after getting back home to town, a lady inviting us all to call around tendered the invitation to me by adding, perhaps as a good inducement, by saying that she had a daughter. Of course, I thanked her in reply. Of course, she was only joking. But there was one, the picture of whom I treasure more highly than all others and in plain letters are written "Sweet Sixteen." You need not think that I don't think you are sometimes only joking, for as our views are very much the same, I often say course expressions that I only mean half in sport. Often have I used words that I have afterwards thought had no meaning to them.

But enough. We were highly favored on Thursday evening the 8th by hearing the celebrated Philip Phillips sing and play on the organ.[32] The people seemed well pleased. I thought when we knew he would sing here how nice it would be for you to be with us and go along. It may be that I may at some time write to you on larger sheets of paper. I also excuse the style. Write soon.

Yours,

L.S. Carpenter

Brushville

June 17th 1871

Dearest friend,

I shall attempt to answer your very *welcome* letter which I received Wednesday, not knowing how interesting I shall be able to make [it] or how well it may be written as I have been busy all day until now (it is half past three) doing housework. I suppose you are well aware there is plenty to do on Saturday and especially when a person is in school all days of the week accept this one. Mrs. Algar is quite an old lady and I feel it more my duty to do the heavier work than if she were younger. She is seventy one years old, but is very smart for one of her age. She is a good principled woman and one that will not impose upon another. I enjoy it very much here. The house is situated so we can see about six or seven miles north and several miles east and west. It is situated more pleasantly than most of the houses are. There are no children and it is very quiet and pleasant. I have not been homesick yet but have sometimes felt as if I should like to see some of my acquaintances for a few hours and converse with them. I have not heard from home for three weeks.

I have only five weeks longer to teach and then I presume I shall return to the old log house, on the prairie.[33] I am very glad your brother leaves with you the assurance of a hope beyond the tomb. How refreshing is the thought that if we but live as God would have, we shall meet the loved ones gone before. I have often had reason to thank my

Heavenly Father that he has left all of *my* friends and relatives that were near to me here upon the earth that I might enjoy their society. When I hear of others losing friends and kindred, I can but fully realize God's mercy to me. Surely "Goodness and Mercy have followed me all the days of my life."

How far is it from Greeley to Camp Collins? On looking on the map I see it is not very far from the mountains. How often I look at that map and imagine I can see you all busily employed at your various occupations. About how far apart do you dig the ditches, it must look odd to see them all over the country?[34] You thought right when you thought I would have liked to have been with you to have heard Philip Philipps sing. It would have been a great treat to me indeed. I have always greatly desired to hear him. I think you must have enjoyed your excursion very much. I think if that lady who informed you that she had a daughter could not have trusted that a country schoolmarm had a part of your heart or all of it, if you will allow such an expression, she would not have spoken as she did, but maybe she will learn the facts in the case some future day.

We are favored with a very good rain last night. Two weeks ago Monday, we had quite a hail storm which cooled the air very much and we have had cool weather since. Some evenings it seems cool enough for frost. Before the hail storm we had some very warm weather. The thermometer stood ninety eight degrees above zero in the shade. I meant to have asked you before if there were any locusts in Colo.[35] There are a great many here, but have done no serious injury thus far. They were quite a curiosity to me at first. You spoke about your writing on larger sheets of paper. Certainly I will excuse the style, and would be only too glad to receive longer letters from you. I thought . . . I could write a longer letter to you but my thoughts seem quite well scattered now and being rather tired they fly farther still. Mr. Rogers has not been here since I wrote. I saw him pass the school house one day but that is all I have known of him lately. Have you heard any thing of Aggie's father since you have been out west? How does she prosper[?] I often think of her, she is such a sweet disposed little girl. Give my best respects to all of your folks and write a long letter soon.

From one who often thinks of you.

Martha Bennett

Home [Greeley]

June 23rd 1871

Dearest friend,

Your welcome letter of the 17th inst. has been received this evening.[36] We are *all* about as usual in regard to health. Not being much change in Peter's health. We received sad news in the first of the week, in a paper sent us from Oskaloosa containing the sorowful news of Henry Howard Coleman's death by consumption on the morning of the 4th of June.[37] He had been staying with his parents for about two months, so Howard has left us. Poor fellow has left, but to enter into a better land than this we live in. His having lived with us considerable, and being a *true* and special friend of mine, it makes me think of many circumstances that have occurred while we were together. But so it is. "We are passing away." May we not hope some day to meet those kind friends some time again? I think so. These four lines are certainly appropriate:

> Brother, thou most mild and lonly,
> Gentle as the summer's breeze,
> Pleasant as the air of evening,
> When it floats among the trees.

In my last letter I failed to answer some of your questions from lack of knowledge and space. We haven't yet heard anything of Aggie's father as to whether he has gone up or not about our taking her away to Colorado. But are in hopes he will sweat it out if he must. Father and mother enjoy good health and we will all like the country if we can make a living. It is a pleasant thing that you can enjoy such a fine view as you can where you are living. In our excursion down to where the Cache la Poudre joins the Platte River it was *midling* pleasant. When we had gotten there and were getting ready for a lunch together my team, which are young horses, got loose while Frank Scott, my cousin and I were wattering them.[38] For not being on our guard, they jerked their halters out of our hands and tried running on their own hook a little while but did not tear their harness any. One of them I found in Greeley town which is about five miles away. Rode this one back to the folks who send expressions of the finest regard in our unlooked for change.[39] This company was composed of our relations and their special friends; *no* one going as a team or some person's girl. Mrs Rea hasn't said anything more about that daughter, and if she should, I would feel like informing her that I have a girl in the east that no other one on earth could take her place in my affections. That she not only has a part but the whole of my heart. And having been blessed, I sometimes think, providentially with my fullest ideal of claiming the heart and at some day her hand. I hold as the most sacred those ties in my heart of a perfect lady in my view. When the train came in this evening, I saw it coming down the hillside. I hoped that it was bringing a letter from that schoolmarm of mine.

The ditches and dykes are different distances apart according to the distance from town, and the dykes are seen the most from their being a ridge of earth thrown up at different heights on which there is a small chanel for the water to flow through. The one we have been working on today and for a while past is one mile northwest of town; [we] are getting most [of the water] through but I fear too late to save our five acres of oats out there as the ground is very dry and they haven't yet sprouted. The thermometer stood [at] 106 last Sunday in the sun. Ditch or canal [Number 2] on the north of town is 27 [miles] the one on the south of town [Number 3], 14½ miles in length.[40] The water sometime appears to be running up hill by the looks of the ground but that cannot be possable.[41] As it is most likely we will stay here some time yet, if not for a permanent home, we have thought some of putting up a house this season on the 80 acre piece north of here across the river and from town about one mile. If so, you and I can have it for our home if we want it most likely. As we have some talked about what kind of house we liked, I would receive it with the greatest delight any choice or oppinion that you could fancy or suggest as your liking. As we don't yet want to put up a large house, but think one that would bear the adding to of a larger portion sometime if desired, it should be the kind you like the best if possable. My preference would be to live by ourselves if we can. Is that your choice? This is plain talk but what is your oppinion? As in regards your letters sent me, what you may say is known only to myself. I do not mean to fix any stated time for my going back there and being united in the sacred bonds of matrimony, as I will leave that to you to choose.[42] If you have any choice some time within one year, this fall or next spring, it may be if all would suit to do so. Please understand that I mean by this writing to know only it may be a belief of the present moment and that you might think a little different after thinking the matter over. This we can find our united oppinions by writing often and long letters. Write just what it pleases you to write.

As there is quite a variety of people here of different parts of the country and oppinions and so forth, I have placed in a rude form a few lines that might amuse a little: "Do not view me with a critic's eye, but pass my imperfections by."

On tomorrow evening and Monday evening, Mrs. [Elizabeth] Cady Stanton and Miss Susan [B.] Anthony will lecture on the subject of women's rights in the Tabernacle.[43]

Camp Collins is six miles from the foot hills and 24 miles from here.[44] Peter lives six miles this side of Camp Collins. There are few locusts here but many potato bugs and worms going for the potatoes.

Entirely yours,

Leroy Carpenter

*Leroy included the following poem at the end of his letter.*

What have we come for,
When looking around on every side,
And see the coming tide
The question often comes to me,
Why do they come so rappidly?

Some come to find a resting place,
Some the wheels of progress trace,
Others to cross the desert wide,
And thus secure a lengthy ride.

Some their lost health to regain,
And thus to soothe an aching pain,
The mind to feed on pastures green,
And see a sight so long unseen.

Many come to find their wealth,
And fancy no loss by stealth,
Need think *their* path to find,
For other men are only blind.

Many come intemperance to shun,
And to live where there is no rum,
To poison the lips by drinking of the bowl,
That enrages the mind and ruins the soul.

Among the number may be found
Those that come for favor and renown,
That their selfish views may find a place,
As if *they* were chief of all their race.

But find they're all alone
That every man's head is not a stone,
The[y] look around with jealous eye,
And only ask the reason *why*.

From distant Maine may here be found
Those who seek for richer ground,
And western Texans have their herds
Grazing on the grasses called *absurd*.

From cold Wisconsin here are seen
The gatherer of hopps so green,
And hot Florida claims its share
Of the richest gold so fair.

Welcome then from farthest east,
The western people here to greet,
The north, too, may have its share,
With distant south, Colorado's purest air.

—L. S. Carpenter

Brushville

July 2nd, 1871

Dear Leroy,

I received your very welcome letter yesterday morning. I am very glad to hear that you are all well, and enjoying yourselves. My health is still quite good. What a blessing it is to enjoy good health. I attended S.S. and prayer-meeting this morning. I have a class of little ones, and a very interesting class they are. Last Sunday there were eleven, the largest number that I have had. When I sat down to teach them today I could not help feeling sad to think of leaving them so soon as I shall have too, for there is no one that I know of to take my place. I feel the responsibility that rests upon me very much, but I am willing and glad to be able to do something in my master's work, and my prayer is, that I might do more. We had a very good prayer-meeting. The S.S. is a pretty good size.

I have heard from home since I wrote to you. They were all well except father. His health is quite poor this summer, as it was last. For several days before receiving your letter I had the impression of hearing of the death of some person. And I *have* heard of the death of Howard Coleman.[45] It is hard to loose our friends but oh! how joyful the thought of their be[ing] better situated than they were in this wicked world, and that we may meet them again, if we but live as *God* would have us. "Meet to part no more" Oh! May God keep us in "the straight and narrow way that leadeth to life everlasting."

I received the book containing a History of the Union Colony and have read it.[46] Reading it does not diminish my desire in the least to see Colorado. From the map and pamphlet, I can form quite an idea of the country. The mountain scenery must be sublime, and I should think the country was pretty also. Accept my thanks for these, for I certainly appreciate them. I admire the principals upon which the Colony are founded. How pleasant it must be to live where there is no drunkenness and where poor society is not known. I think if all of the western country was settled on the same principles it would be very desirable to migrate in that direction, and if it can be ascertained that persons can live in such places with as little expense as elsewhere, the west will not long remain unsettled. You must be careful and not let those horses of yours take you with them on some of their runs or I am afraid I might not receive quite so many letters from Colorado, as I do now. And you must take care not to have them out when you are watching the *train* or you will forget them and they will take advantage of you. How do you like the work of digging ditches[?]

You wished me to make any suggestion I could about building a house. I do not know of any in particular. You will probably know the most comfortable way of building one that will save the most labor. No, I do not care about a large house, any more than we should need for our own use. It would be my preference that we should live alone, and if circumstances were such that we could not be married so soon on that account, I think we had better delay it, not that we could not agree with others, but I think it would be more pleasant for all parties. Why, when I think of *me* having a house of my own, and some one else to take care of, I feel my inability very much, but I cannot tell what I can do untill I try. You will have to put up with a good many mistakes, I expect, for you know your "Little Schoolmarm["] (as Mr. Alger calls me) is not very old in experiences yet. I cannot tell you *just* when I could be prepared to become your wife, as I should like to consult with my parents a little. I feel it better to do so as I am not of age, and I cannot see them now untill I go home which will be three weeks.[47] I hope you will not feel hard that I have not answered your question immediately but I think best to think about it some and give you an answer that will stand without any alteration. Of course I shall exercise my own mind on the subject. I will give you a reply just as soon as possible. I shall go home as soon as possible after my school is out, and will write to you immediately. I may have to remain a day or two in order to get my money.

I think your lines of poetry are very appropriate and good. I will not view you with a critic's eye but will pass your imperfection by. I hope

Mattie[48] will not think hard of me, but I can scarcely find time to write a *respectable* letter to you, and now farewell.

    With much love,

    Martha Bennett

[Greeley] Saturday evening, six o'clock

[July 8, 1871]

Dear Martha,

Your interesting letter has been received on yesterday eve. We are quite well. Peter is a little better. The weather of late has been quite good. That Sunday that I said the thermometer was 106 in the sun, I should have said in the shade. But since then it has been more pleasant generally. On last Sabbath evening about the middle of the night a hail storm passed through town doing much harm to truck patches. We attended Baptist meeting last Sabbath in the morning and evening. But as you said in regard to our ever becoming Baptists, it would indeed be odd. Mr. Brown, their preacher certainly is a good man and I like to hear him preach. Yet, as they believe in immersion as the only real Baptism, and their communion being close[d], I prefer my mother church the Methodists, and as our views are the same, I think that we will stick to the old ship. Your school will soon close. No doubt you will often think of the school house near the road, so beautifully shaded with small trees. I have often thought when working on the ditches on a warm afternoon, how pleasant it must be around your school house. You ask is it hard work to do on those ditches? If a person works fast and without resting any, it brings the sweat and tries the nerves, sometimes to much for health. We don't work any more out there for a while.

    You speak as though your letters failed of being interesting, and so fourth. There could not be a greater mistake. Every one is full of information and news. For instance, in regard to a suitable house to build, "one that is comfortable and is not too costly" implies in meaning as much as many more words strung out. In speaking of the time that I might go back there, I did not intend you to think I wanted to limit any time, but wanted to know if there was any prefference of time with you. So I am not in the leas[t] disappointed whatever in getting your reply. We do not yet know fully as to how much the country will suit us. But are in hopes to like it if possable. Father paid today $400 for another eighty acre lot of ground which is adjoining the one we intend to build on. It is near town and a little nearer the railroad being a few rods over ¼ of a mile from the tracks.[49] Want to put a house on it instead of the other piece as before spoken of to make the homes both good. This is intend[ed] for us (you and I). Perhaps it might suit yourself as well as myself to defer our union until next spring and then you would be of age.[50] We could maybe [be] better prepared to have a house to ourselves and not be too soon for you [to] leave your native home. It is right for you to consult your parents even if you were over age in my oppinion. Certainly, you cannot look at housekeeping as a greater responsibility than myself.[51] To think of myself being a married man seems like undertaking great responsibilities. But time is bearing us on toward the middle of life when we must do for ourselves or something else will come. I will look over those various changes in your management that you mention and you I believe will consider that I am often a blundering, erring mortal and have sympathy accordingly. Some improvements are still going on in town and *good* Carpenters are quite useful.

I would wish you a happy closing of your school and maybe will send you a few copies of our newspaper [the Greeley *Tribune*] if they would interest you and your folks. They sometimes exagerate a little in describing the country for we must remember "'tis not all gold that glitters." We had a fine and happy fourth of July. The Methodists took in $80 for the church by furnishing lemonade, ice cream, etc. Please write soon. As ever, yours,

Roy Carpenter

〰

[Brushville]

July 15th, 1871, Saturday Eve

Dear friend Leroy,

I received your very welcome letter Wednesday morning and would have answered it sooner, but I had an opportunity to go to Davenport with Dr. Russell of Calamus and as I wanted to get some pictures taken for my scholars, I got ready as soon as possible and went with him. He had business there and was obliged to remain over night. I made good use of the opportunity and went over to Moline to visit some relatives of ours living there. I was to meet Dr. Russell at Davenport eight o'clock Thursday morning, but when I got off of the ferry boat, Mr. Bradford (one of the neighbors here) met me and told me he had come after the Dr. and sent him home in the night as one of his patients here was not expected to live. Consequently, I was obliged to wait untill Mr. Bradford had finished his business there and then came with him. It was so warm, and he had driven his team so hard all night to find the Dr. that we waited untill evening before we could travel and we did not get here untill half past ten Thursday evening. Last night I sat up with (Mrs. Curtis) the lady I mentioned. She is very sick, and we hardly have hopes of her. I got three hours sleep in the middle of night, and do not feel quite so drowsy today as I should, had I have had no rest. I cannot go to Lodge this evening, and I send this by Mr. Jed Curtis. I guess it will reach you safely, it is the first letter that I have written to you but what I have mailed myself. If I should mail this tonight I would send you something besides my poor scribbling, but you must excuse all mistakes and crooked lines for this is a very busy day with me, and my hand is not so steady as usual. I am ashamed of this paper Leroy, but it is the best Calamus can afford, and I have no opportunity to purchase elsewhere. I have seven days more to teach and my school will close for the present. It would have closed next Friday but I lost two days by my trip to Davenport and am going to make that time up on Monday and Tues. of the following week. Yes, indeed I shall often think of the Brushville schoolhouse.

How short the six months of my teaching time has been. I can hardly realize the time has been so long. The scholars are lamenting thence when I shall leave them and I would wish it farther in the future upon some accounts.

I am very glad to hear that your brother [Peter] has enjoyed a little better health. The warm weather must be hard for him to endure. Is your father as smart as he was when I was at your house[?] I presume all of you can find plenty of work to do. If you can't, come back to Iowa and I guess you will not be obliged to remain idle long. This morning as I was cleaning my room (in order to leave it as I found it) I had occasion to lower the upper sashes and thought came to my mind, "I hope Leroy will fix our windows as to lower the upper sash as high or low as one would wish it." I think it is so much healthier to have the windows so arranged because one can ventilate a room with[out] causing a draft to strike any one, so as to give them cold by sitting by the window.

I have received a letter from my sister Lucy, living in Illinois.[52] I have written to her twice since I came back here. I thought she had forgotten me but I am glad to see that she has not. She is very anxious to become acquainted with you and asked the question in her letter "Will he take my sister away[?]" I shall have to tell her, yes! won't I? Her health is not very good this summer. Uncle John would not let her have but a few music scholars. He want[s] her to take life a little easier. They (Uncle John and Aunt Rachel) would like to have her live with them as their daughter, but she is too independent for that. She does not like to depend upon anyone for anything. She wrote that she would be home the last of this month. And you may be sure we will make good use of the time, while she is there. I only wish she would bring the melodeon with her and [we] would hear some music once more. Sometimes this summer it has seemed to me I could have walked three miles to have heard some music. This may seem a short distance to you as you like to walk quite well, but it would be as far as I would wish to walk [in] this warm weather. My sister often regrets that she is not near me so she could teach me to play, but as she says we both *will* help ourselves, and of course we cannot always be together.

You spoke in your last about sending me some of your newspapers if they would be interesting. They will interest me there is no doubt and I know our folks would be glad to read them. Father likes to read quite well and would spend considerable of his time in that way, but he works so hard through the day that he needs every moment at night to rest. I presume I shall not leave for De Witt untill the later part of [the] week after next. I am visiting with my scholars the last few days of my school and do not know how soon I shall start home. My school will close Tues of week after next and I may go up to Calamus, the Wednesday after. My friends there wish me to visit them, and I presume I shall stay there untill Saturday morning. If you write you probably will write so I will receive it before I start to De Witt.

I am quite anxious to get home, as I have not seen any of our folks. I spent my Fourth at Dixon a small place across the river [Wapsipinicon River]. Mr. Jed Curtis, the young man who makes it his home here, offered very kindly to take me over to the celebration. He first asked me where I was going to spend my Fourth. I told him I expected to stay here all day. He said that would not do and I went with him over there. We started about nine and came back about three. He went to a dance in the evening. I of course did not accompany him. Give my best respects to all of your family and write soon.

Yours as ever,
Martha Bennett

Home [Greeley]
August 5th 1871
Dearest friend:
I was glad to receive your kind letter. Also a fine photograph closely resembling my eastern friend. I would express my thanks to you even in

this silent medium and so many miles distant. Since my last letter we have been called upon to experience like your recent comment, that of the ["]proof that we are passing away." Our brother Peter died on the evening of the 28th of July at ten minutes after five o'clock instead of the time mentioned in the paper I send you with this letter. A few lines in regard to his life in this letter and perhaps no more need be said hereafter in that respect, unless in answer to questions you may ask, which would be gladly answered. Although zealous in the pursuit of being in possession of some property, yet left the world perfectly resigned to his lot. The evidence of his happy change into the other world were the most clear and evident in the last moments. Conscious of his approaching departure, he gradually ceased to live until the silent body was found to be without life. Father, mother, and Sarah with his own family were those that were present at the time of his departure. By using cold cloths, the body was kept until Sunday at eleven o'clock, Friday being the day of his death. With a good attendance of the neighbors, some from Greeley [the body was] conducted by the Free Masons to Colins [Fort Collins]. A short distance this side the procession of that order dressed in their attire met us, and all marched into their new school house and listened to a good sermon delivered by a Presbyterian minister, a[f]ter which the body was laid in its silent resting place close to Camp Colins. Too much cannot be said in commendation of The Masons and his neighbors for their kindness during his sickness. Some came near fifteen miles to set up with him overnight. And now although with others we have not been the most in conceit of the Free Masons, yet their kindness in his case came right from the heart and not a mere form.[53] Poor Mary, his faithfull and intelligent wife is now a widow. How lonely it must be to be left alone! Her three boys, [the] youngest one about two years old will, maybe, [be] a support to her. She will receive an Army pension of $25 a month and $1,000 life insurance. We are in hopes her wants will be supplied. The neighbors intend to do her harvesting this year.

In performing what you think to be your duty, do not do so much as to injure your health, as you say you are not as heavy as some time since.[54] I believe that there are boundaries to our exertions for others, for often people by exposure loose their former good health, never to regain it. I am enjoying good health, have been working five days three miles west of town for Boyds in harvesting their grain.[55] They want me to help them more, but do not expect to work much more for them as I only get $1.50 a day which is not much for a country where it costs so much to live on.[56] The five acres of oats that we sowed this spring is a total failure as the ditches and dykes were not made soon enough to supply the grain with water. Many hundred acres around town have been lost in the same way this summer.[57] Although where we used to live we did not pretend to live like kings and princes, yet the common comforts were supplied. Such things as chickens, turkeys, eggs, fresh butter and many other things we are as yet deprived [of] entirely, but are in hopes of having them some time, and if I knew that they could not be had here, I would try my favorite State [of] Iowa. However, we enjoyed the eating of watermelons (small, ripe ones) on the 26th of July. They were planted in May. Can Iowa beat that? And would be glad to have you share with us.

If you live with your sister this winter, I am in hopes you may enjoy yourself finely while learning to play on the melodeon.[58] Not saying anything against Brushville, I would give a guess that there are places where you might have better society. The carpenters have commenced building our own house, your house. They think we have a beautiful place to live. There will be a shed 8 feet wide and the length of the house; will be made with the house.[59] This may be a good thing for the cooking department, the other part being our bedrooms and one front room. Will that do, Miss Bennett? The Good Templars had a good time at their metting here that I spoke of, but as [brother] Silas and I hauled away dirt from the cellar in the forenoon, I failed to hear the exercises. There is some sickness in town, mostly the cause of eating too much green victuals. The day that Howard Coleman died, a daughter of our cousin was married to a young man by the name of Bennett. "All of Cedar County."[60] There are not so many people coming now as came in the spring, principal reason being the busy time of the year. The Methodists want to start their own Sunday School shortly.[61] Times are getting a little harder than they were, but all hope for a happy future. Denver City is improving rapidly, if so, why should not Greeley also improve ere long? We retain our former minister for next year, Mr. Adams. Good for us! Philip Phillips while here wanted him to leave for him a home in this colony, Mr. Adams and him being acquaintances. Enough scribbling for this time. All wish you much success and happiness. Write soon.

Truely yours as ever,

Roy Carpenter

At home [De Witt, Iowa]

Aug 11th 1871

Dear friend Roy,

Your welcome letter was received evening before last. I was glad to hear from you again but sorry to learn that you had lost another relative so soon. It is hard to part with our friends, but it must be so, and if we can reconcile ourselves to the separation when it comes, we will be better prepared to perform our necessary duties. I am glad to know that his [Peter's] hopes of another and better world were so bright. How much comfort to all of you to feel that you may meet again. I am glad that he had such kind friends to administer to his wants. I hope his wife will be able to bear up under her afflictions for the sake of her children. How much land does your brother own[?] It is quite a distance from Greeley for her to be, but I presume some of your folks will often go out to see her, for how lonely it must be for her. Now every article that she used will have a little history, that will remind her of him who was her comfort in this unfriendly world. The Free Masons were certainly very kind to her in her afflictions, and "A friend in need is a friend indeed."

When I last wrote I was still at Brushville. I went to Calamus as I intended, and remained there untill Tuesday forenoon. The friends or my friends were rather reluctant about my coming away, especially at Brushville, and were clamorus to have me return and teach the winter school. I told them I would if I could not do better elsewhere. Mr. Millard (our county superintendent) sent me word he would like me to apply for a situation in the Lyons Public schools [Clinton, Iowa, suburb]. Father and I went down Monday, and Mr. Millard gave me a letter of introduction to the Principal. They are to let me know the first of next week. There are one or two other schools I can get by application. Mr. Millard said he did not want me to go back to Brushville for fear I would go to teaching a school of another kind too soon, and he had me started in teaching and did not want me to stop. I told him he need have no fears in that direction. I guess he may think Brushville is not all the best place by next spring, don't you think so?

Sorry, do not think I never mean[t] to let you know the date of our marriage. It is this way, I know father will not be able to help me [with] what I need, and I want to teach on that account and as soon as I ascertain what time I have to teach I can tell when I can be prepared to go to Colorado. There will be a great many things for me to attend to that I cannot do untill I am through teaching. I presume you had rather (if convenient) we would be married so we can be back in time to begin spring work or does it make any difference with you[?] I suppose you would like to have an early start in things next year so as to be better able to prove the merit of Colorado soil. For yourself, it must be a little discouraging to you this year but I am in hopes you will have better success next year, and it may be you can have a chance at some chickens and turkeys and the like. I should think you would miss those things. You had such an abundance of every thing in Cedar Cty [county]. Do you hear from the friend you left there, often? How does that intimate friend (gentleman friend) thrive this summer? I believe his name is Mr. Reeder is it not?[62] I saw so many strangers and heard so many new names while I was out there [Tipton], that my memory may not serve me correctly, but I shall trust to you to correct me if I make any alarming mistakes, as I presume your memory is fresh on subjects pertaining to things around home. Don't you often wish to see the old home[?] Now maybe I ought not to write this for fear I cause you to be homesick, but if you must see it again you can stop when you come out next spring. You have not tried your new home long enough to say whether you regret moving or not. I hope you will [not] be disappointed in your anticipations of a home in the west.

I am glad your health remains good and hope it will continue so for your own comfort. My health is quite good, although not so much so as last spring. I will try and remember what you said about over exertions.

Our Camp Meeting at Camanche [south of Clinton on the Mississippi River] commences Tuesday. We have secured a place for a tent although it is not built yet. I expect to attend some of the time. We cannot all leave at once, and I shall take my turn remaining at home.

Also the Teachers Institute for this County is held at DeWitt, the first week of September and Conference is held at Clinton, the 28th of the same month.

Sister Lucy did not come home, as we anticipated, but she intends coming some time this winter. She had our melodeon with her, but sent it home and Sister Lydia is playing now. This is [the] one that is married and living near us on the farm. I have not been to visit Sister Mary, my oldest sister living near Maquoketa. I want to visit them, if I can find time before school commences, unless I live with [them] this winter and teach the school in their district. I am in hopes to write you next time just where I shall be and what I shall do. I hardly know now myself what I [am] going to do. I want to take my younger sister, Sylvania with me this winter and get her away from the society she finds in this school. We are anxious to get her where she will see what good society is.

I think if every thing grew like those watermelons you spoke [of], you will have a crop next year.

I am glad to learn the Methodists think of organizing a S.S. It is pleasant to attend S.S. It would be *very* pleasant if P. Philipps should take up his abode in Greeley. We would have the privilege of hearing him sing frequently perhaps.

You wished to know if I thought the size house for us that you mentioned would do. I think so, if you do. I guess we will have room enough unless we should get to quarreling and each one have to live in his or her part, then I don't know hardly how we would manage. The idea of building a shed is a very good one indeed. It will keep a great deal of heat out of the house in the summer, and as the [I]rishman said "what keeps out the heat keeps out the cold.["] I suppose your folks are all well. You must give them my *very best respects*, for I send them. Our folks join in wishing you much success.

Yours most truly,
Martha A. Bennett

[Greeley]
August 20, 1871
Dear Friend Martha,
I received your excellent letter on Thursday evening while setting in Mary's house [Mary Carpenter, Peter's widow]. Frank Scott, our cousin, and I had gone up on Tuesday expecting to stack some hay for one sixth as our pay. But they, having broken their mower, failed to give us work. But as Peter and Frank had put out enough of oats together of nine acres, which was reasonably good we found employment at putting it into the stack.

I was glad you left Brushvill with so kind feelings to follow you and hope like success may be your lot in the future, for we know that not many do leave their school with the good will of all. A good proof that you are gentle as well as genteel. As we still receive the Davenport *Gazette* every week, I notice in last week's issue of the Teachers' institute to be held at DeWitt and knew that conference was to be held at Clinton. Am in hopes you may enjoy yourself at these meetings as well as at camp meetings you mention. How far is it from your home to that place last mentioned? Mary is being left to care for her family alone. [She] misses her husband's aid but the neighbors still continue their kindness to her. Her knowing that Peter might leave at any time does not seem the same as though he had been taken away without any forewarning. She has a Homestead claim of one hundred and sixty acres of land, besides one hundred and twenty acres as a Preemption claim[63] that she hopes to be able to hold, so that when her boys get large enough to work, they may have enough land. I occasionally hear from [Tipton] by way of letters from my special friends Alfred Reeder and Delphus Howard. They were well not long since. Delphus wants to commence going to school at Iowa City on the 14th of September. You remember names well. No, I never will forget those two young men, but ever will remember them with the warmest feelings, and would divide the last potatoe with them if necessary. There are a number of people back there that I would be glad to see at any time. You are very thoughtful of my feelings when you may think that to speak of these things might make me homesick. If I live to get back there next spring, I hope to make a short stay near Bethel, and maybe you will make it suit to go with me. That can be fixed at any time. I did *not* think you long in telling when you thought we might get married, and want you to feel at liberty to make any arrangements you may think best at any time. I had not thought of your saving money to use when we unite in the important ties of married life. My thoughts were just these: having found one that I loved, I did not think it a matter of question as to what property you might have. However limited may be my means, my feelings are that you own just as much as myself. Our interests being one, I want you to consider that you have a home out here if we like it out here. It may be that even I might like this country, yet you might not. If so, we might go back into Iowa if enough means should be left (after the fire) to put down a stake.[64]

The workmen are building the house. Many have taken a fancy to our home site, and Mr. Shadak [Shattuck], who is now talking to father, wishes he had so nice a place to live so near town on a farm. I think your friend the superintendent will find that you have some other place to live besides Brushville next spring. It is best to put out the spring crops quite early, if possable. But you make your own conclusions, and I think it will suit me. I believe so. Our house is large enough for us, and if we might quarrel, I'll try the cellar until peace is made. I guess we'll fix that matter. The shed will [be] or is ten feet wide instead of eight, as I wrote before. There will be room, I think, for our relations and friends to visit us, at least by putting them in the garrett when they want to sleep. Mr. Adams, the Methodist minister, preached at half past seven o'clock, this being half past three P.M. and hopes to preach every Sunday here. We had an interesting time on Tuesday evening in the Tabernacle by having the presence of some prominent eastern Agriculturalists and Horticulturalists. Mention is made of it in the paper last sent you. It was my intention, if I did not, to have expressed my thanks to you for that beautiful picture sent not long since. So natural that I often take a look at it when upstairs. Our crop of melons is just about good enough to be nice; better ones than at first. The people are some better than not long since in regard to health. There is now considerable fire in the mountains caused by first getting into the thick bed of leaves, but destroying the prime timber to a great extent. If the people here were deprived of this timber, there would be destitution. The crops that received watter enough this summer have proved a success. Hopes are entertained that by next year, we will have the ditches and dykes prepared for carrying for the crops. I worked eight days for Boyds, and they would [have] liked [it] if I could [have] done their stacking for them. But I must close. Write soon. Sincerely, yours as ever, Roy Carpenter. Greeley, Box two hundred and sixty-three.

Greeley

September 10th 1871

My dearest friend,

Your gladly received letter of the 3rd inst. was received yesterday evening by five [?] but came on Wednesday P.M. as I was up the river stacking hay for Mr. Strouce [Strauss],[65] did not come until Saturday P.M. I noticed in the Davenport *Gazette* since your other letter, that one dark night not long since as six persons living in the country were leaving or going home from Dewitt, their wagon ran into a ditch and upset, all of them being seriously injured, and I felt anxious to hear from you, fearing by chance that either you or your folks might be among the injured party. It is bad for anyone to be hurt, but am glad none of you were of the number. We are well excepting Silas who was taken sick a little more than two weeks ago with the mountain fever, but since of the typhoid fever, being for a few days quite ill, but is now improving.[66] The mountain fever is not regarded as being dangerous unless other forms succeed from it. There are as yet many cases of the former disease now in town so that Uncle James (Dr. Scott) is kept busily engaged at his profession waiting on the sick. Mattie's health is common like (if I may use the expression). Good enough to help eat the wattermelons. As we had a rain night before last, since then it is colder than before and is not a good time to eat melons. However, our turnips are getting large enough to eat, so that we are going for them. There will be a fair at Denver commencing on the 19th and continuing until the 23rd of September. I would like to go if time and money are not too scarce. Frank [Scott] and I have been batching it and sleeping out of doors while stacking the

hay and had good times at it until Friday night when we were favored in
having our awning to get heavier until in the morning it got too much
to be borne when with having wet heads [and] damp sides got out from
under the ruins [?] feeling a little dull but no cold [and] not unwell feelings have yet followed. I haven't had any cold since we came to Colorado.
The fire in the mountains has done thousands of dollars injury but is
now mostly stopped. Knowing your distance from town and being busy
in your work I am not surprised at your not alwa[y]s writing so soon
as otherwise you might. I would be glad [to] get letters often from you
but suit your own convenience *always*. I am in hopes your selection of a
school may prove a good one. You made a close guess when you made
a reply to your superintendent's question about not getting married. I
had supposed that where I first found you was your first term of teaching school. Where was your first terms teaching, there or away from
home?[67] But I guess Mr. Willard will have to give up his Martha to try
pioneering in the West before long, but am glad she has been so faithful
a "school marm" for two years.

So, your mother says she can't let me have that Martha of hers.
Well! That's bad, indeed. I don't know how to think of that for certain it is no other mother can replace to me one that I prize so highly.
Maybe I had better write to your mother about that matter. Or, I am
somewhat a believer in the old saying that "whatever is worth having is
worth asking for." If such is to be the case, what about our new house
on the hill that is built, painted on [the] outside with white lead and
primed inside (painted one coat), the lathing done and is now ready
for plastering, and a little finishing inside afterwards will find it a finished house. But maybe if I am a good child, it may yet be all right.
And it might be your father has something to say on the subject. You
might get his consent and then perhaps both will agree to let you come
out west, for a while at least until we move back to Iowa. Boys used to
work seven years for the parents of a daughter before they could make
their claim good.[68] If that is to be my fate, our house will have to stand

idle a while. Maybe you can fix that matter all right before I go back to your house. Father has some notion of building themselves a house yet this fall just where we would have had ours had we not have made the last purchase [of 80 acres], which will, if so, be one fourth of a mile west of us. Handy won't it be? Your brother-in-law was very kind in making his offer to you of tying the knot if we wished him to.[69] It would be a great advantage, as by so doing it would all be in the family and he might trust us for his pay until we could next year raise some potatoes to sell to pay him with. However, I'll leave you to make that choice. If you would prefer next April on your birthday, if a good day in the week, perhaps it would be as well. You had better thank Harry [Green] for his kind offer. Does the tale in the Greeley paper named "Rosa Robbins" interest you and if so I can forward to you each week a coppy.[70] I don't think much of it. Please write soon. God['s] will to all. Yours in truth as ever,

Roy Carpenter, Box 273.

Monday morning [Greeley]
September 25th 1871
Dearest friend Martha,

Your gladly received letter came on Saturday evening last. It affords me much pleasure to know that you are all well and that you enjoyed your short visit to Rock Island, also your teacher's institute. Father and Sarah are sick [and] quite unwell but are in hopes that theirs may not be so severe as Silas's was. He is getting better every day and is doing some chores. There yet is much sickness in town, mostly of the mountain fever, mostly caused by imperfect ditches to carry the water through town. You need not fear these ditches as being bad to cross over or drive by the side of, as they are not so wide or deep as those that are torn out by rain showers, and are not so crooked.

Fig. 14. The Greeley house Leroy built for himself and Martha, 1871. *CSU Water Archives 09f043.*

No names are given in that *Gazette* as to whom they were, only that they lived in the country.[71]

I did not go to the fair to Denver as we had not finished stacking our hay until Thursday. As to it's being a favorite business of mine, I do it as a part of farming duties, although not playing. The work is pleasant enough when the hay is dry and the weather fine. We stacked about sixty tons. Mr. Strause said that he guessed he'd have to try and get me to do his stacking next year. The price of hay being so high here, it becomes an object to work on the share [to be paid in hay] if possable. And as the roads are so good, it is not so difficult to haul it home.

Our house is now plastered with a little or *some* plastering. I should say white washing. Will be ready to move into. As matters are, we do not expect to build a[nother] house this year, and as *our* house would be empty over winter, we expect to move into it as soon as the finishing can be done. Where we are [now] living is not a good house for winter and [we] are in hopes by going on the hill the family will enjoy better health.[72] But they will go out any time that you and I need the house, so that they will not be in our way. Maybe by so doing, the house will get used to people living in it by the time that we will have the control of it. However, if you and I had needed it, the other house would have been built.

We have been getting some breaking [of sod] done for next year's crop.

Time with me is going away very rapidly. How does it seem to you? I am in hopes that you may enjoy yourself this winter and that your Quaker School may be one that my dearest friend may enjoy to the fullest extent.[73] I don't yet know what I will do this winter. If we are well I may go into the mountains some. Just before leaving [Iowa], friend Reeder suggested my going back there and once more teaching a school in (Old Cedar) this winter, but it is quite uncertain about that as I am much too far away to board at home.

It may be that you sometimes think I contradict myself a little in still speaking of Iowa as my favorite state and yet give (or try to) some of the advantages of Colorado and its climate. My intention is this: I want you to see this country and give the soil a fair trial and then, "as two heads are better than one," we may be better prepared to judge of the merits of this country. We may be prepared to have a permanent home some place on this little earth. I think it is best to stay long enough to fully decide that matter before moving. I am not a believer in this matter of moving around so often from place to place, but having found a *good* home to stay where it may be for our life time.

I do not intend to flatter[74] you when I say that I never had found one that I regarded an equal to you, as one I could love and appreciate until I became acquainted with Miss Bennett. While I know that it is a common saying that opposites should marry, yet I could not love a girl of secession principles, believed in Mormon doctrine, or taught a Catholic school in preffrence to a Protestant one.[75] That would be consistent with the old saying, would it not?

The Baptists had their new church dedicated on last Sunday a week. Dr. Evarts from Chicago conducted the exercises. The people came out largely. I was up to Strauses that day. The church is nicely finished off and makes one feel more at home. There were services yesterday and in the evening as they expect to have in the future each Sabbath. Mr. Brown their preacher intends leaving this week as his people are not entirely satisfied with him. I think he is a good man. He preached a good sermon last evening from the twelfth verse of the fourth chapter of Acts. The Congregationalists expect James Beecher this week, a brother to Henry Ward Beecher,[76] hoping to have their church well represented here, he being their pastor. The new Methodist church is being built rappidly. A new brick school house has been commenced which will be a nice building when finished.[77] Oh, yes, I had those windows to our house as you spoke of, so that they can be either shoved up or let down from the top as you may desire. I am in hopes that you will like our home. I must close. My love to all inquiring friends. With much love to you, I would remain as ever yours. Write soon.

L. S. Carpenter

Monday [De Witt]
Oct 2nd 1871
Dearest friend Leroy,
I was very glad to receive a letter from you Friday evening. Somehow they seem to do me so much good, and I often wish I could *hear* the words expressed. When I received yours I was busy superintending the housekeeping and waiting upon Mother who is sick. She had been feeling poorly week before last but Tuesday she was obliged to take [to] her bed and is still obliged to keep it. The cause of her sickness is inflammation of the bowels. The physician thought Friday that she could get along without any trouble but Saturday night we thought it best to send for the doctor about midnight. He came and staied untill Sunday morning between eight and nine and having gone away Friday, thinks that

she would improve. Left double care upon me, and I have had so little opportunity to be alone to write to you that I have left it untill the present time. We are quite well except mother.

You wrote that your father and Sarah [Leroy's half sister] were sick. I am in hopes they will not have a long siege of sickness. Has your father's health generally been good this past season[?] I am hopeful that Silas will improve untill he gains his usual amount of health, and am glad to hear that you and Mattie have escaped the mountain fever thus far. There is a great deal of sickness in this vicinity mostly colds and fever. I have been suffering with a cold of late and on account of losing some of my usual rest by being up with mother I do not feel so well as I should otherwise. I suppose your health is as good as ever. I have been fearing every letter I should hear that you were sick or something had happened to you but I have been favored with better news so far since you emigrated.

I should not certainly [fear] those numerous ditches if I could have the company of some Carpenters to keep me from falling into them. I think that would be an excellent place for drunkards. They would roll over so nicely into the ditches, and, get a wetting. And I think t'would waken their drowsy powers a little. I am glad you have so much [work] for if our house should get blown away or burned, we could make a house of hay.[78] How would that do? And if you should have a quantity to take care of next year and should need some assistance, I might assist you a little as I have had some experience in that business with father. You may think the matter over candidly and if I can manage housekeeping adroitly enough by that time to find any spare moments, all well and good, if we are both spared untill that time. I am glad our house is so nearly finished and of course am perfectly willing it should be occupied any time you think best by your family. I am in [hopes] you will all enjoy it as much as I anticipate doing so, and I am in [hopes] the house will become so accustomed to people living in it that it will feel no inconvenience thereby. Oh you can hardly guess how I have been laying plans, when we should enjoy *our* home together. I hope that I may live in such a way that there never may be a regret expressed or unexpressed that we ever met. I hear of cases sometimes where the happiness of home circles [is] destroyed by a coldness of heart, and a great many like things, and it is my inward prayer that by the grace of God, *I* may be enabled to be a comfort instead of an annoyance to any companion and others.[79]

Your views respecting a selection of a house are exactly in accordance with mine. I had thought that I should like to see the country, and that we had better give the soil a fair trial. And then if we could do better other places we could go there. I did not think it strange that you wrote of Iowa as being your favorite state and yet set forth the advantages of Colorado, but thought that you knew the merits of Iowa and liked this country, but that you had gone to the west thinking you could do better. And while trying the climate, soil, etc., you discovered advantages of that [region] it were well to mention for the encouragement of others upon the supposition that the country proved what or as you anticipated. I should like to be with you some, if it were not too cold this winter when you are in the mountains to enjoy the beautiful scenery there is there.

I presume the thought of coming back to Iowa to spend the winter among your acquaintances would be quite pleasant to you especially if you could board at home, as you expressed in your letter. I suppose you hear from your friends often or enough to keep yourself posted about matters around your former home. I often think how pleasantly you were situated and what a beautiful home you used to enjoy.

It is pleasant to have comfortable buildings and churches and School houses built near us for our accommodation and comfort. The Baptists are a little ahead of the Methodists in building their church.

I was disappointed in expecting to attend Conference at Clinton on account of mother being taken sick, although I did not desire to go after I saw she needed my care and she told me to write to you. She was glad you had some one in our house so you would not take her nurse away.

Of course you understand that she is rather jovial like myself and only means half of what she says sometimes.

I will not consider it flattery, that you expressed in your last, but the sincere sentiments of a noble and kind heart. And I hope that I may be enabled to return that love so completely that you may never feel any way but what I have a true love for you, as I trust I have, if I know my own mind upon the subject. I never thought much about the subject of persons of opposite views and dispositions being married, but always thought that when I found an honest upright man, or in other words one that suited me, I would accept him as my companion. Such I trust has been the case, and I hope I may prove worthy [of] the love of Leroy Carpenter.

You expressed the hope that I would be pleased with our home. I am inclined to think I should be very hard to suit, if [it] were not from your description, and I am very much obliged to you for fixing the window sashes as you have. You are very considerate of my wishes. I have thought often that I should like to go by the way of Aunt Martha Colemans [Oskaloosa, Iowa] when we take our trip West. What say you? I would like to see her very much. Can you tell me about how long you could remain here after you come or do you not know untill the exact time of our marriage is decided upon[?] The reason I ask is that I can arrange my time in the best manner, as I should like it if we could visit our relatives here: my older sister [Mary Green], an uncle and aunt living at Andrew north of Maquoketa and sister Lydia [Lydia Fox] near home if it would be agreeable to you. It would be a source of pleasure to them. I presume sister Lucy will be at home at the time. She likes the idea of going west very much and is very anxious to see you.

Uncle Coleman attends Conference this year. Father said he spoke very feelingly of Howard's death and made the remark to the ministers that now his sons were grown they would have to bear the burden themselves. He has outlived the most of the family. How old is he, Leroy[?] I should have liked to have seen him. How is your Mother's health now?

Give my love to all and I shall look for a letter soon
Yours as ever,
Martha A. Bennett

Home again [Greeley]
Oct. 14, 1871
My dear Martha,

I received your interesting letter on Wednesday, this being Saturday. Sarah is improving slowly and the rest of us are doing common like. As I failed to answer your question in the letter before the last one, in respect to whether we had or not had rats out here, I will answer that before going further. As yet there are but few if any, at least I have not yet seen any, but most likely they will come as the people become more intelligent, for they seem to be fond of associating with enlightened people.[80] The country has no lack of having enough of that animal that carries with itself such a weight of (not influence), but odor so common back there that bears some resemblance to the oat kurd. There are some mice running over the country keeping company with the Antelope, I suppose. There are about as many rattle snakes as in the prairies of Iowa and of the same kind which disappear as the country gets improved, also other snakes like those we left that are less poisonous. In the summer these may be seen in little towns as they are called out here, the Prairie dog, which as you approach them stand on their mounds and bark at you. Where this house now stands we saw some last summer. But as the country is settled up, they move out, leaving only their long and deep paths through the earth, being not the most favorable to our irrigating process.

We have been having a snow storm which has made it a little cold. That was on Thursday. How was the weather back there at that time?

We have been moving into *our* new house this week, expecting to finish this week. Bringing Sarah over in the wagon seemed to improve her a little.

On Monday last there came by telegraph the sad news that "Chicago was in ruins" and since read the facts which prove fearful in the extreme.[81] When coming home from Ohio, while in that place, standing on the cupola of their court house, I could see a vast sea of buildings below in all directions. And to think so large a portion is now a complete ruins is a sorrowful thought. Many that last week were rich are now poor, that were enjoying good health are now scorched badly or burned to death.

In speaking about going to the mountains this winter, if I should go up there, how I would like to have you along if we could keep from freezing, as they say it's colder there than down here. But if you were along, I think you would have to waken me in the morning as I enjoy staying in bed on cold mornings. Sometimes when I would have to get up early on a cold morning, I felt as if I would rather lay still than to get out on the cold floor.

As to just how long I expect to stay when back there, I do not now just know. We will of course want to call on our relatives before leaving, and I hope may be able to call on our Uncle and Aunt Coleman on our way out here. I am in hopes if the spring favors it to put out our crop or most of it before going back there. If so, we might be at greater liberty to choose our length of staying there. Make the length of your term to suit yourself. As to when we get married, I want you to make the choice, and who we shall employ to tie the knot. And when you have decided as to what kind of a suit you wish to dress in, as I may be to some extent governed by your choice, please mention in a few words your choice. Most, if not all, of this might be found out to be soon enough at any time this winter. Also in regard to whether but few will be invited to our union.

In speaking in your last [letter] about the windows being fixed so that they can be lowered as desired, Mattie allowed that it was not an original thought of mine to have them thus made.

We had our quarterly meeting last Sunday. Mr. Vincent, a brother to F. H. Vincent, author of several Sunday School books, is presiding elder of this district. He is a good speaker.

A sad accident occurred on last Thursday. A man by the name of Robert Wright, while in company with his brother-in-law, was shot in the upper part of the head, resulting in his death in a few minutes. While as you say you have been fearing to learn of some accident or sickness happening to me, I have been in rather similar fears as each letter came to hand. But so far, we have both been blessed to the contrary. I received a letter from [Alfred] Reeder last week. They have been having some sickness in their family. Friend [Delphus] Howard has also been having the fever. Out of perhaps one a hundred that have the mountain fever [in Greeley], no grown persons have yet died. That is better than [it] would be back east. As there is sun on the mountains, the sight is sublime. I am in hopes that you are all well. My love to you all. I would be glad to get a letter from you every week if you could write. From one that loves you.

L. S. Carpenter

Greeley
October 27, 1871
Dearest Friend Martha,

Your welcomed letter has been received. I am in hopes that you are all well by this time. Father is reasonably well. Mother is well, Sarah is nearly recovered. Silas is recovered from his sickness. Aggie enjoys good health. But sister Mattie is taking the fever we think in the regular way, namely by having the headache with fever once a day. But we are in hopes that by taking timely notice, the fever may be somewhat checked in its way. Uncle James Scott [the doctor] was up here this P.M. As for myself, I am well, but while I am well, a spell of neuralgia in my upper jaw on the left side deprived me of near two nights' sleep last week. But how handy it is to have a good mother, for she applied some hopps to my jaw and took the pain away.[82] If you have never had this pain, I am in hopes that you may never have it, for it takes right hold of the nerves and pulls like everything.

Sometimes I fail of answering your questions, the reasons being when I set down to write, I have to set down with the family coming into the room asking me questions, talking and barking around. And a few minutes since, Arthur Clark, a young man whoose folks live near where we lived while in town, while on his way from his claim northeast from here about a mile, stopped in a few minutes. He is a good young man, I believe. It is now after nine P.M. and we all like to stay up a while as the moon is sending down its gentle rays of light. So, if I fail to always answer your questions, please excuse my blunders as they are not intentional.

There have [been] a few died lately in town. Those that have the fever now have it more severely than sometime since.

As to whether I will go to the mountains this winter, I do not yet know. If Frank [Scott] and I go up there, it would be for the purpose of getting out pine poles that are made into fence. They make a good fence when used with pitch pine posts. The matter was proposed by Frank while we were stacking hay this fall, and of course we would keep Bachelors hall if we should go there. I think it's doubtful about my going there, at least very long as it is so far. I will let you know before hand if I do.

You ask if there are many singing teachers in Greeley. It is just this way. Most of the families who have children are to be classed among those having limited means and need to economize their money well. And those wishing to give their children that branch of learning are met by quite a number of that class of teachers, so that the market is well supplied in that line. Further, among the first that came here, a large portion were intelligent people taking the first opportunity to introduce themselves as being successful teachers in "the east." A Miss Ranney, a rich man's daughter of this place, while Mattie was in the yard, wanted to know if we or she could have any pupils from our house, and I suppose she thought that an introduction, needless to say, for she did so by saying that she was a successful teacher where they came from in York state. That's yankee forwardness that I don't admire, do you? So you see these people have really got the grind [?] against any newcomer, although they [the newcomers] may be more worthy.

You need not think anything about your letters' composition, for they are splendid, containing a regular amount of interesting news, and I will gladly excuse anything to the contrary. It is about one and a fourth miles from here over to the M. E. Church, and plainly in view, as our house is perhaps more than twenty feet higher than the town is. From here, the town is plainly visible, the river running a little this side of half way, with the Island Grove Park nearly between here and town in the river about half way. There is where the celebrations are held, and with a good spy glass, you could, I think, make plain distinction of people, unless the leaves are to thick in summer. I can now look into the Grove while there are but few leaves. To tell the truth, you and I have the nicest farm to live on when we get it fixed that is to be found in Greeley Colony. And if the crops prove good, I believe that we will feel at home. Several have told us that we had the nicest sight that they had seen around here. About a mile and a quarter north from here is ditch Number 2, marked I believe, marked on the map where we intend to get our supply of watter for irrigating. This house stands near the south line of the eighty acres. It is expected that there will be a new railroad running between here and town, branching off from the Union Pacific RR on the north some distance east of Cheyenne and going southwest crossing the present RR and go into the mountains to be a narrow gauge road.[83] The surveying is just finished. I am in hopes that it will prove true.

Building is going well enough in town. The people hoping for better times. We the M. E. Church haven't yet started our new school as the colony gave as a present $500 to the first Protestant church that should be built in town. The Baptists got the start of others and received the promised aid. That's why they beat us. Ours will be larger when finished, which is going on. Truely yours,

Roy Carpenter

At home [De Witt]

Sat. evening [November] 4, 1871

Dear Roy,

Yours was received Wednesday evening and duly read and considered. Mother is improving slowly, but cannot do much about the house yet. I took her yesterday to visit a friend near town, and when we come from church tomorrow we intend bringing her home with us. The rest of us are well except myself. My eyes are sore again and it is with considerable difficulty that I write. I presume that if Mother was at home she would tell me I must not write tonight, but I cannot get any time in the day time. And it is so long since I received yours that I must answer or you will think I have forgotten you of late, consequently, you will know how to appreciate any mistakes I may make.

I am in hopes Mattie has not taken the fever yet and am glad to hear that the remainder of you are doing so well.

I have not had any experience with neuralgia and cannot sympathize with [you] as well as I could if I had had some experience with the affliction. [But] I presume I can sympathize [with] you as you can with me for I believe you never are troubled with sore eyes. I have never had toothache nor headache enough to know of any thing about the suffering there must be reduced, and I suppose neuralgia is very much worse [than] either of them.

I had a little bump the other day that caused a little pain. I started to run or skip from the front room into the kitchen and never thought of the door being so low and so happened I jumped right up against the frame of the door rather careless, but "Bridget" was in a hurry and forgot. And I struck upon the top of my head and felt very strange for a few moments. But Lydia brought some cold water and bathed my head and I soon was all right again, except an elevation on the top of my cranium. If you remember the door frame is very low not more than an inch higher than I am.

You wrote of appreciating a good mother's care in time of sickness. I presume we shall never be able to appreciate fully our mother's care untill we are deprived of it.

Your situation and mine are similar in regard to writing for I endeavor to take the place of mother and you know the children can ask unthought of questions about unhandy things. I talk to them and write and then stop and (give orders) as Sylvania says and then write a word or two and so forth. Therefore, I can pity you just right and I will excuse you if you don't answer all my questions for I guess you will have enough to do if you do that always.

Your Yankee teacher was rather forward indeed, I suppose, if she thought she would inform you who she *was*.

I am glad to hear such a glowing account of our home which shows the taste of one who selected the situation. According to your description, it *must* be *beautiful* in the summer or more so than at this time of year. We shall not have much farther to go to church than we did do here. It is a mile to the school house.

If the new railroad goes through, it will be very convenient to get to and from the mountains. I should think there could be considerable money made by the owners of said road, as I presume there will be considerable travel in the summer and fall by persons who wish to visit the mountains. How pleasant it must be to take such trips and to tent out on the mountains of the Rockies. I do not remember whether you write of visiting the mountains or not.

$500 would assist considerably in building a church and it would seem well if every denomination would have as much aid from the public. I presume there is a Sabbath School at the Baptist Church, is there not[?] I have not attended S.S. for three months and it seems as I could hardly wait untill I have another opportunity.

I do not begin school until the 13th. There is preaching at the Low Moor every Sabbath and I presume there will be S.S. at least I hope so.[84] My boarding place is but a mile from Low Moor and I hope to have the opportunity of attending the means of Grace often. I am to board with Mr. Hinman, a Quaker and a very fine man indeed. The family are very pleasant. Sylvania is going with me and will attend school. I expect to take the melodeon and if an opportunity presents itself, anticipate taking music lessons. If not, shall learn all I can myself. I presume Mattie enjoys the use of her instrument very much if she enjoys hers as much as I do ours. According to the advantages we have had it must be a great pleasure to her. Did Mattie receive a letter from me since she wrote? The reason I ask, I did not know but there had been some accident that interfered with her receiving it, as I cannot always mail my letters myself. Do you ever wish the cars [trains] would run faster than they do? I do.

Now I am not going to allow you the privilege of reading two full sheets from my pen, as my eyes seem very thick indeed, but will try and do better next time my eyes permit.

My love to all, write just as soon as possible and direct to Low Moor if you please.

Yours, M.A. Bennett

Sylvania guesses I am writing a love letter, it is so long, she says.

M.B.

Union Colony, Colorado

Nov. 10th '71

Deares[t] friend Martha,

I had this evening the pleasure of receiving one of those ever welcomed letters that always comes from your hand. It was my hope that such would be the case as I was expecting it to come soon. Mattie is improving slowly from her mountain fever. Last week was the severest time of her sickness. As she is not naturally fleshy, this fever makes her quite thin. The rest of us are well. Sarah and Silas are thriving finely on plain victuals. Mattie received your kind letter that has not been answered. But she would be glad to do so if it was within her power. I really appreciate your letters, especially when I know they are written under such unfavorable circumstances.

I once had weak eyes which were soon made good by using Poor Richard's eye water.[85] I am in hopes you will soon enjoy good sight. A few years ago I noticed in a newspaper a suggestion a little like this: Especially when reading, if facing the light, try to have a shade to screen the direct light from the eyes. Also setting so as to have the light pass over the left shoulder. Late studying is hard on one's sight.

In speaking of your bumping your head, I sympathise with you. A few days before Mattie took sick, one evening about dusk when we wanted to unload some potatoes into the cellar, father sent her in a hurry upstairs to get the half bushel measure. She, forgetting that near the head of the stairs is a frame on which setts the patent-chimney, bumped her head hard against one corner, making her head ache and it being the cause of a bump. Poor girl suffered much for a little while. Since then, that corner has been sawed off some, and when you get here, there can be a cushion put there if you think there would be any danger of your hurting your head. We will show you when here so that you can take your choice. But if a person only learns that in a certain place there is something to be shunned, it becomes as natural to avoid it as a miller goes around the holes in the floor of his mill.

I am in hopes you will have a pleasant time in your school this winter, and since you are going to board with a Quaker, no doubt there will be harmony in the camp. But remember, thee must not study to hard for thy learning is already good.

It will be nice to have your melodeon so handy and how I should like to hear you sing and play some. Of course, it would afford me the greatest pleasure to have you improve, but don't take your health to acquire a little knowledge.

Not long since you asked me how old Uncle Coleman is. His age, I believe, is about seventy-two or three and may be a little more. Maybe he stopped with you folks while at conference. You also mention about our leaving our parents who have taken care of and given us continual care and instruction. When we get to keeping a home of our own, of course, it would be handy to have father and mother to give us instruction. Since I have been e[n]gaged, the thought has often [come to me] I would need father's experience in management. But I'll risk the knowledge of Miss Bennett every time and if mother should happen to think that Roy might have got one that knew more about house keeping, I can assure her that I think a great deal of my Iowa wife, and what we lack in knowledge can be made up in practice. No, she will not get tired of your asking many questions.

I have often wondered why it is that so many young people get married just for the sake it may be, to be known as being Mr. and Mrs. When once entering upon that part of life, I believe that real earnest thought and duties are at hand that before were unknown. For then, our parents cared for us; now we will have to care for ourselves. Yet to once have a home of our own, with a feeling that each other is loved on the part of both, that certainly must be happiness. As I have, I think, said before, that I may sometimes repeat in one letter w[h]at was written in another, if so just pass over that repeated.

Alf Reeder not long since wanted to know if I wanted to teach school this winter or not; if so, he would have liked to have known before long in order to secure me a school. It was very kind in him to care for my welfare. As we are so far from there, I could not board at home very well, and by staying here I can see how we like a Colorado winter. We will try and find something to do most of the time if it is not too cold outdoors. I haven't yet been in the mountains but would like to try a trip there at any time it would suit.

The Baptists have their own Sunday School. But we don't attend. There is a Union S. S. that meets in Colony Hall at half past two. Because I did not go very regular, Mrs. Heath wanted to know of me a week ago last Sunday after Baptist preaching what class I belonged to. I had been in Mr. Heath's class a few times but didn't care much for the school and only went occasionally, but to please her I went that day again. Heaths, or himself, is a Congregational preacher and acted as such about twelve years ago in Tipton. He now owns a farm that he wants to sell near Maquoketa (don't criticize this spelling). Well, I'd rather attend a Methodist S.S. Our preacher wants to preach here every Sunday if possible.

Since *our* house is finished, people seeing it from town of course want to know who lives here, so more people know father now than he knows. The other day a man said to him, "So, you are going to live with your son this winter?" Father told him, "No! But his son was going to live with him if he behaved himself." A good joke on me, don't you think, Martha?

You need not fear of tiring me with writing long letters, as it is my greatest pleasure to get one from Miss. Bennett. Please write as soon as your eyes will permit. Your sister thought partly right about your love letter.

With much love to you and yours,

Roy S. Carpenter

Low Moor

Nov. 15th 1871

Dear Roy,

I received your interesting letter this evening, after finding myself antic-ipating a letter when I got home often through the day. Somehow, I knew not how, I felt as if I should get a letter from you.

I am very well now and my eyes are better only they feel very dry sometimes, but that is not very bad.

I am glad to hear that you are all well. Tell Mattie I was not in any very great hurry for her to answer my letter, but thought if it had been delayed, I would write another, and will be glad to hear from her any time she is able to write. I am in hopes she will survive the bump on her head for I have not thought of the bump on my head since I came here.

I have a very pleasant boarding place and as you remarked there is harmony in the camp. Mr. Hinman is a very accommodating man. It rained Monday morning, and was bad walking all day and he took us to school, and brought us home in the evening. He is a real jovial man. Mrs. Hinman is one of the quiet, kind, women you find once in a while. I brought my Album down stairs last night to show the pictures to them. He looked at them, but after he finished he said he did not see the one he was looking for, and I had laid your picture off of the Album when I brought it down (for I have it on the outside so it will be handy to look at). Then I had occasion to go up stairs again and I brought it down and asked him if that was the one. He looked at it quite a while and then said *that* looked *like* a picture that was [of a man of] some intelligence about that. And he thought that would do pretty well for a picture. Then he asked the name, but I told [him] I had not agreed to tell him that. I only wanted to see if I had a picture that suited him. He did not find much out, any more than to look at the picture. He has an idea that there is some one at Calamus that resembles your picture. He said he expected he would see some one this winter that the picture resembled. He likes to try and plague me, but is not the man to noise any abroad, so I did not fear to show him your pictures. If I show it to any one outside of the family they ask the name and of course keep a look out to see if they can discover any[thing] new, so I am generally a little careful how I exhibit and keep it to view, myself. If you will allow me to flatter your *picture* as well as yourself a little more, I will tell you what Harry said after he had looked at it about five minutes.[86] "I tell [you] Martha, there is a good deal of common sense there, pretty sound head." But then you know it does not matter much to me whether people should flatter your picture much or not as long as I am better satisfied with the original than any one I have seen yet. Although, of course, I like to have you judged well, by your looks, as they have no other way of judging you.

Mr. Heath you wrote of I have heard Harry speak of as being in the [Union] Colony, and he said he wanted to come back here as he did not like Colo. I don't know how he heard it.[87]

I suppose you will be very glad to be permitted to attend a Methodist S.S. again. I know I can appreciate the S.S. here for there is one every Sunday at half past one and preaching at half past two. I attended last Sunday, and there is quite a good S.S. Mr. Newton of Camanche is the preacher. His text was taken from Math 25, 2 "Five were wise and five were foolish." He preached a very plain sermon using the parable to a good effect and admonishing to always be ready for the coming of the Bridegroom. It was, as a little girl said, plain enough for almost any child to understand. I am very glad there is a S.S. and preaching for it is so pleasant to attend those services every Sabbath. I was invited to join the Bible Class and did so. Our lesson for next Sabbath is Math. 13, 20 to end of the Chapter. The Church is built in Gothic Style, 35x50 with a cross on the steeple, "which I do not admire." The steps are arranged so that the people can drive up and step out on the platform and drive right on back of the church and hitch their teams. There is room there to turn around and drive round the other side of the Church and the ladies can step from the platform into the wagon on that side. Mr. Hinman has a share in the Library and very kindly offered us the use of the books.

The S.S. anticipates having a Christmas Tree and all those who attend from the present time untill Christmas will receive a present. I think I shall attend, would not you? I must be conjuring up some presents pretty soon for some of my nieces and nephews. If I give any I should have to give to all for I cannot tell which I think the most of.

When I left home, Mother was not very well, but able to manage with the assistance of a girl which she expected Monday. We left Saturday afternoon. Sylvania is with me. I had four scholars Monday and eight yesterday and today I suppose I shall not have more than fifteen or sixteen at the most. So I shall not be compelled to study unless for my own advancement. I think the books I shall study most out of school will be mainly Housekeeping and Music, two very useful branches as you will observe. The former the most important, the latter certainly pleasant. I expect I can take lessons of Mr. Gilbert of Camanche. He has been giving lessons in this vicinity and I am in hopes I can take of him this winter. The Schoolhouse is very comfortable and everything that is necessary is supplied, wash pans, towel, soap and Mrs. Hinman [gave] me a piece of looking glass that I put a paper frame on and we use this to see how dirty our faces are. Handling coal is dirty work and I went to smooth my hair today and observed a beauty spot on my face from the coal. The school house is about a mile and a half south of Low Moor and my boarding place a mile south.

I have not connected my subjects very well, but the family including Mr. and Mrs. H, [their] little girl and Sylvania have been talking around me as they chose and I may have forgotten something. But please excuse all mistakes and write soon.

Yours as ever,

M.A.B.

Low Moor

Clinton, Co., Iowa

Greeley, Weld County Colorado

[November 22, 1871]

Dearest Friend Martha,

I received your welcomed letter this morning but it came yesterday; but we didn't get to the office yesterday. Mattie is improving somewhat. She can now get up some. I appreciate to the fullest extent your expressions of real friendship. And be assured that I will not deem it flattery to speak of your thoughts and so fourth. I may be a little fortunate if others beside *the one* I love think well of the person in the picture. It may be that it was fortunate that I am not possessed with personal beauty, for as the Grammar has it, "beauty often spoils the possessor of it."[88] But when there are so many in the world that are real homly, I am fortunate if I look common like, don't you think so? Allow me to tell you something. When we were living in town near Clark's, one afternoon the old lady called in and while looking at some of our pictures failed to see my girls. So that didn't suit her. She had supposed that somewhere I obtained [?] somebody. I don't know why as I had not told her so. As Mattie knew that your picture, or rather "Sweet Sixteen," was near the top of my trunk, [she] ran upstairs and brought it down and showed it to her. And she said after looking at it a while, "That picture looks like a lady that is prettyer than any I have seen in Greeley," and some other like remarks. I knew that I thought so, but of course don't always say what I think for others would think me partial. So I feel fortunate in earning the affections of one so worthy.

Friend Reeder in a recent letter wanted to know my future prospects and explained his own, and I told him in a few words my intentions or hopes. Was there any harm in that?

Delphus Howard has been having a spell of the typhoid fever at home this fall, so that he failed of getting to the University School this fall, but intends going this winter, as he is now well after seven weeks [of] sickness.

Mr. [and Mrs.] Heath were a little disappointed in one thing at least by coming out here. A strange [?] railroad man had told him while back there that if he would come out here he would give him the contract of building railroad depots along a road that has not been built. As he is a carpenter by trade, that disappointed him very much. Do you know how he was liked back there[?] We think of him as a good man, but [he] is a little jealous towards the Methodists here. His son brought a young wife out when they came out here. But she, the young wife, got homesick and got so bad in the subject that she made him go to Wisconsin where her folks are living with her. So much for marrying a giddy girl! He would have staid here if she would have consented to do so. Of course, we all feel a little natural attachment to our old house, but it sometimes becomes best for us to make a change, and I think we should let good judgment go before mere fancy. I hope you will not think me too radical in this point of feeling.

If all the inmates of good homes that of late have been ruined by fire in the union, were to take it to heart about their loss, how many insane asylums would have to be now built? There are bounds to everything, it seems. A young (not old rather) man lost his wife this fall in Greeley, and he went deranged and remained so for several days, but of late has recovered. How true the saying, "Let reason once become dethroned and it makes mad men of us all."

It affords me much pleasure to know that you are so comfortable situated as you are this winter. And in studying the subject of housekeeping, Mrs. Harriet Beecher [Stowe] has written some on that subject, a few extract[s] only that I have read.[89] And although I didn't like all she says on some subjects, yet she says some good things. I have no fears but that you will do well, so don't be too studious. It would be a nice thing if you could have some chance of music this winter, for you would enjoy so well whatever you would learn. [It is] not everybody that can take the instrument from home when she goes away, as I understand you are doing now. I hope we can afford one of our own if you want it.

This is Tuesday [November 21, 1871] at between 3 and 4 o'clock P.M. Sarah says she generally waits a few days after receiving a letter before answering it. So do I, only in getting a letter from you I want to answer it for the next mail if I can. In looking into our box, if I see a white letter, then it seems as if I were going to get a feast right there, for they are richer than gold to me. I am not joking in saying this.

One thing I want you to tell me if you will. That is, have you [had] any trouble in reading any of these letters? If so, I will take more care in writing them.

Some of our folks in Iowa and Ohio want us to leave here and go back there where there are, or is, so much fruit and corn to eat. Reeder wants me to go back there this winter so that we can enjoy ourselves together and eat of the apples that the orchard we left has grown this year, which is about 80 bushels.

Wishing you happiness, I must close but want to write soon again. Am as ever yours,

L. S. Carpenter

Greeley

December 4, 1871

Dear Martha,

I was the happy recipient of a letter from you this morning being *Monday.* Your letter came on Sunday evening. I am glad to know that you are enjoying yourself so finely. You rather escaped in not being asked whether you intended to teach next summer or not. (Now Mattie is talking about Mt. Vernon.)[90]

Yes, I am in hopes that we will so enjoy ourselves together that we will not get homesick about our Iowa homes. But we would be glad to visit our friends back there if we get along well out here. I would have been glad to have been with you on Thanksgiving day if you refer to last

Thursday. And would like to be back there about New Year's day, but cannot be there.

I have often thought of the remark you made not long since; that I wish the cars [trains] would run faster than they do, then I could hear from Low Moor sooner. And if it was not so far, I might get to see Miss Bennett oftener (is oftener a proper word[?]) Silas tries sometimes to plague me [tease?] a little as he thinks, by saying Calimus knowing that you used to be there.

When I wrote last about friend Howard, I failed to mention that he was then well and was in Rushville, Illinois studying telegraphing with his brother who is there pract[ic]ing or is an agent at that place, but intends going to the University School this winter.

I think you mistake a little when you think the Greeley ladies must be homely if you are prettyer than any of them. Because they may, some of them may, be good looking and yet you be (good) I mean better looking or beautiful. I do think that you are handsome. Don't think that I am flattering you, for I do think so. I could not change my affection to another person any more than to deprive me of my heart's dearest treasure, for I could never hope of finding another lady that so suited my ideal in the fullest extent if I ever had an ideal. One thing I know and you may know that Reeder and I used to agree on, and that is I could never marry for policy.[91] I believe that is the reason why there are so many divorces. A young man who had waited upon a lady in Greeley for some time went to work in a town near the mountains west of Denver, and while there, another fellow received her company. And not long since he received in the place of a letter a small box containing her engagement ring without even a reason why for so doing. So he stopped his work and came up to Greeley at once to look after his fair friend. But she told him that as Mr. Farwell was better off and she could have a better home, she told him that she thought that it was her right to do the best she could and gave him no further reasons. So much for an unfaithful love. I would not give three cents for the love of either a lady or a gentleman who when in good health make property the questions of marrying. I hold that personal virtues are the only true criterions [*sic*] by which we can judge of others' worth.

When I last wrote we had about two inches of snow. Of late, it has been falling at times until it is about a foot dee[p] of settled snow, and quite cool at nights. This morning the thermometer was 9 degrees below zero. As stock are dependent upon the bare range in winter as in summer, it is very hard o[n] stock and there is danger of great loss when some men run from ten to fifteen thousand head of cattle.[92] We have no cattle yet. Have only two horses and sixty chickens. We have a good stable and chicken coop that father and I made this fall. While the deep snow is bad on stock, it is a good time to hunt antelope and jack rabbits as they can't run well. The people get plenty of this game now. The driving storms from the east have drove [so many] antelope from the east, that they are plenty here. Sarah counted 125 in one drove one morning last week and at the same time there was a drove of about 300 in another drove near ditch No. 2. Last Saturday a neighbor, young Englishman, and myself got on our horses and chased until we got three antelope. These are nice to eat. Jack rabbits are about twice as large as those in Iowa and are good to eat. There are a few prairie chickens. By going into [the mountains] a person might get some deer and elk, bear, wolves, and a few mountain lions for a change.

With the exception of a little cold, we are well. Silas and Sarah are thriving finely and will be in good order for the spring market if they don't eat too much beef and potatoes.[93] We use coal entirely for fuel except kindling and had a little bother to learn how to use it. Did you have any trouble to use it in your school room? We don't like it as well as wood but don't take as much work to procure it.[94] We get it for $7 a ton.

I should not think it very far from your school to your home near Dewitt. You may notice some mention of the Greeley Lyceum in the *Tribune.* The members are mostly of the older men but give a good entertainment every Thursday evening. There has of late been a Literary Society formed mostly composed of young men which meets on Friday evenings. By giving 50 cents, I became a member of the last mentioned as that is the initiation fee.[95] We are in hopes of having a good time this winter. I have no trouble at all in reading your welcomed letters. Uncle Coleman [Oskaloosa, Iowa] does not preach to the darkies this year. They enjoy good health and would be glad to have us live near them if possable. As yet there are not many fruit trees in or around Greeley, but the people next spring intend to set out quite extensively, and ourselves $40 worth of . . . fruit trees. We have enough potatoes, turnips, some cabbage, onions, beets, beans and the last watter melon was fed to the chickens the other day. The snow when melted we think will be a benefit to us farmers next spring. We are sometimes a little troubled with a mouse or two. But if they trouble you, we will have to use Dr. Bennett's sure death to vermin. The Methodists haven't yet organized a Sunday School as the Union S.S. meets each Sunday at 2½ P.M. in the Baptists' [church], the Methodists on the 24th of December, if they can, the same day as the new one in Tipton. I must close for this time. I have had the fortune so far of myself of mailing the letters to you in the post office. Write soon. I am yours,

    L.S.C.

Greeley
December 26, 1871
Dear Martha,

It no doubt will seem strange to you at first to receive two letters so near the same time, but when I give my reasons, maybe not quite so strange. In the first place, in my last I failed to answer all your questions, the reason being that I had only read your letter once and that just before writing. Lately, as the weather is cold with so much snow on the ground, without having any sled to use the snow with, we are quite at leisure, and odly I like to talk to you.

No doubt you enjoyed yourself on your visiting at Calamus and on yesterday it being Christmas. You spoke not long since as to whether I expected to make many presents on this or yesterday. I didn't make any presents for the reason that none seemed to be needed. It has never been with us as with others a practice to make any big fuss in these special days, but if we felt like it [we] would have a gathering on any day (excepting Sundays). At the same time, I like to see folks enjoying themselves finely.

You need not fear that *all* the antelope will leave before you get out here, but they may not be so plenty as formerly as a great many have been destroyed by idle hunters who left them lay without using them, and many were too poor to be fit to eat, that is of late.[96]

I think your way of curing a bad cold is quite good, but as to my "shutting my peepers soon after retiring," I seldom do within well quite a while. I often lie thinking of something that has transpired during the day just gone by. But you need not correct yourself by using mother mustard of wife [sic] as the one who might help me to cure the cold, for I hope in about that time [to] have a good wife to take care of me in sickness as well as in health as I expect to do to my companion.

No, I am not afraid of making you vain by telling you that I think you are handsome or if you did know, it would not feel in danger of making you vain, or that I will have a proud wife in having the love of Miss Bennett.

It would be well if possable to make a complete visit to all of our friends before leaving back there.

In regard to the melting of the snow so fast in the spring, as [there is] no run off, there is but little danger as the ground is of a sandy nature so as to sink away about as fast as it thaws. While so much snow is against fattening of stock, yet this snow will be a benefit to farmers as it will wet the ground for early spring if it goes away soon enough. But as our letters are exchanged so soon [quickly] we can find out so as to know about matters at the time. One thing is certain: I would like to put out our crops if possable before leaving as they would be more likely to do well, and I would not like to have our time limited as to our visiting around, would you? I want to plow some as the winter set in too early for us to do it in the fall. On both eighties there will be about forty-five acres to be put out [planted] in the spring.

It seems curious to think how soon a letter can be sent back to Low Moor. I have received a letter from you within three days of starting, so that if we were both on hand at the time of arrival, and could send an answer with the next mail, our exchange could be completed within one week. I received a Clinton *Herald* not long since and have read it all over. I don't mean painted it all over. We received one in the fall containing a list of the [Methodist Church] conference appointments, thinking it came from Uncle Coleman's, but at first they [Leroy's parents] thought you had sent it and laughed at me; it was directed to father.

There was a good time last evening at the Baptist Church in the distribution of the presents on the Christmas tree. The house was crowded full, more than could find a place to sit.

I told you a little story, as the little school boy calls it, when I said that the Methodist Church was about one and a quarter miles from here as it is all of a mile and a half. "But I didn't go to do it" and won't do it again. But the roads are so good, it won't take us long to go to church. Do you want to ride, or walk down to church? As the winter has put a stop to most kinds of work, the M.E. Church will not be finished or dedicated until spring, so maybe you can yet be at the dedication. The Methodists are to share with the Baptists their church until ours is finished.

In coming to a new country, you often wonder no doubt what we will live on. I may before this in part may have told you. To begin with, there is splendid flour made at the new Greeley mill, as white and fine as can be found in the West, and is called "snowflake flour." Although this is not a corn country, yet plenty of meal can be had as shelled corn to be ground into meal. Most of this corn is sent from Nebraska and some from Kansas. Do you like eatables made of corn? We once had (back in Iowa) a man that said that corn was only fit to be used by hogs and that [was said] when we were all using it but himself. That was plain talk we thought, but some do not like corn in any form. We are very fond of it. All the vegetables that can be raised in Iowa can be raised here and be a better crop as they are larger and sweeter. Buckwheat is raised here so that we can make the buckwheat cakes fly if we want to. A good hunter can get antelope and jack rabbits in the winter, I mean in the summer, as well as in the winter, but as I am not a hunter, you must wait until I can learn (if I ever can). As both the Union Pacific and the Kansas Pacific [railroads] are or have of late been locked with snow, the mail has not come regular of late. But we hope better for the future.

Mattie wants me to tell you that she will write to you soon as her hand has been unsteady until of late. Our love to all of you folks, but remember that I am yours only.

Carpenter

Low Moor

Jan. 3, 1872

Dear Leroy,

I now seat myself to write the first letter of 1872 to *you*, although it may seem rather late to be answering your welcome letters. Yet when you know that I did not receive them untill yesterday you will not write them quite so much. When I last wrote I expected to go to Calamus before Christmas, but I found it would crowd me so much that I would not enjoy my visit and could not have returned in time to sing with them at The Tree as the cars did not run Christmas. That is only one train each way to carry the mail, therefore I postponed it untill the Thursday *after* Christmas. I went out on the half past eight train in the morning and

I thought I might get a letter from you and went to the post office to get it and there lay the mail bag on the steps and had been there for an hour. So, of course I could get no letter. Mr. Hinman staid there untill the mail was distributed and received your letter for me. He said the train was about a hundred rods away when he got it. I enjoyed my visit very much. I staid in Calamus untill Friday and then the Harris's agent took me down to Brushville. It happened that I got down in time to visit the school and as my time was limited, it suited me admirably, for I could see the most of the scholars. Oh dear, what a terrible sight of kisses I did get and I suppose you won't feel jealous if I tell you I kissed some of the boys will you? There was Spelling school Friday evening and of course I saw more of the young people and Lodge Saturday night. And I attended Sabbath School in Bethel so I saw the most of the people. I told them I should have to come back Saturday evening unless some of them were going to DeWitt Monday, as the trains did not run as usual. And as Elder Curtis (the one who lost his wife) was calculating to come down he offered to bring me. I accepted of his offer and we came down. When he offered to bring me he said it would take three days to tell me what he wanted to and the thought that he intended asking me to come and take the place of the wife he lost last summer while I was there, flashed upon my mind. And for a moment I hardly knew whether to go with him or not. But at second thought concluded I would, as my mind could not be changed. It would do not [no] harm as I knew him to be a respectable man. I know the people will raise a terrible gossip about it, but what do I care as long as he and I both conducted ourselves properly? And he said if I did not care, he would let them talk, but he said when it came to their talking of he and [the] other woman getting married that he would disdain to be seen in company with, it touched his feelings.

We had got but a short distance, he made the remark that he had lost a wife that suited him. Yes, I told him, I had often thought of his situation and realized that Mrs. Curtis was such a woman as we could

not often find. And some how I don't remember in what way our conversations ran upon his children and I said I had often thought that if I had a settled home, I would like to have Emma to live with me. She is such a nice little girl, so loving in her disposition. And he replied by saying if I came back to Brushville to live, I might have her.[97] I told him I never should do that as I expected that would be the last time I should see Brushville. And then I told him in plain words that I intended going west to a home in the spring. Well, he said, he had made up his mind that he was doomed to disappointment and sorrow for life. His family are living with his brother and [they] are so coarse and swear and use [bad] words, women and all, that it is a source of trouble to him, all this about his little children being under such influences. His wife was so different in her way, and would have brought her children up so differently if she had lived. He said that that ride was the most like living again of any time since his wife's burial. They all sympathize with him as best they can, but he says they were brought up in the back woods and are so rough in their nature. He does not know what he would have done if he had not received a word of encouragement from some little folks now and then. He said no one knew how much a kind word would do and a great deal more that I will have to tell you some other time. I felt so sorry for him. His feelings had almost driven him to dispar. He said if he could not find a good woman, he would have to bind his children out and would go to California, he thought, and get among the mountains and get in some danger and his life be taken and that would be all right. Poor man, I am in hopes he will overcome some of his feelings. Now I will not weary you with any more details of my visit untill at some future time.

Facing page: Fig. 15. Bennett sisters, left to right by descending age: Mary, Lucy, Lydia, Martha, and Sylvania. *CSU Water Archives 09b025.*

Well, about *my* Christmas presents. For a joke, Mrs. Hinman put a nice potato masher and pudding stick and butter knife on the tree for me. The knife was marked M.B. and also a sheet of music named "Only a little Brook." You may have heard it, a very pretty piece. And for New Year's, a pickle fork and two holders to use around the stove and a lamp mat and collar and two hankerchiefs and breakfast shawl.

Our folks guessed pretty well my wants. I got or made presents for all of our folks and intended making some for Mary's family [the Greens], but have not succeeded. This is probably the last Christmas and New Year's I will spend at home. We expected Lucy home but was disappointed, but I guess we will all get together in the Spring if Providence permits. Mary was not able to come home Monday. Her health is not very good. I got home Monday evening and came down here yesterday and read your letters before I got my cloak off, but could not answer them last night for my eyes pained me so badly, I could scarcely hold them open. And I am bad enough scratching of this as it is and if I had undertaken it last night I can't tell how much worse it would have been. My eyes pain me tonight. I have been riding [traveling] so much lately and lose considerable rest that I feel all the effects in my eyes very much although every other way I am well.

You could hardly guess how much I weigh. That is the best way I can tell you how much better I am than I was when I came home after my summer school. Mother is pretty well now. I am in hopes I will prove a good hand to care for you in sickness as well as in health. I doubt not that you will prove as good a one as I. It would suit me better if you should put out the crops before you come as I shall have so many little things to do I will have a better opportunity to prepare. And as you observed, I should not like to have our time of visiting limited. As we cannot visit [Iowa] often, we will have to make a long one while we are about it.

I will try and have a letter to put into the office about the time I receive your next, as you suggested. I did not send the first *Herald* to you, but did the last one. I received the last two papers you sent with your letters and [have] not read them all yet, but will soon. Now don't get impatient at my letter but write soon.

Yours ever, Martha

Low Moor
Jan. 7th 1872
Dearest friend,

As my feelings seem to indicate, I will now write to you. I have attended Church and S.S. and read and meditated and think I will spend a short time expressing my thoughts to you. We heard a very good practical sermon today and I hope we will all be profited by it, for now or in future life, as I hope we may always receive instruction from the pulpit as well as any other means for religious instruction. How pleasant it is to be situated so we attend all the means of worship instituted by our church. The church will seat over two hundred and is generally comfortably seated and the attendance at S.S. is very good. Mr. Newton (our pastor) is a very pleasant man and always delivers such practical discourses. I am in the Bible class and we have a very good teacher.

I wrote so hurriedly before that I did not tell you all that I had intended and I had so much to say about my visit to Brushville that that took considerable space and I could not reply to all your thoughts expressed, but will endeavor to do so now. The Tuesday after Christmas, Mrs. Hinman had an old peoples party and Wednesday evening I attended a young peoples party. I enjoyed Mrs. Hinmans party very much, but the other not so well as I was not very well acquainted. Mr. Hinman's daughter was invited also and we went with a load from Low Moor and going to Calamus the next morning, of course, kept me on the motion very well.

And from your letter I notice that you have been enjoying yourself attending a wedding. I, like you, think we will leave the decision as to the length of the ceremony with the minister, although I think I would not care to have it quite so short as two minutes.[98] They could not have given all the directions included in the ceremony as given in the *Ritual.* You see I have been looking over the directions and etc.

I suppose it was quite a disappointment to them, his being sick and then having been detained.[99] There was a couple married at Low Moor and the bridegroom was so sick he could scarcely sit up while the ceremony was being performed and as soon as the minister finished, the doctor came. It must have been very unpleasant.

One of my friends inquired how my beau was prospering? I told them very well. How do you like courting? You are the cause of certain phenomena. I cannot tell you now, as I have not thought but little about it, but if I arrive at any conclusion about it or receive any instruction upon the subject, I will write it.

I shall not consider that you desire to test my knowledge, if at any time you wish to ask me any question. Could not those miniature lakes, rather mock lakes, be produced by the reflection of the sun's rays upon some smooth surface?

Now I don't know as your health would permit you to sit up as late as eleven to write to me very often. But, I have often wished I could write to you when there was no one around for I get fairly interested and the girls will be seen and something about which they desire my opinion or something else. Now Sarah ought to be glad that you are so well pleased [with] a (little school marm's) letter, don't you think so? Although you may not think I am so little if I tell you I weigh one hundred and forty one. My cloak being on made some difference, I suppose.

Mr. Algar did not have a chance to call me by this time when I was there [at Brushville]. I am very sorry Miss Pease has thrown herself away as you wrote. I do not remember her, but am sorry for any one that is so bound up in another person not to see their faults and to think they have none. She will probably repent of the step when it is too late.

I suppose you wish for some kind of a sleigh so you could take a ride. I know we think alike about that. You would like a ride. Instead of lying awake after retiring, I "close my peepers" but dream all sorts of things and about most every thing that is transacted during the day just past and if there are pleasant dreams, I don't mind it, but when they are so bad, I can't bear to think of them, I would rather not dream quite so much.

So you got a place just far enough away from the church that you could not have an excuse to walk. I am glad of it and also glad that I can be there at the dedication of the new church. And you must not tell another little story like that again. A quarter of a mile biger [bigger] than it ought to be.

I guess we can find enough to eat in Colo. And as I stoop to eat what pigs do, we can have some corn bread. And you can teach me to use the gun and I can do the hunting and you do the work in the house. Woman's rights, you know. And we can eat corn bread or buckwheat cakes and antelope and rabbits and lots of things provided we can raise a garden or *tend* one so as to raise anything.

Can you read any of the story, "Rosa Robbins" in your paper? I have kept track of it enough to have my curiosity excited to see the end of it although there are some parts I do not like very well. I noticed quite an enthusiastic account of voting for the post master in the paper. Pretty good, I think.

We (our folks) attempted to have us all at home New Years, but Mary's family could not come as they were not well enough and I could not get home untill evening. And Lucy could not come at all and that was the way it went, but if we try it in the spring, I guess they will not stop for any excuses. If they do they will be disappointed, I guess.

The Irish are trying to master us in the instance of a schoolboy the other day [who] stabbed the teacher because he did not hear his arithmetic everyday. There were so many classes, the teacher could not do justice to them by hearing them recite every day and heard them every other day. The young paddie¹⁰⁰ or young man came up and demanded that he should hear his lesson then and there and the teacher laid his hand on him and told him to be quiet, but he made for a fight and during the time seized a dirk knife from under his coat and stabbed the teacher in the arm. And when some one told him where he had hit him, he said, he wished he had struck him somewhere else and told his fatherinlaw (the teachers) he wished he had struck his heart. Young American or Ireland pretty fast, I think, don't you?

Tell Mattie I will wait untill her hand gets steady and hope she will recover her strength entirely soon. I suppose if you could take a sleigh riding it would improve her. Oh how nice to ride like lightning—oh, slow lightning I mean.

Now Mr. Hinman is telling me so much to tell who I am writing to, and I am writing something else. If I make a mistake he says he will bear the blame. Now as you say, I often think of you and often think of how we may enjoy ourselves in the future. Respects to all.

Love to you,

Yours as ever, M. A. Bennett

Greeley

Jan. 9th, 2½ P.M. 1872

Dear Martha,

Your ever welcomed letter came yesterday evening and would have been answered before this, only that I had some notion today of going up to where Frank [Scott] and I made hay last summer after a load, as I have been of late doing when the weather would permit. And I would rather put *your* letters in the [post] office.

We are *all* well "I thank you." I am glad to know that you have been enjoying your visits of late, and that those presents you received were so suitable to your feelings. As father bought a pair of bob sleds week before last, we have been trying to make good use of the fine sleighing that yet is ours to enjoy, as it is expected that any time the west winds may thaw and leave us on the soil again. I expect to go after another load of hay tomorrow and come home the day after as it is to long a trip to go and come in the same day with a load.

Your speaking of Mr. Curtis makes us realize how hard it is to loose a dear friend and how a few kind words revives the drooping heart to hope on and take courage. How natural it is for us to forget that our fellow mortals have feelings similar to our own. The only way that one can judge of others' feelings is to imagine ourselves in their place for a while and then that true sympathy of feeling is felt. That is what was felt when Christ wept over the departed soul.

The people are enjoying *good* health, and those that had the fever are getting fat and may be ready for market by spring. As I did not have the fever, I am not fat but enjoy the best of health and am in about middling amount of flesh. In fact, never have been of the *real* fleshy nature. In speaking of your own fleshy nature, I think you can generally judge of health by the weight. As I have sometimes guessed of the weight of others quite close by their looks, I will give a guess that you, if about as fleshy as when we parted to be about twenty or twenty-five pounds over one hundred. Now I may not be guessing near your weight, but what do you weigh? And I believe *our* weight is not very much different, and maybe you weigh more than I do. I only guess. When mother was married, she weighed only 102 pounds and I believe enjoyed good health. My not being heavy, I have sometimes thought was an advantage in getting around. People that are not the most fleshy generally escape an attack of sickness more often than the opposite. For doing farm labor, a man need not be fleshy. If I had my choice, I would prefer solid muscle to flesh, but a little of both are a good thing. Mattie and Silas just "go for" the eatables after their fever.

It does not effect any jealousy in me to know that you kissed some of the boys at Calamus, as I know that I have a better prize in having your heart's affections. And if kind providence permits, I hope to have both the kisses and the affections. After that wedding that Sarah and I were at in town lately, the married couple kissed each other, and then we *all* kissed the bride and shook hands with both of them. I had intended asking you what was your oppinion on that subject, and now since we are talking on that subject, what do you think on that subject? The Bible says, "Salute the brethren with a kiss." When I used to go to school at home, we played kissing games sometimes, but I have sometimes thought it a foolish custom, unless between lovers when by themselves, and suitable to children when playing "ring around the rosy." When one body meets another, how natural it is for them to kiss each other. And now, why should not men follow the same practice? Wouldn't it seem odd for men to kiss each other when they meet? But so it was when the prodigal son met his father. He fell on his neck and kissed him. When shaking, I like a firm grip and regard a loose hand as lacking real feeling. Frank Scott said that it was the custom in Greeley for the newly married couple to kiss each other and then for the friends to follow suit. What do you think, Miss Bennett? But enough on that subject on my part this time for I am afraid you will think that I am getting kissing too much in my mind.[101]

I wish you a happy new year. General Cameron has returned from the east where he has been "talking up" for Greeley and Colorado for four or five months. His home is in Greeley. Last Saturday evening when the General was giving a good talk to a well filled house in the Baptist Church; at the close, others made remarks, and all *very* interesting. But to cap the climax, an old gentleman was telling how men were boasting to him, while down in the Platte River how they could get all the whiskey they wanted in Greeley, and he hinted that he did know where it came from, but young Meeker, the editor's son, got up in the audience and told right out the person's name that had been selling this forbidden beverage by saying that it was Dr. Burnhill who had been selling whiskey. He owns and is keeping a drug store in town. This brought on a unanimous cheer from the people. That seems like handling the trespasser without gloves. I think it was good for him, but quite severe.[102]

I sympathise with you in your having sore eyes, and while it is my *greatest* pleasure to get letters from you, yet do not task your eyes as an expense to yourself for my pleasure to read what your eyes have suffered in writing to me. I felt anxious again to receive one of those precious treasures (letters) fearing that something special prevented your writing and have been doing as you told me to, to look in our box every time I went into the post office. Hoping that you are well, I am yours for life. "To be continued."

Your own,

Roy

Do not think that you are bound to read all that is in the Greeley *Tribune* when you get them. No doubt that is a nice piece of music that was given you, but I am not acquainted with it. Have you [had] a chance to learn to play it?

Over the river [home on north side of Poudre River]

Jan. 14th '72

Dearest Friend,

Your interesting letter of the 7th was received yesterday evening. There is much to entertain me in all your letters. Like yourself last Sunday, I have just returned from preaching and S.S. in the Baptist Church. The Baptists have got their new preacher. His name is Mr. Donegal. I think he is a good man and gave us a good discourse on the subject of our duty and proving the importance of our preparing for the other world and discarding the universal doctrine.[103] The Methodists join in using the Baptists' church at $1.50 a Sunday until the Methodists finish their church. I sometimes read your letters on my way home. But yesterday I read your letter in a store and came near busting out in laughter and maybe you felt amused when you red about how near I guessed about your weight. I guessed it about near one hundred and twenty-five pounds. And when your weight is one hundred and fifty-one pounds, you will think I am not good at guessing. The truth is I am more used to guessing the weight of men and not of women. But maybe you have grown taller and more fleshy than when we separated last spring. Do you know how much you weighed at that time? You may think it curious when I tell you that your weight is more than mine ever was, but a stout, hearty wife will be a good introduction to Colorado. And when we come to these ditches, I may carry you over and then you may carry me over. Will that suit you? When you come out here, I do not want you to either get the fever or get homesick.

You spoke about having so many dreams when you retire. I sometimes think for some time after going to bed. Last night I dreamed that I was preaching from a text somewhere in Iowa [?] but before long stopped because I could not think of anything more to say. But [I] seldom dream of anything that troubles my sleep. After going to sleep or "shut my peepers," I enjoy the quiet repose until morning.

I didn't [get] to tell you a story about the distance to our church in town, and if you will not whip me this time, I won't do it again. The new Presbyterian Church is to be dedicated next Sunday and if you were here, we could be together.

I would like to have dropped in while you were all enjoying the Christmas tree and singing very much. I suppose you sang alto. We have a singing class tonight that has no special teacher that is to be paid. But the members take turns in leading. The object is for a mutual benefit for all and only to pay 5 cents for admission. Now if you could join with us, we could learn together. We meet every Saturday evening.

The sleighing is yet fine and I have finished hauling our hay down from above, but it seems so far to haul hay, about 18 miles.

You ask how I like courting. I enjoy middling well one kind, but another kind can never get tired of this: that of setting by the side of a

Miss Bennett, and then I could never tire of that kind of courting. How would you like the last kind of courting, Martha?

Friend [Delphus] Howard has had one of his sisters at home go blind in one eye from having the typhoid fever. He is now going to the State University at Iowa City. Like a little boy I must tell you every little thing. We have had four hogs sent us from our neighborhood. One of these is to be ours. Do you think that will be enough? Father has bought a cow and things begin to seem to be like home.

You asked how I thought of the conduct of the young paddy in your neighborhood. I think that if the teacher had, after finding that he was determined to have his own way, just tapped him and settled him on the spot, it might have done him good. How do you get along in your school? You must be well fed at Mr. Hinman's if you enjoy such fine health. If Mr. Hinman bothers you while writing, just tell him that you write for a change sometimes. I am glad that they are so kind to you, for you know that just as you are treated, it is my pleasure or displeasure.

Yes, my dear, you may learn to shoot, for I want you to know how to defend yourself and shoot game if I am not at home. All that is to be done is put a load in and pull the triger by sighting straight and then you will hit the game. I believe in giving the woman some chance. The legislature setting now at Denver made Greeley a visit yesterday PM.

Oh, yes, somehow Sarah must have told Mary [Carpenter, Peter's widow] my sister-in-law about you and my intentions, for she often wants to know how my school marm gets along back in Iowa. And me to understand that if she is a Democrat, that I need never bring her up there for she is a warm Republican.[104] But I think that will all be right. She has a melodeon and sometimes plays in the evenings.

Now our old friend of ours by name Mr. Bailey came home with father, mother, and Sarah from church and have been talking about everything, and he made mention of a young lady living in town, Miss Bennett. I thought it seemed natural. Excuse my scattered remarks.

Yours in the past, present and for the future. I must walk to church as they have gone home by sled.

Roy S. Carpenter

[Low Moor]

Thursday Eve, Jan. 18, 1872

Dearest friend Roy,

I received your very welcome letter only about five minutes ago, and as there is prayer meeting at Low Moor tonight and I want to go, I will write before I go and mail it myself. I have been looking and looking for a letter from you and was very glad indeed to receive one.

I am well and am prospering very well with my school and time is flying away so swiftly, that I can hardly account for it. I am glad to learn that you and your friends are well and enjoying life as well as you are.

I am glad to hear that you have a pair of bobsleds for you can accomplish your work with so much greater ease when there is snow, than with a wagon. The snow is nearly all gone here and there are no more sleds in use at the present.

Well, you would hardly guess that I weighed one hundred and forty one pounds, you would? I had my cloak on and that made some difference in my weight I suppose, but that is more than I ever weighed before. Indead, I enjoy very good health, you don't doubt it.

Now when you haul hay you must not fall off the load and hurt yourself.

Yes, it is certainly very natural for us to forget others feelings in thinking of our own, and how little do we realize what Christ must have felt and suffered for us, his teaching us to feel for our fellow men.

I received a letter from Mattie not long since, and it was very acceptable. She sent a plan of our house, which was just what I wanted. Do you suppose I can ever move around fast enough to keep our mansion neat[?] How conveniently it is arranged and how pleasantly situated from your description. I think you have a very good idea of comfort in the laying out of houses, and Mattie is a very good hand to draw plans.

Mrs. and Mr. Hinman were saying [they] thought my letters needed pretty promp[t] answers and now Mr. Hinman just handed me another letter from you. He said he thought it would take my appetite away to get two before supper and I will stop and read it before writing any more.

Well now I am through and feel considerable better only I have so much to tell and so short a time to tell it in that if you can understand and comprehend very well. I believe there is some trouble at the [post] office, for your first letter was mailed the tenth and this is the eighteenth, but your second one came in three days. The postmaster is so careless with the mail, I wonder we get it at all, and if they would change the office, I would be very much obliged to them indeed.

We had a splendid sermon Sunday from Math 10:6, I believe. "Thy Kingdom come," and such a sermon as reminds us to be up and doing with a heart for any fate.[105]

Yes, you need not fear about those boys getting any thing more than friendship for the rest is (out west) I know.

Well about those kisses. I am sure I should not object to the bride and groom kissing each other, but now you better not kiss another bride very soon, unless you ask me. You see you must love, honor and obey. I always kiss my friends when I meet them (ladies, of course) and sometimes the *men* kiss *me*, but I do not like the kissing bees, do you? If any one kisses me, I want to feel that they mean it for real friendship. If not, I don't care about their kisses. And like you, I like to take firm hold when I shake hands. Now wouldn't it seem strange for men to kiss each other, but it would be just as well for men as women to kiss each other I think.

I have been visiting some since I wrote last. I went home with Mr. and Mrs. Heilman Friday evening and staid untill Sunday, and then came to Sabbath School with them. I enjoyed the visit very much. They are a young married couple and seem to enjoy life very well. They are very nicely situated on a farm, have built them a large house, and everything convenient. There are five rooms downstairs and five up and a hall. Rather too large a house for one couple it seems to me, but "everybody to their notion."

Last Friday evening we had an oyster supper at the church.[106] They made about $40 and there were not very many there either. The young men took the old ladies to supper and the old men, the young ladies. I went with Mr. and Mrs. Hinman. We had a very pleasant time indeed.

Yes, you are right about Mr. Hinman treating me well and feeding me good. I feel perfectly at home to do as I like. Sylvania feels pretty much at home here, too, but she is more of a home girl than [I] because she has not been away from home but little.

I shall have to stop now but will write again soon before you write again, and will take it a little more deliberately and maybe you may be able to read easier. But write as often as convenient and remember I am yours.

Truly as ever,
Martha A. Bennett

Greeley
January 2[4th], 1872
Dearest Friend,
Your welcomed letter was received yesterday evening. I attended the dedication of the Presbyterian Church yesterday A.M. Mr. Jackson from Denver conducted the exercises. His text was the sixth chapter of Corinthians. A very good discourse, but not lengthy. I will try to tell you just where his text was before long as it has slipped my mind just now.

There was no begging for money after the preaching, and the church was paid for by and from the east. The house was filled more than full as some stood up.

You asked in your other letter if I read any of Rosa Robbins. I have thus far read all of the story or tale. Some is sharp, but not all as portions have but little sense in it. Gustus in saying that he was post office scribe (for love letters) made me feel a sympathy for him.

We have been having some more snow on last Friday night, and the wind since then has been putting it into drifts.

Mattie received an interesting letter from you last Friday. She tried to make me believe that there was no use in my writing to you as one out of a family was enough and that she could tell me all the news. That would not suit me at all, as I find *every* one of your letters interesting to me as well as those she gets.

I made a miss look [*sic*] when I thought your weight was one hundred and fifty and I noticed afterwards that it was one hundred and forty-one. That is a good weight for any one. You, I believe, get your growth earlier than some do. There is a difference in families about that. As to my guessing, I reconed [reckoned] that of you last spring for the present. Do you know how much was your weight last spring?

It generally takes one year or more for the eastern people to become used to this country, called out here acclimated. And strange to say, the same of horses also.[107]

There is a company of about 25 men in town that is formed calling themselves the road and timber company, who intend going into the mountains to get out wood fence posts, R. R. ties, and send or drive them as it is called down the Cache la Poudre River when it rises in the spring.[108] It is expected that the river will be *very* high about June as more snow has fallen in the mountains this winter than for many winters before. And if you get here in time, we may see another Mississippi River.

I would be glad if you could call around some Saturday evening and help us in the singing association to sing. We have an interesting time at each meeting. The people are great at turning out at all these public gatherings. For the last two meetings of the Literary Association I have not been there on account of being too busy or deep snow to walk through. But a number of them was telling me Saturday eve that more came to the meeting than to the Lyceum.

Well, I have been getting vaccinated in today a week ago and have been in hopes to get a little sick from it but yet don't feel any so inclined, but may yet feel it if not soon. Uncle James [Dr. James Scott] will try it again. The papers have of late been telling of many deaths by smallpox in the east, and as I may go there before long, I thought it best to prepare myself for the worst. Now if it would not hinder you in your school teaching, I believe it would be a good thing for you to get vaccinated, for the smallpox proves fatal to as many as any other contagious diseases and it would be a big event if one looses their life from neglect. So maybe that you have [already] been vaccinated. If so, very well.[109]

A few of our folks would like to know when I am going back to Iowa and of course I do not know, and if I did would not tell them *just* when. Those are matters that I do not like to make known to anyone yet.

I have got all the letters that you have written to me since we began corresponding and sometimes [I] read some of them and it seems so much as if you were talking to me. Taking them all in number, about 23 or 4, it would make quite a chat. It is my intention to keep them while I live, if possable. I was reading the first letter the other day and noticing the similarity with those I now get from you, but of course being as yet new acquainted, was more formal than the present ones. We uns all learn our ABCs before we can read.

The subject of women's rights is now before the Lyceum and is being argued with much zeal on both sides. As I do not remember your oppinion on that subject, what is your oppinion on that subject?[110]

Business at present in Greeley is quite dull, the winter keeping people so much at home that but little trading is done. When the spring comes, it is expected that business will be more lively. I think the reason why my letters come so irregular to you is hinderance in the R. Road, making them come in the same mail by one [train] ahead being hindered a while. But so far, none I believe have been lost either way. It seems to me as though time goes faster this winter than [the] one before.

The mountains are visable and Longs Peak now seems to be smoking from some cause (Mr. Bailey said that a fire on [it] was thrown off not long since, making it not so high.) I don't know. At 12 AM the wind is blowing and the sun shining.

I am your absent lover and correspondent.

L. S. Carpenter

Low Moor

Jan. 23, 1872

Dear Roy,

I will now attempt to pen a few of my thoughts, hoping that they will entertain you for a short time. After I mailed your letter Thursday evening, I went to prayer meeting and found a few persons there. We enjoyed ourselves very much and as it was light and good walking, we got home safely.

Saturday I spent ironing and baking and so forth. I told Mrs. Hinman of my intentions and she takes every opportunity to teach me the secrets of housekeeping and I am very glad she is so kind, as I am not with mother and need to improve every opportunity I have in that line. Sunday, I attended the usual services of that day. We had a very good sermon as we most always do.

Last evening we all went out to spend the evening. We visited a young married couple, or they have been married a year. We enjoyed ourselves very well. And this evening I am spending writing to you. It is very cold today and I feel like staying near the fire tonight, as it is not much warmer.

I had begun to think something serious had happened to you before I received the letters from you as it was so long before I received them. I don't see why I did not get the first one sooner unless there was some mistake in the postmaster, for I got the second one three days after it was mailed and the other one, eight. And you may be sure I was glad to get them when they did come, and I hope they will let them come right through here after.[111]

I think young Meeker did come down pretty plainly, on the Dr. "Served him right."[112]

Some time last spring, I weighed one hundred and thirty eight. That was just before I went out to Brushville to teach the summer term. I do not think I have grown any taller since we last met, but heavier. I don't know whether I shall consent to carry you over the ditches or not.

I am sure I do not want to get homesick when I go out to Colorado, and do not think I shall, but can [not] tell untill I try it.

Now you do pretty well to dream you are preaching. I hope your sermon did some good. How much I should like to go with you to your singing class. Yes, I sang alto at the Christmas Tree. I should like to have had you attended then. I should think the class would be considerable benefit to you all. It will keep you in practice and that is what we all need.[113]

I am glad you have finished hauling the hay for I suppose it took you two days to get a load, didn't it? I like to ride on a load of hay. It is so comfortable when I don't tip over.

I believe I should like the last kind of courting you wrote of very well, better than the other. Then we could say so much more in a short time than we can now in two weeks. That is too bad about your friend, Howard's sister going blind from the fever. It is good she did not loose her sight entirely. I am very willing you should tell me every thing you want and then I should never feel afraid of telling you the same.[114]

You must feed your porker good and not let him squeal all day. I should think you would appreciate having some milk to use as you wished again, after being obliged to do without so long until someone would sell you some. If cattle cost so much out there would it pay to buy here and take out there? I suppose the freight would cost more than the difference in the price.

I wrote Mattie that we might engage a car and put our live stock in one end, and dry goods and ourselves in the other, would you like that? I would not. Tell your sister [sister-in-law], Mary [Carpenter], I am coming, Democrat or not, and if you won't want us to quarrel, you must keep us apart. How does she enjoy herself now? I am glad she has an instrument and shall want to go and hear her play some time if you will be my escort, will you my duckie?

When Mr. Baily, (your friend) spoke of Miss Bennett, you did not say, who, did you? There are so many families by the name of Bennett, but they are not related to us.

Can you tell the time you can come out and when it will be convenient for you[?] I shall be making my calculations for some time in April and you may be able to tell when you can put the crops in so as to come. I shall [have] a great deal to do and if we could ascertain when the time [is], I can work up to [that] time. You have given me the privilege of setting the time, but your circumstances you shall have to tell nearly the time of putting in your crops and then I will set the day. How long do you think you can stay out here? Do you think of visiting any of [our] friends other than around Tipton? You can not get through short of three [days] out there, can you? May be I exaggerate, but every one will want to see you and may not consent to let you off with a call. And I don't know how long you can stand to visit with my relatives.

We are expecting Lucy home soon and then I expect she will begin to fix me for my trip and if she should fuss me up so you would not know me, but take her for me, what then? But they say we are very alike. Maybe you would not discover the difference and it would be as well for you, but poor me. What would I do, stay behind? I expect at any rate, you would get some one who could play enough, if you would furnish her with an instrument.

You know, of course, I have some quilts to piece, but sometimes take that kind of work to pass away the time. And people say, Why you are getting ready to get married. Of course, I tell them yes and I think it right to get ready before hand. There is a Mr. Gulick at Low Moor that has tried to attract my affections to himself or has told some that I was just the kind of woman he wanted, a member of the church, could sing and so forth. And they say that he and I are going to get married, although he never comes to see me. And I should just as leif they would think so as long as nothing I say causes their thoughts to run in that direction, for I can work away and they will never know any different untill next spring. He is one of those fellows that means all well enough, but is awkward. And I always feel so out of patience every time I go to meeting. He wants to stand right by me and talk as if I enjoyed it, but I shall not hurt his feelings in any way unless he wishes to become more familiar. Maybe he will have his eyes opened some time. I always treat him just as cool as I can not to be rude, but he never takes [the hint]. Did any young lady ever try to have you understand she would like to make you think she thought you was a model man when you did not care any thing about her? How disagreeable.

I am in hopes I shall receive another letter from you this week, tomorrow or next day. Give my respects to all friends inquiring and if our folks were here, my folks rather, they would send theirs to you. Write soon and remember I am yours ever,

Martha A. Bennett

Greeley
January 31st 1872
Dear Martha,

Your looked for letter of the 23rd inst came to hand yesterday evening, being six days on its journey. We have been having some real winter weather of late. Yesterday a week was a nice day until about three o'clock PM, when all of a sudden a tremendous wind from the southeast sprang up, snowing from above and blowing that [snow] that had fallen the night before. And so strong was the wind that the house could not be seen four rods from the house.[115] Old settlers say that they never saw a worse storm here.[116] The morning and day was a cold stormy day and on Thursday morning the thermometer stood [at] forty [degrees] below zero making it terrable cold. Since then sometimes the wind has blown so as to fill up the R.R. track and on Friday PM I went over and helped the Greeley men in number about 100 throw the snow out of the track. We were volunteers this time. The snow had to fly out of the way in a hurry, and not until yesterday eve did the north mail get in, and a big one it was, too.[117] This morning the weather is clear and pleasant. There was a letter put in the office a week ago and you no doubt would have got it 'ere this, had the cars been running. Father, Mattie, and Aggie have gone down to town in the sled.

You ask as to whether I know about the time of my going back there. As there is much snow on the ground, this must be melted first and soaked into the ground before the cropps can be put into the ground. This will depend upon the weather entirely. I do not expect to help finish all the spring work before going back there as that would take all summer, but would like to put in the wheat, oats, and a little truck, early potatoes for you to cook in harvest (maybe). I would like to be there in April if possable. As the sun is quite warm out here, I don't want you to work too hard or be in its way to tan those white hands of a little school marm. But you said not long since that you could pitch hay and such work. Now it will be very handy to have a wife to help me so much, and

Fig. 16. Train stuck in snowstorm, Longmont, Colo. *CSU Agricultural Archives, from records in the Great Western Sugar Company collection.*

you say that you like to ride on a load of hay, but not if it would be like it was with me not long since as a man was coming towards me with a cow, my left side horse scared and jumped to one side into the deep snow and away went the load over on that side, but as it was tied on, it stuck to the sled. The man got off his horse and we made the team pull it up in its propper place by hitching them on the other side from which it fell. No hay lost (or but little) and nothing broke or hurt and only took a few minutes. You wouldn't like that, would you?

As to whether I would know you from your sister Lucy, or not, time may tell, and if it so happens that I take the wrong girl, you can let me know just before the knot is tied and then I can have the benefit of having two kisses. Now, I never have had a kiss from you yet, but want one when we meet, if not in a too much public place. What say you?

That young man Stout likes just such a woman as you are for a wife. [He] must not be in too much of a hurry for that will not do, as I have claim on that young lady that sings and belongs to church. And the world would not [ . . . ] either if it were offered to me, so that he need not trouble himself any more. [Not clear what Leroy is saying here]

You ask whether any young woman ever thought I was a perfect man? There used to be a girl by the name of Susan Cristman in our neighborhood that different ones told me that she strongly thought that I was just the chap for her and one day she came up to the house to see me, and as I had to go for the cows, or something, out the way she went home, I walked with her for a piece of the way. While we were crossing that pasture after coming in from the lane south of the house, she said she "wished we had to go six miles that evening." I never told anyone, only our own family about it, as I did *not* want to make sport of her feelings, and the young folks would have thought it a good joke on her. I differ with some persons in this that what is told me through innocence by another that I am [not] to make sport of their expressions or pleasure. For although a little foolish it is mean to give it to the public for their pleasure.[118] I told a number [of people] that told me that she loved me, that I would rather she bestow her affections on a more worthy object. She was a good, honest girl and her parents were respectable Methodist people. But she was not smart enough or fast [enough] on foot to entertain me, I mean clumsy while walking.[119]

That young man will have to "get his eye teeth out" as young men call it when they mean that a fellow is young and green and must learn what it is to be wide awake and mind what he says and does.

I do not know how long I could stay there [Iowa], but maybe can tell better after a while. One thing certain, I do not want the folks to get tired of having me around if I can help it, but want to call on them if possable before leaving. How long would you like to stay among your friends? It may make some difference as to how the roads are about getting about among the people. I very often think of you and would have liked very much to have been with you in your singing entertainments. I want Mrs. Hinman to be very kind to you and learn you all that you want to know. I am in hopes that you will not get homesick out here and

I believe you will not as you can see so far. I want to get a spy glass if I can get a good one and can spare the money. Mary has a good one and can see for a long distance. When the fire was in the mountains this fall, it looked nice at night through the spy glass.

I told you in the last [letter] that I would try and tell you where the preacher's text was in Corinthians, but will try sometime maybe when we are together as I do not just remember now. There was a hotel and furniture store burned down in Evans last Saturday afternoon.

My vaccination did not yet, has not yet, had any effect, but I guess the material was not good, and must try it again I suppose. Do you know how many weeks of school you have left? How far is it from where your school is to your house, or do you know?

The Duke Alexis passed along here in the cars on the 17th of this month in the afternoon. There were six palace cars in the escort. They moved along very slow compared with other passengers. They did not stop at Greeley.[120]

Young Heath's wife that went to Wisconsin with him got the typhoid fever and died not long since. If she had have staid here most likely would have got well as nearly all did. I do not know who that Miss Bennett in town is as I have never seen her to my knowledge. There is a Dr. Bennett in town but don't know him. It is a common name, as Carpenter is a common name. You will not have to make a very big move in your initial letter "B" to that of "C" after [a] while, will you? Space forbids further at present. I would like to call in some evening first rate, but you need not look for me soon, my dear. With the same feelings of love as ever for you, I wish you to enjoy good health and appetite, hoping soon to learn from your interesting pen, I send my first love to you, hoping for many happy days together hereafter.

Yours as ever,
Roy Carpenter

Low Moor
Feb. 7th 1872
Dear Roy,

I received your very welcome letter this morning and very [glad] I was to receive it. Mrs. Hinman was telling me what to write and I forgot to insert a few words. I am glad you did not get blown away in that storm you wrote of for I should miss getting *some* letter often, very much. I suppose you have received the answer to the last letter before this by this time. I wrote Saturday evening and mailed Monday, at least in a day or two. Sylvania brought the letter this evening and you ought to have seen her wink and point to the *C* on the envelope.

I have been making some molasses candy for I have a very bad cold and cough, which is uncommon for me. I often have a cold in my head, but never a cough. Mrs. Hinman doctors me with candy and I am very glad, for it is so sweet. I don't mind taking it very much, as I like any thing sweet. There are so many persons that have a cough now, and I have a barking school. Mrs. H. says you won't need any dog, for I can do all the barking.

You asked how many more days there were of school. There are just six weeks with the remainder of this week, which will be about the 20th of March.

There are several of our folks that [we] may have to visit and if any more time is left I may call on some of my friends. There is Mary's and Lydia's and Uncle John Gilmore and Mr. Balls. You don't know them now but may before long.

I declare, the time is *very* short untill you will come. Yes, you may have a kiss when you come if it is not too public a place. And as that young man that likes me is not at home yet (as he went to Wisconsin) he may be home untill I go home and then woe be to him if he comes out there to see me.

Oh, yes, while I think of it, I saw a notice of Elder Curtis's marriage to a lady of Mechanicsville in the Clinton *Herald*. I hope he has found some one that will be kind to his children.

I don't think I should have been very badly frightened if I had been on that load of hay with you, and if I had have fallen off, the snow is soft you know.

If the Duke Alexis did not stop in Greeley I suppose you did not see him. I guess you will not have six place cars to attend you on your journey when you travel west, will you? As long as the cars ran so slowly, I should think he might have stopped to let you take a look at him for a minute. Now that was right for you to help clear the track. Did you get a letter after working so hard? If you did would you as leave work at that rate again?

You were considerate of Susan C.'s feelings, I am sure, and acted right in respect to telling any one. But didn't you feel a little mischievous over it? She was going to have you understand how she felt about it. All very well, I suppose if both of you had thought alike, but as you did not, it caused you to feel differently. I guess I did not see that individual when I was out to Tipton.

I don't think I shall get homesick in Colo. And do not intend to think of it if I can avoid it. And if you get a spy glass and I get very homesick, I can look back east for a while and maybe that will suffice. But I have been away from home so much that I hardly think I shall get homesick. Lydia says she is afraid I will never see our folks again, but Mother says if it was some men, she would never expect to see me again, but as it is you she does fear, but that she will see me some time again.

It is seven miles from Mr. H's to our house and our folks have been over it so often that if you should come early and I should not be at home, they can tell you the way over here. Did Mr. Heath return to Greeley after his wife's death?

No, I shall not have to go very far to find my initial paper after I find C and that will be easier to find than my initial, I guess, for the druggist often tells me, that that letter is sold more than any other. Would you rather have waiters or not when we are married?

Have you set out any fruit? If not had we better take some when we go or can [we] get it cheaper where you are? If you have a large trunk you had better bring it and we can pack our things in them pretty much and they will go free and that will be saving, you know. I speak or write of these things now because after a while there will be so many things to think of we may forget something. I forgot to tell you it has been so stormy the last two Sundays that we could not go to church at all and although this may be not very interesting to you, my head is so thick with a cold, I have to write something to fill up the sheet and any thinking powers are somewhat removed.

Does Agie's father ever write to you any more? And how does she like the country? Tell Silas when I come, I will try and keep him busy if you can't, and remember me to all your folks.

Hoping to see you before long and still enclosing my affections to you. I remain,

Yours in life,

M. A. Bennett

Low Moor

Feb 3rd 1872

My dearest friend,

I received your very welcome and interesting letter this evening. I fully sympathize [with] Gustus [character in the "Rosa Robbins" serial printed in the Greeley *Tribune*] now in getting sick for letters, for I have been watching and waiting for, Oh, it seems so long, to receive a letter from you and imagine everything in respect to you, but at last concluded the delay was caused by the snow on the track. Your letter was mailed the twenty-fifth of last month, and I guess you done your part, didn't you? I mailed a letter to you a week ago Thursday evening, and had my mind all ready for a letter from you. Then, I did [not] get any, and Thursday evening I thought *surely* I would get one, but no letter for me. I went to prayer meeting and enjoyed [it] as well as I could, and concluded there was no use to worry a bit, but wait patiently untill the cars saw fit to bring one for me. I told Mr. Hinman when he went to town today to bring me a letter, and he did. Wasn't he good? I think so.

I am very glad to learn that you are all well. Tell Mattie she must not hinder you from writing, but she may write as often as she finds time to do so. Were you aware that you dated your letter January 2nd?[121]

I hope they will not dedicate any more churches untill I come to attend, although I am glad you can attend the exercises. I should like to go with you. In one of the papers you sent me, I [saw] the mention of the dedication, and it also stated that there would be no begging for money. You are something like me in recollecting texts, for I am very apt to forget them, when I wish to remember them.

It has been very cold this week and stormed so badly Sunday that we did not venture out of the house to go to church. It is quite pleasant today; the snow is nearly gone, but I think I never saw a wagon track so smooth. It is such good walking, too.

The Cache la Poudre [River] will be of great benefit to the country, indeed, if they can use it in the way you write of. I hope it won't rise so as to float a part of the town away, or is there no danger of that? I believe it flows *through* the town, don't it? I often imagine how beautiful the country must look.

If I can stay when I call to sing with you Saturday evenings I will come some time, but if I cannot, I won't come. That is all. How much more pleasant public gatherings are when there is a *general* interest taken.

Yes, I am vaccinated several years ago, and therefore won't have to be vaccinated now. It has been reported that there were a few cases of smallpox in Clinton, but I don't know how true the report is.

I have every one of your letters, and my portfolio was so full I had to put some of them in a box for safe keeping.[122] Your mind and mine

Fig. 17. Low Moor train stop on the Chicago and North Western Railroad. *Author's photograph taken in the fall of 2005.*

are alike in keeping them, or each other's. It may be pleasant to look them over some day which will be a very pleasant way of refreshing our memories of former days. I counted yours once, but have forgotten how many there were, but I know what was in them, I guess.

You desire my opinion of women's rights. I have never exercised my thinking powers very much upon the subject but think that if women can retain their modesty, and be esteemed as highly as true women are by their fellow mortals, that they may vote. I do not think it will make much difference except in the liquor question that I think would receive a severe blow from the increase in the number of votes. And I certainly think women ought to receive as good compensation for a certain amount of labor performed equally as good as a man.[123] If every woman votes as her husband or parent, of course it will only, may [only], double the number of votes on each side, and that is all. But if every [woman], or the majority of women, vote as their own minds dictate, I am not prepared to say what would be the result, *except* in the liquor question.

I think time never sped on swifter wings [for] me than this winter, but it is spent pleasantly by me, and I hope by you, also. The main reason for me is I have to improve it so well, that it seems shorter.

We have not been home since New Year's, but received a letter from home yesterday. Father has been quite poorly, and Sam, my cousin, got his limb disjointed the other day. He jumped out of the sled and was running along by it and slipped, and the sled ran over his limb. It was set, and he was improving consider[ably] when they wrote. That big sister, Lucy, of mine has not come home yet. What shall I do with her? But I need not call her big, for she is no larger than I.

Well, today I have been doing housework and the like. Last Saturday, Mrs. Hinman put me at the baking. She says I must learn to cook. Don't you think she is right about that? I do. She tells me so many things I can only remember by close attention so many important items, and when it comes to an impossibility to remember, I write it down. Oh, I forgot to tell you: Mother sent her love to you when she wrote.

There is an Englishman near that had a cancer taken from his breast that was seven inches long and three wide. How much he must have suffered from it! There is a doctor liv[ing] in Princeton, Ill. that makes that his business. There seems to be a good many cancers around here. The man I spoke of was very poor, as he has not been in this country but a short time, and the people have been assisting him. Mr. Hinman took a cord of wood to him today, and he said he scarcely ever saw anyone so well pleased as they were. I could not find anyone to give me music lessons and I am trying a little to teach myself. I have so many things that are more necessary to do, although not any more pleasant, that I cannot improve as I might, but I try and practice a little every day, and every little [bit] helps, you know. I would like two hours a day very well, instead of part of an hour.

You must excuse the appearance of this letter for the paper is not ruled plainly, and I cannot see the lines without straining my eyes. Next time I buy, I will notice the lines, I guess. I will send you some of the papers we take. I think the *Watchword* is about the best temperance paper I ever read. The reading is so interesting and instructive, and it is not all temperance. The *Country Gentleman* is pretty good and Clinton *Bee*, also.[124]

Now, I must close my letter for I guess I have written as much as you can take care of for once, and hope the wind will not blow the snow on the track any more for our sakes, unless it is for the best. Respects to all and love to you.

I remain yours sincerely,

Martha Allen Bennett Low Moor

P.S. Pleasant dreams. I know I shall have them now.

Greeley

February 12th '72

My Dearest friend,

Your interesting letter of the 3rd inst has been received on yesterday evening (Sunday eve) PM old style I may say. This morning I take my pen in hand to let you know that we are all well and am in hopes these few lines may find you in the possession of the same blessing. I have been waiting and expecting a letter from you for several days and had intended to write you again if I did not soon learn from you. You must remember that one of those letters remained in the post office fully one week before it le[f]t town, so that may be the reason of its not getting to you sooner, and it's being dated Jan. 2nd as you say. Besides, there has been great interruption on account of snow on the Union Pacific R.R. By this time I hope you will have received your reply, or my reply, to some questions. The quickest time of exchanging letters was when the evening (Sunday) I wrote about Mr. Baily being here and receiving one from you the following Sunday evening. I intend gazing [at] those papers you sent, being three of them a good survey before throwing them aside.

You are mistaking [*sic*] about Greeley being divided by the river, as it is entirely on the south side and several feet higher than the river. The town is in what is called a second bottom land, and your house is on a third grade, or still higher and the highest in this part of the country and is called [the] bluffs. So that many have asked me, how do you like living on the bluffs [during] this cold weather. I sometimes tell them that it is healthy to live where we can catch all the brainy breezes, and then they laugh some. Quite a number have supposed that our light in the front window was a star, it's shining so brightly. So that you can make your light shine when you are at home out here. And maybe you can think it if not say it when I am coming from town: "there's a light in the window for thee." When hauling that hay in the morning, I could see our house about 15 (fifteen) miles, looking like a little speck on the snow.

Yes, my dearest, you may go and see Mary, and if you can't get along together, I will try and compromise the matter somehow. She is getting along very well, or midling well as there has been so much snow and cold weather that people could not come to see her and thus making it lonesome. Some of the winter she has been teaching some children or a small school.

I attended a festival at the Barnum house on the evening of the sixth, Tuesday evening last, for the benefit of the Congregationalist Church. There was about one hundred there and [I] had a good time. Like some other young chaps, I went alone. It takes money to attend these gatherings, you know, and I don't often attend them.

I am sorry your cousin got a joint put out of place and am in hopes he may soon recover from the injury.

I am in hopes the wind will not blow any more snow on the R.R. track so as to hinder our letters from going through on time. I forwarded to you two papers last week. In one there is a description of the late terrable storm. Try and read it if you have time. If you do not get the other letter let me know, and I can write it over.

My first vaccination did no good, but the second one is doing finely, but not making me sick, only a little dizzy for a while and making my arm some sore.

Our snow is not leaving fast as most of our winds come from the north. But we are hoping for its leaving us soon. The people are enjoying good health and are looking for better days in the future. My health is choice.

Do you attend a Good Templars Lodge this winter or have you become tired of the institution yet? Some that had been going stopped as they became tired. I don't care much about it and don't like to spend much money for anything. A young man last Monday eve wanted to take in my name into the Lodge (It meets in the new Presbyterian Church) in that evening and said that no one would vote against me. I told him that if I concluded to do so that I would present my certificate. But as summer is coming on when I must work on the farm, I don't think it worth while to join. We have nice times in our Literary Association sometimes, but maybe that will stop going when it comes time to go to work.

Well, our time of correspondence is coming to a close, and we must soon try what it is to provide for ourselves. I have known of some young folks that thought it but sport to get married. I do not think so. I[t] certainly is the *most* important ceremony we go through on earth (aside from religious exercises). I have not, like you, read in the Ritual the ceremony of matrimony, but we can read that over together before hand if we think best, I suppose. But few preachers go through all of the form set down. I have not been in favor of a lengthy ceremony, but thought that about five minutes was long enough to tie the knot.[125] What is your oppinion? What is your oppinion in regard to bridesmaids and groomsmen on that or such an occasion[?] Where there is a big display made they generally do so, but I don't know much about it. There was a young man by name, Dan [?] that was married not long since at Low Moor, mentioned in the Tipton *Advertiser*, and as the lady's name was Martha, Sarah said that Martha was married and what was I going to do about it? I asked for the rest of the name. Well, she said she was married any how. *Well*, strange to tell, shall we dig a *well*?

As yet we have been hauling our watter from the river in barrels, excepting what snow was melted. I enjoy good sleep these nights, and as you say you enjoy nice dreams, I believe you do. But I seldom dream much. Mattie will be glad to write to you at any time, she says, and will not be in the way of my writing. Now if you *please*, write soon, and you need not fear of tiring my eyes by writing long letters, as they are richer than a feast to me. Much love to your folks and happiness. I remain your hopeful lover.

Roy Carpenter
Love to you

On the bluffs [At home, Greeley]
Feb. 15th '72
My dear Martha,

I received a very interesting letter from you dated February 7th on Tuesday evening, and would have answered it before this only that I thought you would rather get them not so near the same time. By having them come more regular at times, it will, or would be, more convenient for you to answer. How is your mind on that subject? I am sorry to learn that you have, or had, such a bad cold, but when you get here, I am in hopes you won't have any more colds. But it affords me *much* pleasure to know that you are so kindly cared for. Mr. H[inman] need not think because you can bark so loud now that you need always do so; and thereby need have no dog to watch, for you must not be kept out all night waiting for thieves, for that would make me lonesome in the house by myself. And you might catch cold out of doors so much.

A good way to stop a cough is to grind some pepper and put it in some warm watter and take often a teaspoonful, as that soothes the irritated tonsils. You are mistaken that because of your cold that your letters are ill composed. No, they are *all* very interesting to me. The last letter came unsealed, so that I took it out as you put it in the envelope, and it was not marked Low Moor as all the rest were. But I don't suppose anyone read it; if so, no harm done.

I was misinformed, or we were, that young Heath's wife is dead as she is *not* dead and they are living, I believe, in Iowa.

You asked not long since if it would pay to buy a cow back there and ship out here. I don't think it would unless it was an extra kind [meaning unclear], and we could not think of having her in the same car with us as she might bawl out and scare us sometimes. But she might be tied behind the cars, maybe. While we were at Grinnell, Iowa, we saw a family and one or two horses in a freight car with their goods in, and all secured nice enough as it was pleasant weather and things looked comfortable. I have a common sized trunk that I might take back so that we might put in some things, and if I hadn't enough to fill it, you could put in some things. It is all right to speak of these things at any time as we might forget them if not spoken of at the time. It might pay to bring some fruit out as I think they can be bought cheaper there than here. I will enquire before going back. As I spoke about those five dressed hogs sent from Tipton, they were all fine hogs, and it would have paid us if we had have had a car load sent out, as several wanted to buy those sent out to us. But father said you and I might have one if we wanted it. We have *no* live hogs yet.

As for Susan C., I know you did not see her when you were out to Tipton as they have moved out to the western part of Iowa. But she never interested me any somehow. And if Mr. young fellow calls on you, he can soon be let known that his hopes are all blasted by a few words.

I am in hopes Mr. Curtis has done well, but think he was in a little hurry, don't you? I never believed in being in too much in a hurry about marrying. The duties of a married life are quite important, I think. Some young folk, as soon as they fall in love, go and get the knot tied. Well, the honeymoon is soon over[126] and then, where are they? They are married and must make the most of it. And then I have sometimes thought many deceive themselves in regard to what it is to be in love. I think both parties should become acquainted and love because they like each other's ways, oppinions, and be independent of circumstances. I have known some young men that wanted *capital* when they got a wife, and nothing but a beautiful lady [who] could play on an instrument and sing nice would be the only kind they wanted, and never seeming to think what they were themselves, whether worthy or not. But we often see young ladies marry a young man that is in principle a scoundrel, and they knew it, too. This has always seemed strange to me. And some young women after having been told the many faults of a young man, yet continue to love and even marry. Now love and marriage are both natural to young folks just starting in life but to marry is more than to only love. I look at the act of getting married as the all important act of life. But such talk will make you tired, I expect.[127]

The Duke Alexis did not stop at Greeley. And I would rather have been those that were with him than he, as General Sheridan and others composed the unit.

If I should happen back there, I should want to see my dear girl as soon as possable of course, and think I could find the way well enough, but doubt being back there before your school is out.

Well, the snow is melting quite fast and the sleighing will soon be gone. Yesterday (Thursday) and the day before, I hauled a load of coal from Higley's coal bank twelve miles northwest from here.[128] Frank [Scott] staid all night Tuesday evening. He has been cutting three thousand poles for fencing in the foot hills this winter.

I have been reading some in the *Watchword* you sent me not long since, and find it to be an excellent paper. By this time, no doubt, you have received my letter. Speaking of receiving them. You suppose that *all* will be glad to see me back there? It is this way: I have some friends, but I know very well that a few there could rejoice in nothing more than that extreme poverty could follow me through life. And such, of course, would rather never see me again. And *I know* that there are a few that I would rather [ . . . ] never see their picture on earth again if possible. Because if I am a friend, they generally soon know it, if not, the same way. Father, mother, and Mattie have just gone over to town. I am in hopes the cars will not be any more bothered with the snow and that the rest of our letters may go through in three days. Now, as you are my dearest treasure and my dearest friend, I hope soon to see you. And I send my love to you. Yours as ever.

L. S. Carpenter

Colorado

Low Moor

Feb 16th 1872

Dear Roy,

It is just four days since you took your pen in hand to inform me that you were well. I cannot say so of myself, as I am still suffering from a severe cold. I still have a cough, and that is very unpleasant in school, and out of it, too. Otherwise, I am enjoying myself. I suppose you have received the letter I wrote dated the 9th, I think it was. I felt very glad tonight when I received your letter and soon had devoured its contents, and would inform you that Sarah was mistaken, for I still remain single and expect too for a few days longer. I have not heard of the marriage of the person you wrote of. I received the papers you sent me last evening and read not only the account of the terrible storm but all other news contained in it. I *do* enjoy reading so much and generally read every paper of consequence I can find. I think the *Tribune* is a very good one. There are a great many good articles in it, and I class it with the

*Watchword* that I sent you. The last one that we received it seems to me is *better* than the others, and so it seems every time. (This ruling on the paper is so faint that I am going to write just as it comes.)

Yes, I will remember that one of those letters remained in the office over a week and that it was not your fault.

I have just been listening to a *splendid* story in the *Watchword* about temperance, and if I can, I will send the paper to you. Do you take the Clinton, no I mean Davenport and Tipton papers, besides the Greeley paper? If so, we will have a nice time reading the news. You can read, and I will listen and sew, or knit your stocking, etc.

Now, really, I thought the town of Greeley was divided by the river, but I see I was mistaken and glad, for they won't have so much water in town as I thought. Quite a mistake in me!

I had an invitation to a party this evening, but as I had no *beau*, I concluded I could remain at home, and am very well satisfied now as I can read and answer your welcome letter. The party was at a Mr. Kistner's and I presume most of the company will be persons I am not acquainted with, and I had rather remain at home. I did not receive your letter untill seven o'clock this eve.

I am glad our house is so high, for if you forsake me this, I can sit and look upon the scenery and clouds, and maybe watch for you when you return. Now if you take me to Mary C's [Mary Carpenter], I want to go when she is teaching her small school. I suppose you won't object, for you know I am an old hand at it and always like to visit such places. You can leave me there and go back home and keep bachelors' hall in our house, and she and I can have a fine visit. Did you tell her what a young no nothing I was, or leave that for her to find out when I come? You know, if you tell her and have her ready to see such a looking fright, she won't be shocked, but as your folks have seen me already, they don't have to pass through the process again.

Now don't think I don't appreciate your judgment (for you know what you wrote about it), but she [a Miss G. mentioned in a previous letter from Leroy] would think me of considerable consequence if such a gentleman as you should select [me] for [a] companion. But now I have written enough of such nonsense, and now for something else.

Sister and I went home Friday and staid untill Monday morning. Lydia and one of our neighbor girls came after us. While we were enjoying our Sunday, who should come in but Lucy and Uncle John. They were not aware that the time of trains had changed on the D. St. P. RR[129] and had to go considerably out of the way, consequently did not get home untill Sunday. They started Saturday. Uncle John made me promise that I would come over and see them when the *time came*, and I promised. So you are bound to go under my promise, my dear. Ha, Ha! Lucy is going to stay untill May.

Now you must not keep all your money untill your trip (provided you have enough) for I want you to enjoy yourself and spend enough to keep your purse from bursting open. You must not save it all for me. You mind, now.

Well, mother says I am getting worse and worse every day, so you will have to put up with it, for she ought to know. But be careful, or your mother won't let you bring me out there to boss you.

Cousin Sam's ankle is all right now and [he] is as much the limber boy as ever.

I do not attend any Good Templar's Lodge, because there is none here. They never appear to accomplish much good in the matter of temperance, and I often think if everyone would carry a *Pledge* with [himself/herself] and induce others to sign and then help them to *keep* their pledge, there would be more good accomplished than there is by some of the orders. For instance at Calamus (and I suppose it is so in other places) they would take the Obligation which is for life, and I know of several that have violated it several times and still pretend to be honest and so forth, and when they were away from the Lodge Hall, then "now for fun boys." The trouble is their consciences are spoiled so badly, they do[n't] care for the Obligation.

Ah, yes, every day of our lives is a leaf in the great book of responsibility and more so than ever when we fill it with a record of our union to another for life, and how can we do but to trust in our heavenly Father that he will prepare us to meet the responsibilities of our lives with hearts made better by his Grace, and minds fitter by his teachings for the many changes that we are subject to. How wretched would be the lives of his followers if they realized for one moment there was no God. But thanks be to him, we know there *is* a God Almighty, All seeing and Merciful, and may neither *you* nor I nor *anyone* be brought into that state of mind which says there is no God in whom to trust. And how lightly do those esteem the sacred ceremony [wedding] who think it a mere sport.[130]

Before receiving this [letter] I wrote for your opinion about attendants. I should prefer to have them, and if you wish to bring any of your friends, our house is small, but if they can put up with a little room, bring them in welcome. I would like the ceremony just long enough to say and do all that was necessary, and I hardly know how long that would be, as I have not attend[ed] many wedding[s], and never being especially interested, did not observe. If our letters come as soon as this one did, very good. This is all at present. Very much love from yours truly,

Martha A. Bennett

P.S. Remember the *Tribune* said, sign your entire name when you write to friends or lovers in the east.

Martha

Greeley

February 21st 1872

Dear Martha,

This evening's mail brought another of those ever welcomed letters. The weather is fine and the snow is slowly melting away, and each day brings to view the soil that we will soon have to till. Some of these warm days makes me feel like having, or as if I had, the "spring fever" or lazyness. Our sleighing has gone and we are again using the wagon. The roads are in some places muddy but are drying up. Times are yet dull, but [we] are hoping for better days.

But this is not talking much like a love letter I guess. In your other letter you speak of imagining my thoughts while we were throwing the snow out of the R.R. track, as that of expecting to get a letter from the *east.* Just so it was, for while so doing I hoped the mail would bring a letter from you. But after the snow was out, we rode in the engine house into town. And I asked one of the engine men if there was any mail, and he said not, as the north road was blocked up like this one, so that I had some idea about the matter. I watched the track quite closely for some time, looking for one of those nice letters.

Maybe in my last I said nothing in reply to our having waiters on the *big day.* If I did, no harm in repeating it in this epistle. I have heard quite often of that being the case but have never been at such a wedding. As you say, it is your preference. I, of course, will willingly comply with your desire. Do you think of inviting many to our wedding? It may be that certain parties would go from Bethel, our home, down on that vacation if they were not too busy putting in their cropps and felt welcomed. It is best to talk over the matter well before hand. Now I want you to write just as you think best about this matter As our affairs need not be made known to any other than ourselves if we think best to have them so. And *you* are the one to boss the matter entirely. The lady must have her choise before the man, and as that will be *the* important event of our lives, let us try and have it be a happy time that we can look back upon in after years as a pleasant event in our history, when we were made wife and husband.

I wish that cold would leave you so that you might enjoy yourself better. I would like [it] if I knew of a speedy cure. But the taking of ground pepper in warm watter I have always found the best to stop a cough. When you get here, I am in hopes no more colds will trouble you, as I have not had a *bad* cold since we came here.

You need never fear that Mary or any of my folks will ever think anything else but that Roy has been fortunate in getting Miss Bennett for a companion.

Now it is said that lovers generally flatter each other before they are married, but after [a] while, they cease to do so. Now, I am not at liberty to surmise as to what your folks will think of your husband, but I, of course, would rather if (true) that they would think well than to think that you did not do much. So I won't be quite so green as the fellow that I once heard of that asked the young lady, "What do the people think of me?" calling her by name. She told him, "I think you are a fool." Good for him, wasn't it, Martha? And then we have both of us heard of a married couple being jealous of each other. How foolish that is. [I] once told Howard Coleman when in conversation that if I ever got married that I wanted to get a wife smarter than myself. "That's it," said he. I have *never* changed my views on that subject yet. And so George Reeder once told me "you are too particular" when speaking of the company that I liked—lady company. But I do feel as if I am fortunate in having your affections. No flattery. And if you feel at home in like or similar views, we are both fortunate. I have always thought that a married couple ought to always think more of each other the longer they live together, instead of less as they seem sometimes to do. The cares of life may increase in life, but true love should prove true to itself. It is said, "True love seldom runs smoothly." But if you find that I am not perfection, don't take the matter to heart, for I have always known that I have my faults. But in giving you my hand, I also give you my heart.

So, your sister, Lucy, has come at last, and as you have said, no doubt [she] will begin to fix you [up], and if you desire, we hope to call on some of your relatives. I would be glad to see any or all of your friends. Now, when you get here, do not think that I am going to take you around and tell the folks that you are Mrs. C., for I have paid but little attention to women since we came to this colony, and if you want to get introduced, maybe the girls, Mattie and Sarah, can introduce you, as I am of a quiet turn, and as friend Delphus Howard[131] once told me, that I was hard to get acquainted with. Not because it is my intention so to be, but because it is my nature, maybe. One thing certain, if a person is naturally quiet, it would be only worse than folly to be talkative, as it would only be blat[t]ing nonsense, you know. But I would like to be social if possible. To appear natural is the best attitude for any person. It was just as easy for Daniel Webster to be himself, as it is for this boy to be his humble self, if I may draw a comparison. But I think a person may improve himself in anything.

I will send you a copy of this week's *Tribune* and in the local column, you can see our affairs mentioned full as much as we know ourselves.[132] So that you and I must not get too proud if we are above other people (on the bluffs), and other people look up to us, for you may be sure they will know us. When I was down to uncle's this P.M. the time that there was a social gathering of the M.E. Church ladies, aunt was reading about us in the paper and joking about who would do my cooking, another lady joined in the talk. And I told them that I would give $25 for a good wife to keep house, and that lady said that she could get me a wife for less than that much money. Of course, I made no mention about my intentions, but thought they would find out before long. And by bringing my Iowa girl out here, I would feel all right.

Now, I read your letter on my way from town, and do not remember maybe everything you mention, and as all the folks are setting up I don't like to get out the letter and read it in their presence. Somehow, I would *rather* read your letters by myself if possable. But if I leave out anything this time, I'll try and mention it next time.

Although the days are getting longer, yet time is going more rappidly than I ever saw or felt it go. Now, as Mrs. H[inman] is training you to keep house, if you learn how to make good bread, I think you will have learned the principle thing in keeping house. Oh! I forgot that you already [know how to bake] and when I was at your house, you had such good bread which likely you made. As for spending my money, I have to spend a little but must be saving, and as to saving it for you, I, of course, am doing it. I don't believe in a young fellow need be going with many young ladies while away from his dearest, as people become estranged from their former love by forming new associations. Sometimes. So, I have not waited on any lady since we came to Greeley. We had a good time as you will see in the paper on last Friday evening in the new M.E. Church. As I said only a few words at the last, I am not mentioned as having had or made a speech on that occasion. The house was filled so that not all could find seats, and there were about four hundred people present. Young Gipson, the president, wanted me to make a speech and I told him that I might say a few words. The temperance subject was discussed, the ruling thought of the townspeople at present as you will see mentioned in the *Tribunes*.

I am going to try sending three of these small sheets in one envelope. As of late, I have been sending two larger sheets as they hold more words. But I will close for this time. I am in hopes that you will soon get over that *bad* cold. So, good evening to you this time, sweet repose and perfect rest is my wish to you. My love to you.

Leroy Swanstedt Carpenter (not very often I write my middle name)

(To be continued)

Low Moor
Feb 23 '72
Dearest Friend Roy,
I received your welcome letter last evening. I went to prayer meeting and enjoyed it very much indeed, for I always enjoy the exercises of

such places. There are but few that attend but there are a good many members in town that might attend if they felt disposed. I am glad to hear that you are well and the rest of the family.

You are very considerate of my convenience not to answer my letter so soon. It does not make much difference as to whether I receive them near together, only that I had rather hear from you about once a week than to have both come at the same time as I can not hear from you oftener than once a week. I have nearly recovered from my cough, and am very glad I escaped any further difficulty from it than I have. Yes, Mrs. H[inman] cares for me very well. It is good to [have] such friends. I am much obliged to you for the remedy you wrote of and will try it some time when I have occasion.

I am quite sure that I have sealed all the letters I wrote you but may not have done so, but you received the letter as it was and that is all that was necessary as what was in it was of not much interest to strangers.

Well, Mr. Gulick has come back from Wisconsin, and I suppose I will have somebody to stand by me after church is out untill I get in the wagon to come home. I really felt a little out of place with no one to stand by me last Sunday, and if he comes and says anything about my staying near Low Moor to live, I can find words to tell him why I won't.

Yes, I think Elder Curtis was in a little hurry about getting married, for it was not four weeks from the time I saw him untill he was married. I don't know as he had been acquainted with his wife before that time or not. I have not heard anything of her yet.

I received a letter from the parents of one of my scholars at Brushville the other day. The little boy was sick when I was out there, and they said they would write and tell me if he recovered. He was delirious then and did not recognize anyone. They wrote that he had recovered, also that five of my older scholars had been converted, girls that I have often prayed for and talked with upon the subject of their souls' salvation. And it certainly causes me to rejoice to know that they see the necessity of serving God, and they wrote that they often prayed for me in their prayer meetings. "Surely, it is good to serve the Lord."

Our ideas are alike upon the subject of marriage, and Mr. Algar's expression was very much [the same] as I think he said he did not believe in loving unless there was something to love a person for. And as you wrote, I don't understand how one person can consent to marry another unless or when they know that the opinions and motives are so far inferior to their own. You have express[ed] my ideas upon the subject so fully, by expressing your own, that I will not occupy further space by writing mine.

Now, you manage nicely to get Father, Sarah and Mattie over to town when you want to write. Ha, ha! I cannot blame you much as it is much more pleasant to write when there is no one around to bother or talk than when everyone is chatting to suit their fancy. "I speak from experience."

I should think that [ . . . ] the Duke Alexis would be well satisfied with traveling by the time he reaches home.

Well if you find when you get here [that] you have forgotten the way to our house, just inquire for W. H. Bennett's daughter and maybe someone will have compassion on you and tell you, or when you land at DeWitt, go to Mrs. Farr's and she will tell you where I am.

The snow has gone and the mud has come, and I know how to travel through it, but it is not very bad yet. The turnpike roads are dry and we get along very well.

If you have to haul coal when I come, I shall have to do as a young man's wife did that we are acquainted with. She came to his home, and when he went for coal, she went with him. They hauled it about twenty-five miles but could not make a trip in a day.

I should think that your friend Frank had cut enough poles to satisfy his appetite.

I am glad to hear such a favorable report about the *Watchword*, for I look anxiously for it every week.

I must write you what a knock I got the other day from one of my boys. Oh, scholars! I allow them to toss the ball in the schoolroom sometimes, and the boy that stood opposite the door bounced it just as I came in and it hit me fair in the eye, and it seemed my eye went *in* my head. For some time it was very painful, but I doctored it with snow a while and it has come all right now.

Might I inquire the cause of your having such bitter enemies in your neighborhood? It cannot be very pleasant to have persons feel this toward you. I won't want to visit them for fear we might not agree.

I don't remember whether I wrote you or not that mother said that if you wished to bring any of your friends that they were welcome, and although our house is small, we will accommodate them the best we can, and she says you must calculate to stay at our house some time as they want to get acquainted with you before you take me away.

I have not decided what color for a dress I shall get yet, as I want to talk with Lucy a little about it and have not had any chance yet, but I will let you know when I do decide.

Have you heard from Uncle and Aunt Coleman lately? How are they enjoying themselves now?

One of the school directors near here wanted to engage me to teach the summer turn. What do you say to that, Roy?

Our quarterly meeting begins tomorrow.

The spotted fever[133] is raging in Clinton and Lyons.

Now I send my love and bid you good night, hoping you [have] much enjoyment in the days to come, and sweet repose. Write just what you like and I won't get tired reading it. From yours,

Martha Bennett

Low Moor, Iowa

Low Moor

Feb. 28th '72

Dear Roy,

I was the recipient of a letter from you last evening and I did not answer it then as mother and Lucy were here and had to talk so much business, I could not compose myself to write you. I am very glad to hear that you are all well and enjoying life as you are, only that it is too bad that you are suffering from the spring fever, and think Dr. Scott had better prescribe for you before you get worse.

The roads are dry here now and we are not compelled to [go] near our rivers to and from school, of which I am very glad, for I dislike to fuss with them.

Just three weeks and school will be out. The spotted fever is raging around here. [There was] a death occured this week in Low Moor. The child took, or was taken, sick last night at eight and died at noon today. I shall close school tomorrow noon to attend the funeral. I am allowed a day to visit some school, and I have used half a day already, and there is no other school I care to visit, and will use the remainder of time in that way. How suddenly death comes, and how necessary to be prepared for that important time. There is considerable sickness in this part of the country. I am very much obliged to you for the remedies you have written of for my cold and will use them any time I have the opportunity, but as the cough has left me entirely, I will not use them now, and I hope we will not have any more colds in Colo.

Now, really, I don't wonder that the ladies were surmising as to who would do the cooking, for the Editor put that in pretty cute about the Carpenter houses, don't you think so?

No, I won't feel proud if people look up to us when "his son lives in the house he now occupies," and be careful that his son don't [feel pride]. But I am afraid you will pay more than [$25] for your wife, and I don't know whether you will ever get paid or not. Time will tell.

Yes, I can make bread but cannot tell whether [I] will have good luck or not every time, and [I] can cook a few other things. When you can't stand it any longer, we will go down to your mother's for a change, and then we will get a good meal, surely. Did I understand you that our house is nearer town than your father's, or not? If so, we can stop on the way home and get supper, and then you can sleep well after eating good victuals.

Lucy was here from Sunday until this morning, and we had some music worth listening to, if I am any judge. Practice has perfected her.

I sent my turkey home, one that Mr. H[inman] says is my Christmas present. He told me that I was to select three of his chickens some time, and he would present me with them. It will pay, won't it, to take a few?

Certainly, I will excuse you if you don't answer every question, for I, like you, would rather read your letters when I am alone. I can enjoy them much more. How do you manage when you read my letters on the way from town? Let the team find the way themselves, or have someone drive for you[?] Suppose they should run away and you should loose the letter[?]

You wished to know if I was going to invite many to our wedding on account of the size of our house. I shall invite only our relatives and a few of my very particular friends. You may not know who my relations are. There are my two sisters' famil[ies] and an uncle at Bellevue and our family at home. We have some cousins living in the interior of the state, and maybe a few of them (one or two) will come, Mr. Ball's family, the ones Lucy lives with, and some of our neighbors, only a few. Now you can use your judgment about inviting some of your friends. We wish you to feel free to invite or bring some of your friends and to share equally with us. I would rather you would have some of your friends. Mother wishes you to use your judgment and feel as if you were one of the family. We were talking over our affairs last night and can't see how I can get ready before the last of April, or if it will discommode you too much, I will have to do more when I get there and go with less ready. Now, don't understand by this that I wish to put you off, for this is not the intention. Our time is so short after school is out before April begins that I can't accomplish much. How will it suit you, Roy, or you can tell better in a week or two, perhaps, than now.

I hope we will never be guilty of flattery now, and then stop it after [a] while, or to flatter to obtain each other's affections, for I would wish our affections towards each other to increase in after years, and, like you, wish our wedding day to be one that we can look back to in after years with a great deal of pleasure. I certainly think a jealous couple must be the most unhappy persons in this world, and if I were not *assured* that I could trust you out of my sight, and you me, I would rather our affections for each other would be severed forever than to think that either of us were jealous of each other. But I do not apprehend any such trouble. [I] do not have such fear, for you have been away so long that I might have become sure of nothing of the kind if I had not *known* better from my acquaintance with you. Do not fear but that our folks will think *well* of you. At least, I don't [have such a fear], and like your folks, they will think me fortunate in claiming your affections. I have often expressed my views as you did: "I always wanted a companion that had a mind superior to mine," or that I considered as such, and I have never *changed* my mind yet either about that subject.

Well, if both of us are quiet, who will do the talking? Our folks often tell me I must be more sociable, but I don't like to talk unless I can say something of some account, so I listen to others talk. Well, if you *are* hard to become acquainted [with], when anyone forms your acquaintance, they have formed one of some consequence. How *much* better anyone appears if they don't put on borrowed airs.

You may talk to the ladies. I won't worry if you do. Nor have I allowed the attentions of any gentleman this winter. I don't care for any. You will have to go to considerable expense for me, and I only hope I may be able to repay you in some way for it sometime.

I received the papers. Have not read much in them yet, but no danger but what I will for I *love* to read.

I am pleased to learn you enjoyed yourself so well on the Friday evening mentioned and only hope you will enjoy yourself every day. I would like to have [been] a little bird when you spoke. Those three sheets were not too much and arrived safely. Mr. West and Meeker are having quite a lengthy conversation on the liquor question through the columns of the *Tribune*.[134] My wish to you is enjoyment of this life and the life to come. I send my love to you. Please write your middle name a little plainer for me again. I will write mine. Martha Allen Bennett. Tell Sarah she must not plague you at all.

Allen

Greeley
6th of March 1872
Dear Martha,
Yesterday I received your good letter. We are yet well and (excepting Silas [and] Mattie who have just improved from their vaccination), young Temple and I expect to finish digging the cellar which is 17 x 22 feet. Although the ground is about as hard as your cellar was, yet the sun does not shine as warm as last summer.

I believe you need not loose time by attending a funeral that is in your school district.

You will live a little closer to town [Greeley] than our folks, and we have a better view than they have, being a little higher.

As to my fever this spring, I received a good one in using an Irishman's pick and shovel in making the new cellar.

I of late have often thought that it would put you to some inconvenience to get ready in a few days after your school was out. And I will not think you are doing anything but right to take enough time in getting ready. And it may suit me to wait a few days longer than I had thought at first, but will try and let you know in time if possable. Brother William[135] in Ohio was married the day he was of age.

A kind offer [of] Mr. H[inman]'s to give you those chickens as a present. It might pay to bring a few nice ones out here, but would cost more than it would pay to bring out *commercial* poultry.

As I expect to attend the Lyceum tomorrow evening, I want to put in [the mail] this letter at that time, and would [have] liked to have put it into the Post Office sooner, only I do not now go so often to town.

I always write such scattering thoughts as happens to enter my mind as I am writing. The way I read your letters on my way from town is when I am walking and not riding. Not long since as I was reading one of your letters, a man was driving his team in a sled at a rappid rate and told me to jump in while he was passing, but I preferred reading your letter than to ride and not read any. Our team when used are generally more gentle than last year and have yet never run off with the wagon or sled, for it would have made them double bobbs [double bob sleds] if they had. Hence, the necessity of extra care. Their not caring much for the cars [train] makes them easier to drive.

The snow is leaving some every day and will ere long be gone. But we are not sorry at all.

Yes, Meeker and West have been having a lively time in discussing the liquor question. But am in hopes they are through now.

We have our next quarterly meeting in the Baptist Church next Sabbath. It seems curious how rappidly time is passing off this winter. I can scarcely see where it has gone to. And soon you will close your school and bid your schollars a good by with fond recollections of the past. As to your taking a summer school that is offered to you, you can, of course, use your own judgment as seems best. But if you want to you might intimate to the director that there is a schollar out west that needs your valuable instructions and that you thought some of taking a trip out west where the white snow is seen towering high above the dark form of ledges of rock that he [would see at a point] many feet lower than this snowy range. Now, use your own pleasure in answering all civil questions. And if that young gent needs a housekeeper and wishes you [to be] serious, you can intimate that you are fond of a little change of climate, and like once a time a year to go for some antelope meat, jack rabbits and so fourth and most likely he will begin to think you are going where the "Wood vine never turneth."

I don't expect as fine an escort as Alexis received but will try to be content without so much pomp and show. A person only needs enough room to make them comfortable and that is all they can use. The prospect is fair of getting a new R.R. soon not far from here.

Well, I cannot yet tell as to whether or not I will bring any friend or not to our wedding, as it will be a busy time on the farm at that time of the year. Please let me know when to direct letters to DeWitt instead of Low Moor, so there need be no mistakes made in sending letters. I would, of course, be glad if I could call in to make your school a short visit, but will be busy until my leaving here and [it] may take me several days to get from here to DeWitt, and may go on the Kansas Pacific R.R. through Kansas City to see more of the country by so doing.

The people here are enjoying excellent health. Mrs. Stansby [?], Uncle Scott's sister-in-law is dangerously sick from brain feebleness as her constitution is quite delicate.

We have a good assortment of preaching on Sunday, and as it is a free country, [we] can take our choice of meeting as we see fit. I have often thought what a curious country [the Union Colony] we live in. On the east there is a stretch of hundreds of miles where but few people live. On the west the massive forms of the mountains, and a desert north and south for many miles. It is hoped that the cropps will be good this summer as this snow will dampen the ground. They expect to make some improvements in town this summer and some in our neighborhood. As I hope to see you ere long, if there is anything that I attempt to write, but you can't read, just remember it. My middle name is Swanstedt. But not Greeley, Colorado as you say yours or a post is Low Moor.

Ever yours,

L.S. Carpenter

Low Moor

Mar. 7, '72

Dear often thought of friend,

This evening came and with it a letter from you, and welcomely it was received, as I had been looking for one from you for a few days. I am very glad to learn that all of you are well and still liking Greeley life.

And you and Silas are digging up the Greeley soil again, are you? I hope you won't find it so hard to stir as to make you too tired or affect your comfort. Well, you won't have to write a great many more letters at night, and you won't have anyone to bother you by talking to you. I can sympathize with you for I have had to write all the letters I have written with a couple of noisy girls talking with Mr. and Mrs. Hinman. We won't have to pen our thoughts much longer, and [will] have no one to talk around us. I am afraid my tongue will bother you sometimes.

Are those German brothers good musicians? I noticed a short sketch about them in the paper speaking well of them.

Mr. West and Co. are having quite a lengthy conversation about liquor [in the Greeley *Tribune*].

I wish you could have heard Lucy laugh when she read about Mr. C.'s sow living in the house he now occupied.

I *supposed* when you asked me about my suit that you were asking to know what *color* to get for yourself and [I] cannot tell yet what color I should get, and you will have to get what you like. Of course, if our suit[s] were of colors that would contrast well, they would look nice when we stand up, but presume blue black or black will look very well with the color I may wear.

Well now, as men are calculated to have stronger minds than our sex, you must not be led away by any questions I should happen to tell you to ask. So, if I should write any more such questions, treat them as you have this one, and no harm will come of it.

You have accounted satisfactorily for the present for your enemies at Bethel, and those that make such remarks about others are often the *weakminded* ones themselves, and if he was acquainted with your family at all, he did not act the part of gentleman very much in referring to Silas. As you say, he was *jealous* of your ability.

If you are going to have me read, you will have to do the mending. I should just as leave you would exchange work as not, and as I like to hear *you* read, we will have to take turns at it. Will it be too late for me to plant some flower seeds when we get there? One of my scholars' mothers offered me some nice ones if I would come again to see them. I think I will go.

I wrote in my last about my not getting ready before the last of April, and have thought often since maybe it would keep you from home when you would be needed most. If it would be so I can leave a few things to finish untill I arrive. As I am rather young, I had not prepared as many things, as a good many have, for housekeeping, and therefore, consequently, thereby it takes a little more time to get ready.[136] But when I get home and get Mrs. Farr out to help me, I tell you she will make the work fly, and between she and Lucy to manage your poor, slow Martha [who] won't know how to do anything more than to keep out of their way. You must make up your mind to [accept] slow people, for such they always call me. When I was small, they used to call me grandmother, for I was so slow and particular. If we thought best, we *could* get ready a little sooner than the *last* of the month. Now please write what you think of it. I will have all my friends on command for the occasion if needed.

Do you intend building your father's house right away? Don't hurry them out of *our* house for I can live with them well enough, and if it would be more suitable to them not to have to move so soon, well enough. Do just as you think best, and I will be agreed. Did you say their house was, or would be, a quarter of a mile from ours? I have forgotten what you wrote about it.

I *will* make some allowance for you, but would not object to getting three such sheets as you wrote before *every* time. Next time we buy paper, we will have to get the largest size. I guess my initial paper will last me untill you come. If so, I won't use so much, only when I write home to our folks, or to tell mother how you treat me. I cannot write on it with any comfort. My eyesight is not good enough to see the lines by candle light unless the paper lies in a certain position.

There have been two deaths in this neighborhood since I wrote. One, the child of a couple. They were married a year ago New Years. They lived at his father's and all the family thought so much of it. Of course, it was a hard trial for them. The cause [was] the spotted fever. The other was the wife of one of the neighbors. She was buried Sunday and left four small children motherless. A young lady near Calamus with whom I correspond wrote that she attended church at Brushville once since Elder C[urtis] was married and that his wife was there, but he never introduced her to them, but went right home. She was quite well acquainted with the Elder lot. She thought his wife appeared like a very nice woman.

School closes Wednesday of week after next, and unless you answer pretty soon, maybe you had better direct to DeWitt. Oh, dear! I will have to go five miles for a letter then, instead of one. It will take longer to get them, won't it? But I suppose I can stand it for a few times.

Mrs H[inman] says I will keep some of our folks trotting to town all the time toward the last of the week. They are all sleeping now, and I just begin to think right. It has sleeted, rained, and snowed today, and of course, blowed from the east, leaving four inches of ice-like sand to travel through on the ground. But Mr. H[inman] did not let *us* travel through it, for he took us to school and brought us home.

Come in some evening and I will sing the piece I got off the Christmas Tree for you as I have learned it. Music is of so much pleasure to me. Lucy is going to give me some instruction when I go home so that I can help myself to learn better.

If you come the K.P.R.R. [Kansas Pacific][137] you will have the advantage of seeing another part of the country. Does this road run to Burlington or farther north? I never traced it all the way through but know where the principle part of it runs.

How had you rather do when we travel, make our farewell visit at home before we go to Tipton or after? How time speeds along on swiftest wings. My love to all your folks, and I still remain yours and hope you may be able to read this while enjoying good health.

Truly yours as ever,

Martha A. Bennett

Greeley

March 12th 1872

Dearest Friend,

The letter that I received yesterday evening, I read while coming from town in our wagon, and the team didn't run away either. Well, as I forgot to attend to one errand while in town, I had to go back after dark, and young Horsley, an Irishman, staid all night. No chance was given me to answer your letter yesterday evening. And today, I have been taking a half ton of coal up to Mary's through the wind, and my eyes feel a little dim this evening. Your letters as ever are easily read and seem not to need ruled paper, for they are straight and nice. Now you are getting to sharp for my dull comprehensions in suggesting that if you read (as I suggested) for me to do your housework, for you must know that I am no house keeper. And you ought to make a little allowance for a country boy. I guess you'll find a little time to read aloud. I had never noticed that you was a quiet lady, for I had though[t] you [a] very interesting person to talk to. But when they say you are so slow, they had better not be too sure, for I don't think alike with them on that subject. When I was in my teens, our folks used to complain of my being so slow. I couldn't help it if I was, could I? And if you find me too slow, just say "Hurry up!" and then I can tell you when I am so slow.

When I asked in regard to your suit of clothes, I referred to the *color* only. Most likely, my suit will be of a dark complexion; is that the fashion in Clinton Co., or have you noticed of late? In my oppinion a lady generally looks well in a purple colored suit if [the lady is] of fair complexion.

Now that our house is set upon a hill, it will become us the more to set a good example to those below us. (My pen writes too heavy) The new house will be about a quarter of a mile west of *ours* and not quite so high on the hill, but is to be one and a half stories high, and will most likely be built before long. But I guess there will be enough room in this one for us all until theirs [Leroy's parents] is finished. And then we will make them hustle out of this one in a hurry, won't we Martha? We noticed in the Davenport *Gazette* that the spotted fever was raging in and around DeWitt. I am sorry to learn of its presence and feel a little uneasy as to your welfare. Am a little afraid that you may get the fever, to. I have often thought how true the words in a stanza in the Methodist hymn book:

Dangers stand thick through all the ground
To push us to the tomb,
And fierce diseases wait around
To hurry mortals home.

Mary and the family were not at home today, but most likely had gone up to Fort Colins.

I haven't sent you the late numbers of the Greeley *Tribune*. Nothing special of interest is in them. "Rosa Robbins" isn't very brisk just now. Fox and Augustus have both joined the rebel army.

The weather is nice with the exception of too much wind for comfort. The snow is leaving.

We had another quarterly meeting last Sunday at the Baptist Church. Mr. Vincent, our presiding elder, preached to a full house in the evening. Mr. Adams preached in the morning. Father, Sarah, and myself attended in the morning. After preaching, I waited for S.S. and then went to S.S. at the Presbyterian Church which meets at half past two o'clock. Then, mother Sarah, and this boy went to hear our elder in the evening. So, you see I attended two preachings and two S.S.s on Sunday. It kept me quite busy to attend all my appointments.

You ask if the German brothers are good singers. They are good singers and are well liked in town. There is no putting on airs or arguing with them. They are going to live on this side of the river ditch, as they are commencing to build, but will not be as near town as we are, as their claims are about two miles west from here and some farther north than our house.

Well, it is getting to be about time that Mr. G[ulick] pops the question to you if he expects to get you for a housekeeper. And poor fellow; his cake is all dough this time, and will have to try again.

In speaking of my enemies at Bethel, don't understand me [to be] claiming any mental greatness. I meant, or referred to, his two-faced system. I have never asked anyone to flatter me in any way. But why this direct contradiction of his own words? That he was fooling of me hence, we knew quite well. And if no preventing providence [intervenes], he may have a chance to remain so if we succeed well out here.

Now I am pleased to learn that your sister, Lucy was amused at seeing our new home made mention of in the *Tribune*. I have an idea that she is but another model lady like my Martha, and don't mean any flattery, but really think so and will be glad to see my new relation.

Yes, you may reserve some of those initial envelopes if you choose to inform your folks how unkind I am to my dear girl. Well, if I can't love "that little school marm," who can I love? Or, if I fail to prove true to her my chance would be poor to find another that would have me, and that I could love as a wife. One thing, bear in mind, my dearest, that is I am far from being perfection, and if you ever thought so, don't continue to think so, for I am only a poor living mortal, and have often thought when thinking of myself, how strikingly true is the Scripture when it tells of the depravity of the human heart.

As the sing[ing] class of late meets in the evening, Tuesday evening, I have not of late attended. I am in hopes the discussion between Mr. West and Meeker has come to a perpetual end.

You ask if we will make our final adieu at your folks before visiting at Tipton. Now I would like to know that we could make it suit to call at Tipton. As that would be off the route to be convenient, it seems unhandy to bring our things off of the R.R. Aside from friend Scott living in Tipton, we have no relations in that neighborhood. We have an aunt and cousin on my father's side, living about seven miles south of Mechanicsville off of the R.Road again, but no doubt it would be best to leave for a stop left in the east as we go west, and leave going back over the R.R. again. As I hope to get my clothes at Tipton (or expect to), I want to try and get a little money there if possable and may make a call on some of the folks some miles distant from Bethel. Now don't think that I am contriving any plan so as to look at our going together at all places on our wedding tour as any trouble at all. But how I would wish that we could give them all a call and that we could be together at any place. Don's wife and child living at Clarence I would like us both to visit before leaving if possable.[138] We must make a call at Oskaloosa at least before leaving Iowa. I can come by Burlington [R.R.] I believe, if there is any object in so doing. But as I am not well posted yet, am not sure whether it will be on my route or not. Anything that I may at present write may [be] very far from having the best way. And merely mention these things and want to know your desires always *first*. Please mention your thoughts without reserve. Remembering always that I am your boy at Greeley, Colorado.

Carpenter

Any part that you can't read, pleas tell me of it and I will try and do it better the next time. Yours for life,

L.S.C.

Low Moor

Mar. 12th, '72

Dear friend Leroy,

Your welcome letter of the eighth instant arrived at its destination this evening and was duly received and its contents processed. We are all well and enjoying life pretty well. There was a very bad rain, hail, and snow storm last week, making snow or sleet-like sand to walk through or worse, and if Mr. H[inman] was not kind enough to take us to school it would be very hard walking. It is about three inches deep. I am glad you are enjoying life so well and are getting over the fever for it is a very disagreeable complaint.

Oh, dear! I can't half think of anything to write to you. That is just all there is about it. My mind is so confused, I can scarcely gather the pieces *up as it were*, but nevertheless, I will try and give you a little pleasure by writing a few sentences from this unworthy pen of mine.

There is a great deal of sickness about here: the small pox, spotted fever, and colds in general, but your unworthy friend has been spared through it all without one day of severe sickness. Mr. Hinman's daughter came home from school with her face all swelled with erysipelas,[139] and so it goes, a great many complaining.

I read the most of your letter as I came from school. Mr. H[inman] came after me and brought it for me, and as the girls did not come home untill tomorrow, I could read it without any quizing. You know children can do that very well. Mr. H[inman] says those are good fowls he offered me.

You write as I do; whatever comes into my mind.

I thought you were going to say, "You're reading my letter and the man came so fast you did not know it and he ran over or against you." But I might have known better as those sharp eyes can keep track of teams and letters. Keep the team gentle so I can drive them easy.

The time has slipped by *very* fast for me and it is just as well, for it won't seem so long untill spring for either of us, and when any[one] does not keep looking forward to some particular time in the future, but lives for the present, time flies faster.

Don't you anticipate a great deal of enjoyment in the Quarterly meeting you spoke of? It is a good thing to have the choice of so many ministers. You can have a better chance to decide who suits you best.

Yes, only six days more and I will close school [March 18] maybe for the last time. The recollections of the past are pleasant, and I often think the teacher's lot is rather [lonely] for when we become attached to our pupils [we] have to leave them. I sent to Lyons the other day and got some cards for them, some of the handsomest ones I ever saw.

I heard that the county superintendent was wondering why no one could hire Martha Bennett to teach school this summer. Don't you? I suppose everyone from Low Moor to Calamus will know of my getting married before it comes to pass, for I told Mrs. Harris of Calamus that I was corresponding with you, for the minister there wanted to pay some attention to me and I told her the reason I did not want it. She told her husband and *he* told a good many others, and I don't know how Mrs. Coal, one of our neighbors knew of it. [She] came over to Lydia's and told her all about it. Now I think Willie must have told them for I told no others that said anything about it, or would say anything. It is so trying to think you have a friend and find often them not to be such.

When I get home, we will talk the matter of time over, and I will write you about it. We will get home Thursday of next week.

You will be content with your little school marm for company, I hope, on your return to the land, "where the fish jump into the pan already to cook." [On the train] We will take two seats and make a little room for ourselves, unless the car is so full we cannot.

I am sorry to hear of the illness of your uncle's sister-in-law.

Yes, I hope the snow will dampen the ground enough to make the crops a success without too much labor, for I presume every landholder needs all assistance possible from snow and rain as very probably their means have become somewhat limited by living through the winter. What a pleasant time of the year it will be to travel when the fields are clothed in green and all Nature rises to proclaim the greatness of their Creator! Tell Mattie I should like to hear from her once more before leaving Iowa, but perhaps her time is occupied in some other way. Maybe I ought not require it of her. How does your father stand the western climate, and does your mother still enjoy good health? Tell them I often think of them and send my love to them.

That young gentleman is not quite so friendly as he used to be. I guess a little bird has been whispering in his ears to keep still, [and] that I did not care about him. I hope so, for I don't care to tell him myself.

Now, Roy, can you pardon me for this poor excuse of a letter, for I can scarcely think at all and the next one I will try and make more interesting. If you [see] me careless, say so; if not say what you think always and that will suit me exactly, and I will endeavor to do the same. I am obliged to you for the corrections you made in the writing of my name. It would appear rather strange to some, I suppose, unless they knew I meant it for the name of [the] Post Office. Would you like to be called by your middle name?

Write a good long letter if you please, and remember, I remain yours,

Martha Bennett

Low Moor

March 19th '72

My dearest Leroy,

This morning I sit down for the last time in Mr. Hinman's house to write you. Your very welcome letter was received yesterday morning and read with much pleasure, as I was sewing on the machine and putting a quilt together. Of course, I did not sew very much untill after your letter was read. My hand is not very steady and you must excuse mistakes if you find any. I should have answered your letter last evening, but I had made arrangements to visit one of my scholars and thot best not to disappoint them.

The snow is nearly gone and it is rather windy in the evening, although it freezes every night hard enough to hold anyone up.

Tomorrow I will teach the last day of school that I may ever teach in Clinton Co., Iowa. The County Super was very much astonished when in my reply to the question, "Will you apply for the Low Moor school?" I answered, no. He said he thought they would make up an extra purse of $50 or $60 for me. I tell you, they are after me now. I don't want them.

We do not here of so many cases of the spotted fever as we did. This a physician told me the other day was only a very severe form of the typhus, but there is a new disease called cerebro spinal meningitis, or break neck that is pretty fatal but caused by taking cold, and if a mustard plaster is applied immediately, it generally relieves the patient.[140] I have taken pains to find out about these diseases in case I should be taken. Now, don't worry, Roy, for if I should be taken [I will] do all in my power to have it stopped by a good physician, and that is all we can do.

It would be a great deal of pleasure to me to read aloud if I can, so I shall not object very much.

You had better not send any more of the papers unless there is something very particular in them, but keep [them] untill I come, as I shall be so busy I cannot take much time to read them, although I should like to very much.

I have not noticed very particularly about the color of gentlemen's clothes, so I could not say anything about it.

Now, your folks are perfectly welcome, of course in our house and untill they are ready to go, I would like to have them stay. I don't know whether it is for a very selfish motive or not, but it really would be a little more convenient for me [if they stayed] a short time. I can get things straightened a little.

Now, you must not stop going to church and S.S. after I come, as a man did that was married here this winter. After they were married, they both stopped going to S.S., and he was not at church last Sunday, but I love to go to S.S. so well, if you don't take me, what *shall* I do? But I am not going to worry at all about it, for it won't make it any better.

Mr. Gulic[k] does not bother me very much any more. Sunday I was standing near the door and he stepped so close to me to ask me when I would leave these quarters, that if I chose I could have kicked him without any trouble, and you may be sure I took one long step back in a hurry. No, I don't think he will pop the question this time; may wait until next.

I shall not think you wish to speak of your mental ability in the matter of your neighbor at Bethel. Only wish to show how changeable his mind is and how he contradicts him[self].

I shall never have an occasion to write to our folks anything except how *well* you treat me, and Roy, I only hope I may be able to return your affections in such a manner that neither of us will have occasion to ever regret our union. I shall remember what you think of yourself if you will remember the same of me, that I am far, very far from perfection, and you may not be surprised to find many mistakes attending my course through this life. But one thing certain, if both of us live to make others happy (by others I mean each other as well as our friends) we will not see such great faults as we might.[141]

I shall not think you wish to deprive me of the privilege of visiting our friends near Tipton, if you do call on some of them, for it will be impossible for us to call on all [of] them if we should like to. I should like to call on your sister-in-law at Clarence very much as I have heard you make mention of her several times, and of course, we must call on Mr. and Mrs. Coleman, for if it had not been for *her*, we should not have found each other. Certainly, we ought to express our thanks to them and call on them. Suppose we arrange our visits after you come. How would that do? It will suit me to visit just where you want and you just where I want to, I suppose. When I get home and talk with our folks, I can tell better then what to do and will [be able to] write more satisfactorily then, but I must stop now as it is time for school. But I remain more than ever to you as far as I am concerned.

From one who loves you,

Martha Bennett

P.S. Please direct to DeWitt and excuse haste.

At home [Greeley]

March 23, 1872

My dearest Martha,

I received your interesting letter yesterday evening. The weather is splendid but freezes some at night. We are well. All of your suggestions are in direct accordance with my own views. We can tell much better when together as to when and where we will visit, and in fact can't tell much about the matter until we can converse with talking. It takes so much time and ink to express one's views on paper that we can make that matter all right when we meet. I will have to first go to Tipton to see about my clothes before going to your house, unless you prefer for me to do otherwise. If so, please mention it. As the saying is, you took the words out of my mouth when you say that I will go where you want me to and maybe you will do the same for me. And if I don't mind, you just do as if I was one of your pupils: take me by the ear and tell me to come along with you. What say you, my dear? Now, it must be a disappointment to the superintendent not to have Miss Bennett any longer for a school teacher. Well, I appreciate the responsibility that is resting on me to be kind to my young wife who is so good a teacher. No doubt the people between Calamus and Low Moor often inquire if that young Miss B. is going to get a man as smart and good looking as herself and quite likely [they] will find themselves deceived, and will conclude that the young lady could have done better at teaching and [could] have waited for a better chance. Well, I *know* one thing: there are some that are jealous of my place in claiming the affections, and at no distant period of time, the hand of Miss Bennett. I refer to my old neighborhood and fancy the cynic's expression, "Well he couldn't have got her if his aunt hadn't helped him." How handy it is to have a good aunt. I have never heard of anyone that has said so, but am so well acquainted there that I can well imagine such to be the thoughts of a few. Now, of course we *must* call on our folks at Oskaloosa, and may express our thanks to uncle and aunt for their [our] introduction. But I will mention now what at any time in the future I would have done. After coming home from your home the first time, I wrote to Aunt and tried to express my thanks for their kindness in our introduction, but don't understand me to presume that I wished to have them think that you would have me, for I only referred to the introduction. And I want you to cease thinking about hoping that you may repay me by diligence for the money spent on you becoming my companion that you mentioned of late, for you own just as much of *our* little property as I do, and [you] are *under no* obligations to me at all,[142] and I propose marrying because I love the person and not your money. And [I] had intended to tell you to let me know if you need any money. If so, just mention it. "Better late than never."

Mr. Adams and a Methodist lady with him came up here on Wednesday to get the promise of milk and eatables for the M.E. festival to be held next Wednesday evening in the new M.E. church. You are invited to attend. Mr. Adams allowed [that] since our folks are going into their own house ere long, maybe that he could have the benefit of marrying me to some one of Greeley's maidens, but I intimated that there wasn't much chance for him on my part but asked him what were his charges for the uniting of a couple, and he laughed and did not say. Now, you are to choose the day, the minister and so fourth in our case. If you prefer the evening to the daytime, it will make no difference to me. Many prefer, as did young Welch's, to be married n the evening.

It is the intention to start the M.E.S.S. a week from next Sunday, and we will try to attend at least some of the time if at the right hour. I will, of course, excuse your haste in writing, but can read easily your letters. Excuse these scribbled lines. Do I understand you that you think best that we should have attendants?

As our time for corresponding is nearly at a close, anything you think of just mention it. As for myself, by present appearances, I can best leave here before long, and if [it] will suit you, tell me if you can guess about the time. The exact time of the wedding, I think, need not be known until I get to your house or about that time, unless you prefer otherwise.

I had expected Mr. G[ulick] would make some further indiscretions to you, that he took a fancy in your mind. As for that kiss, that doesn't belong to him, and [I] think him a little foolish to ask a kiss of you as that belongs to lovers only when done privately (plays being excepted). He will soon, I hope, know who the fortunate fellow is. One thing please remember: that is that I am being tanned some from work-ing outdoors of late. On that account, it would suit me to go back there quite soon, as I don't want to be as dark if I can help it, as the red man that not long since roamed over these plains. I am of that complexion that is easily tanned.

I will try and not worry myself about your being among the spotted fever, but have often feared for you. Is that disease contagious, or do you know?

I think that by next week at this time, we will have finished putting into the ground our wheat and oats, and after that is done I can leave at almost any time. Father expects to hire some person to help them in set-ting out our trees and shrubbery. If it is convenient to you, please write often. I have several things to talk with you about.

Yours in love,

Roy Carpenter

The moon shines so brightly these evenings that I cannot sleep so well as when [it is] the dark of the moon. If I have failed to answer anything in this letter, please write it again. Most likely my suit of clothes will be of a dark color. I love to read your letters and their authors.

At home [DeWitt]

March 30th '72

My dearest Leroy,

Your very welcome and interesting letter was received yesterday and duly appreciated, for it has seemed so long since I heard from you. The letter came day before yesterday, but as mother and I were at Lyons and did not return untill yesterday, I did not enjoy the unspeakable pleasure of reading it untill yesterday afternoon, and I should have answered it last evening if I had not promised to spend the evening at one of our neighbors before the receipt of your letter.

Now, I am so liable to misplace the modifying clause where it should not be placed. Read it as if the last clause was often promised.

We are having a steady cold eastern rain today and are in hopes it will do much good to the soil.

We are all quite well. I am not entirely rested yet from our ride to Lyons.[143] Mother and I drove the team, and the roads being a little rough, it seemed to tire me considerable, or caused me to have the back ache which is a new complaint for me.

I am very much pleased to know that our views are similar, and will not abuse you if you don't do just as I wish. Certainly, I will go with you wherever you wish me to, and as you are going to Tipton after your clothes, if there are some persons there you wish to visit that will make the number too large for *us* to visit, why don't hesitate to visit them at that time, for unless you have considerable time, we could not visit all without spoiling our visits with some that, perhaps, you would rather visit when I was with you. Of course, I should not object to visiting all of your friends with you, but I merely suggest this so that you may see that I am not particular.

Yes, the superintendent will be considerably disappointed if I don't teach, but I wonder if *he* would if he were in my place. Of course, not. You see, it's an *accommodation* to him to have me continue at it as he knows my qualifications and does not have to *trouble* to examine me and can depend upon me. No flattery; only a natural standing up for oneself, you understand.

Well, if people should judge that Miss. B. has made an *unwise* choice, and has not found a companion equal to herself, *she* thinks she has found one more than her equal, and if *she* thinks so they and we ought to be satisfied. Those folks that are jealous of you might be glad if they had as good an aunt to help them as you have, or to introduce them. Of course, *all the aunts you have* could not have made the match any more than Aunt Martha [Coleman] if *we* had not have seen fit.

As you so kindly wish me to cease thinking of my obligation to you, I will and will not refer to it again if unpleasant to you. You are very kind to offer me money, but I have not needed any and do not at the present, and as you told me once before to ask you if I needed any assistance, don't trouble yourself by thinking that you are too late.

Did Mr. Adams think you were getting so old he needed to assist you in getting a wife? If he did, he was very kind to do so, wasn't he? But you tell him you have a housekeeper engaged for the summer.

Thank you for the invitation to attend the festival, but as I have not any *beau*, I guess I will not go.

I have concluded to have my brother-in-law [Mary's husband] perform the ceremony, and I would prefer to have you write to him to that effect. His address is H. H. Green, Maquoketa, Jackson County, Iowa. [I] think he may think I have forgotten that he is a Reverend if we don't have him do so.

I think that the twenty-fifth 25th of April will be the most suitable time for us. By *us* I mean my folks, and as your[s] are very accommodating generally, I presume it will suit you also. I suppose you will have to come a day beforehand, as you will have to go to Clinton for the license. We will meet you at the depot whenever you will be there.

Marshall [Fox, Lydia's husband] told me he wanted the job of taking you down to Clinton. That is the brother-in-law that lives near us. You must not hire your way out here.

I have not got my dress [made] yet, but will send you a piece when I cut it. It is a narrow black and white striped.

Mother says to tell you we think of having a cold tea instead of wedding dinner and wants to know if you would prefer dinner. Yes, I would rather have attendants for the afternoon, and if we go any place the next day, if you have either of your intimate friends that you would wish to bring, do so and tell him that we live in a poor house and he may have to take it camp meeting style, but he will be just as welcome as if we lived king's style. But if you have no one that will come, we could invite

Mr. Young of DeWitt. You remember him, of course. I will have Lucy for bridesmaid and you choose just whom you will. If you have either of your friends [who] will come with you, or be groomsman, we will meet him the 25th at the depot whenever he comes.

You had better make a heavy vaile to wear over your face, and you won't get tanned. Ha, ha! That's the way I do.

Mr. G[ulick] did not get the kiss, but he might have got it.

I have enjoyed our correspondence very much indeed, but hope our lives together will be *more* pleasant to both than our courtship [has] been. Since school was out, I have been quilting and riding and attending to things generally. Our folks have given me quite a start in things to keep house with. Write once more, if not oftener, and remember me ever, as I often, very often, think of you. Your letters are a feast to me, for I *love their author*. From

Martha Bennett

Greeley
April tenth 1872
Dearest Friend Martha,
It has been several days since I last wrote to you and last received one of those ever welcomed letters that of late have been coming about once a week. I went down this evening to the Post Office, expecting to get a letter from DeWitt; was disappointed. Now it may be that tomorrow's mail may bring the looked for intelligence. I hope so! But one thing that I did not mention, and that is I expect to write the last letter as that may mention when or near the time of my going back there. If I get a letter from you soon, I will try and answer soon, and if it is your last letter, please mention it so that I may answer and avoid your sending and not my getting (excepting of course those sent to our folks).

Father has a bad cold, but the rest of us are well.

Cousin Frank came down from his claim near Mary's last Tuesday, and I went with him into the mountains where he has been cutting pine poles the past winter. The boys have a log hut where they stay when not at work near their work. Got there Friday evening after driving over very uneven places. But the joke of it was we found ourselves introduced into the direct presence of a native of that country, that thought it a free country and was enjoying the comfort of the comforts of a good shelter and a warm cot to sleep in. You have seen and heard of this species of animal no doubt ere this. Is of a nice color and is a cat, but has by some means had the title of Pool [Pole] prefixed to his name. Now, either he or us had to leave the shanty. But we thought our rights came first, so summoning all our courage up, Frank got his firearm ready, and while I held two candles, he finished the chap after firing three loads of lead. The rest of our trip was enjoyed by finding about four inches of snow that had fallen during the night and was real winter on Saturday morning. But came down to his home that day (Saturday). It had only rained a little down here at the time it snowed up there. I came home yesterday (Monday). There [are] more storms in the mountains at this time of the year than during the winter months. The scenery is very interesting to one that never saw big hills and massive piles of rocks, but the largest mountains are further up into the Snowy Range. This range presents a beautiful picture on clear days. But I hope ere long your *own* eyes will see this picture of nature.

The festival in the new M.E. Church was a success, taking in about $210 that night. This is used for carpeting the aisles and pulpit. As I was up to Mary's on last Sunday, was not at the opening of the church. Mr. Thompson, the Presbyterian minister, preached in the A.M. services, Mr. Adams having a headache. They want to establish a S. School.

No doubt you are very busy these days, and if so, I would not want to put you to the trouble of writing many letters, unless you want to, but as I have been receiving letters so regularly, I am afraid that these unworthy lines may find you suffering with that spotted fever. I am *very* anxious to learn of your good welfare. Am waiting for a letter from you.

It may be that my last two letters failed to reach you. If so, just mention it if you will.

We have been putting out our oats and wheat but have to finish this week. And if I *knew* you were ready, I would try and start next Monday, but will wait further knowledge from you before starting. If I get a letter from you stating that it would suit you at any time, you need not answer this, for I have as yet, I believe, received every letter that you have sent me.

I am getting some tanned every day as the sun shines most of the time, and the wind blows briskly occasionally. It may take more days to get there than if I were going on the Union Pacific R.R., as my route may be to St. Louis and up the river. My object would be to see the country and will have to stop at Tipton. If they will have to make my clothes after getting there, it may take me longer than I would like, but [I] will have to wait until they are ready. I have sent no orders yet, and it would be no use in so doing, as they will have to take my measurement before thinking of furnishing my suit. These lines have been spoken plainly and [I] would not excuse them so, only that they are matters of fact, and as I am addressing one that is interested in my welfare, and you know that I only love you. I often think of you and cherish the hope that we may meet ere long, both in good health and trusting in a happy future. If you haven't received those last two letters, please reply to this quite soon.

Remember your absent lover,

Roy S. Carpenter

Understand that you are to take your own time at getting ready and I will try and come at about the proper time. I do not know whether it will suit any young man at Bethel to go with me down to your house. This is a busy time of the year.

Mrs. Stansberry is no better, and as her complaint is the heart disease, [she] may pass away at any time.

〽

Greeley

13th April 1872

My own dear Martha Bennett,

Yours of the last date has been received yesterday evening. I never have been more pleased with a sample of clothing of any kind than that of your dress material. It is a model in every respect. And now the next thing is, can I get a suit of clothes that will compare with yours? I am afraid that your good judgment will prove to plainly of your wisdom. Maybe I had better get a suit of ladies' cloth, or fine calico trimmed off with a blue ribbon. A good saque might make me a *good* covering over my breakfast stole.

But a little sober. Mrs. Stansberry died on Wednesday morning the tenth inst at four o'clock A.M. [She] was buried at ½ past two on the eleventh. The day was very windy, especially the P.M. As I don't expect to receive any more letters from you (but I would be glad to) I will finish our correspondence with this letter. The time has passed pleasantly and rappidly to us both. One year ago yesterday P.M. we landed at Greeley. How short a time it seems to me. I am glad to know that you are so fleshy, and your folks need not wonder or plague you about it, as it only proves that you have been well kept (fed) and that you are ready for market.[144] And if you are fleshy and in good order, I love you just as much, for as we are soon to be made one, you can take one of me a little better. You weigh at least ten pounds more than I do. But my health is *perfect*.

As to writing plainly to you, I have always observed or tried to [be aware of] the fact that letters often fall into the hands of other persons. And maybe not our friends who might make sport of and expose them to others. For written in ink, they are indelable unless destroyed. But it is a fact that as we are soon to be made man and wife, the desguise will be thrown off, and we will concourse together as we see fit and it will be no person's business. For to the married and the world, the curtain is drawn, and they have their own liberty to choose what may and may not be made further. Of course, propriety is *always* to be observed even in the married state, but this is a matter of their own choice. While you may have been known as "the little school marm," the world will soon learn that you have become Mrs. C., and then you are at liberty to go with me when and wherever you may choose to. I love you as I love no other female, and hope my affections will retain their needed love, etc. during the time of our honey moon. True love should only grow deeper the longer we are together.

Unless you have grown taller, I believe I am a little taller than you are, but you are more heavy set, or built, than I am. But I am glad to know that I am to have a wife of some flesh, as we may be more comfortable together.

In my last you may notice that I have written to Rev. H. H. Green, Maquoketa, Jackson County, Iowa, and I wish you would, if not already done so, to inform him of *our* desire. Maybe he did not receive that letter. I wrote the next day after you first spoke of the matter to me. Be *sure* to have him on hand to join us together, my darling and sweetest treasure.

As Marshall [Fox] and I will need one day to go and get our license at Clinton, and I had better see you (maybe), I can't go to your house and to Clinton the same day. I will try and get to DeWitt on the first passenger train that day on Tuesday before *our* Thursday. On Wednesday, he and I may go for our license, so that on the 23rd, I will try and get to DeWitt, on the 24th to Clinton, and the big day the 25th. I will invite friend Reeder to accompany us on the floor as groomsman, but if he can't come, may have to do without any attendant. If such should be the case, you may invite for me any young man excepting George Young. I can tell you on Tuesday. I expect to leave here on next Monday the 15th (fifteenth) at 4 P.M. After getting to Kansas City, will go the nearest road to Iowa and not go to St. Louis, as I haven't time. If I had time, would have liked to take a boat ride up the Mississippi River. Mr. Adams intends going on a visit east the weak after I leave here. His wife went several weeks ago.

I am in hopes you have got my last letter. I was surprised to know that some of the town people, not our relatives, knew of my intending to go east, and yesterday evening I was asked about it, and [I] told them that I was going on a visit and had a little money coming to me there. But when we get here, they will think that I have had a good errand back to Iowa.

As before mentioned, I want you to take your own time at visiting back there. But we will try and make out our programme when together. Expect to stop over next Sunday at Bethel. If it will suit you, we will come in the Union Pacific R.R. as that is some nearer than the other road [Kansas Pacific Railroad].

Our Literary Society after next Friday evening, will adjourn until fall, my dear. I expect you will get, if not already, get tired of my addressing you as my dear. But please don't think hard of me doing so. We received four letters yesterday evening. One from J. W. Reeder, Tipton (to myself), from Oskaloosa to mother, and from Jud Scott, Tipton. I expect to take only a hand trunk of Sarah's back with me. Maybe after getting to Kansas City I will change my mind as to the rest of the way. Don't know yet, but want to get there in time. If I am hindered with getting my clothes at Tipton, will try and let you know in time, as it is not possable for me to have them until I am there for them to take my measurements. Hope to get there about next Thursday.

Now the letters from me are yours forever, and you may do what you see fit with them. I will try and keep yours in my own hands. No one to my knowledge has ever read one of your letters sent to me. They always seemed to sacred to my feelings to alow other eyes to read them. I want to put them in a bundle and lay them where they will be safe, as I expect to keep them through life. And if when I am gone, others wish to know how to write a good sensible love letter, they might do so by reading one of those from Miss M. A. Bennett to this boy. If you see fit, you may destroy my letters, or any portion. Am I right in saying that:

Love binds, love wields, and love controls
Nothing but love will satisfy the soul
Original.

Yours for all time to come. Good evening and good bye with corresponding.

    Roy Carpenter

Your dress will look nice on my girl and she will look sweet to me. Our love to all of your folks and much happiness to all.

    L.S.C.

# Postscript

FOLLOWING THEIR WEDDING ON APRIL 25, 1872, Martha and Leroy visited friends and relatives, had a formal picture taken while they were with the Colemans in Oskaloosa, and then headed west by train to begin life in the Union Colony. The home Leroy had described to Martha, now vacated by Leroy's parents, was awaiting them. Here were born their three children: Alfred Bennett (1873), Delphus Emory (1877), and Fred George (1881).

Daniel and Nancy Carpenter moved to their own home a quarter-mile away. Sarah married Revilo Loveland in 1872 and no longer resided at home. Mattie remained with her parents until 1879 when she married Harlan Bosworth of Fort Collins. Silas, a committed bachelor, helped his father on eighty acres adjacent to the land worked by Leroy. At some point, he built himself a home fifteen miles east of Greeley at the end of Ditch Number 2 (Barnesville) where he farmed and engaged in stone engraving and sculpting until his death in 1929. Agnes Murray eventually moved to Fort Collins where, at the age of thirty-five, she married C. L. Duvall of that community.

Upon arriving home in 1872, Leroy attended to the crops he had planted prior to leaving for Iowa. From previous experience, he knew that nothing would grow in semiarid Colorado without consistent irrigation. As with other farmers who were learning the art of irrigated agriculture, Leroy spent many hours figuring out how to make Cache la Poudre River water flow through the ditches and laterals onto his lands. Out of necessity he became acquainted with the priority system of water rights, including the obligation to make unused water (return

flows) available to neighbors. He learned how to maintain and improve the irrigation system on which he was dependent, and to time his own diversions through a head gate without drying up the neighbors' fields. The knowledge and experience he gained eventually attracted the interest of his son, Delphus (Delph).

Ongoing and ubiquitous problems related to equitable apportionment of limited water supplies in the West convinced Delph that being a water lawyer was a more attractive career than farming. He attended night classes at the University of Denver, earned a law degree, won election to the state senate, and made a name for himself as a successful water attorney and interstate streams negotiator. The 1922 Colorado River Compact stands today as a significant monument to his innovative thinking. For Delph, this work was as much of a pioneering endeavor as the frontier experiences of his father and grandfather.

Martha learned to keep house while pregnant. Her first child, Alfred Bennett, provided his mother with all the burdens and pleasures of a young wife. But in addition to keeping a home for her family, she dedicated significant amounts of time to the Methodist Church, attending services regularly and teaching Sunday School classes. The routines of life changed little when Delphus Emory and Fred George arrived, but increasingly she missed her Iowa family and worried about her widowed mother.

William Bennett died shortly after Delph arrived. He had been ill for some time and had been residing with his daughter Lucy in Davenport. The cemetery record states the cause of his death as "dyspepsia and intermiddling fever."[1] It was painful for Martha not to be with her father when he passed away, and as she learned of the births of nieces and nephews, she determined to make a trip home. In April

Facing page: Fig. 18. Leroy and Martha on their honeymoon, 1872, Oskaloosa, Iowa.
*CSU Water Archives 09b012.*

Fig. 19. Delphus Carpenter as Colorado state senator, 1911. *CSU Water Archives 09a022.*

1880, with Alfred and Delph in tow, she boarded the train from Greeley to Cheyenne. There she connected with the Union Pacific Railroad to Omaha and the Chicago, Milwaukee and St. Paul Railroad to Davenport. The trip was difficult. She and the boys got little sleep for several days. Arriving in Davenport, she wrote Leroy that she planned to spend time with sisters Lucy and Sylvania, meet new family members, and care for her mother. Afterward, she would visit sisters Mary and Lydia, some old friends, and the Colemans.[2] It was a two-month visit, during which Martha and Leroy again exchanged letters containing news, gossip, and expressions of affection. Leroy repeatedly insisted that Martha take time to enjoy her family without worrying about him,

Fig. 20. Alfred (seven) and Delphus (three), photographed on a visit to Davenport, Iowa, 1880. *CSU Water Archives 09a002.*

but as the days turned into weeks, she expressed an increasing willingness to return to Colorado.

The tone of these missives is different. Leroy is more preoccupied with the weather, irrigation problems during a drought, and local matters that are mostly incomprehensible to modern readers. But his letters were of great comfort to Martha. She wrote of the joy she felt over the opportunity to show off her boys, to meet her brothers-in-law and their children, and to be able to purchase goods for her home at cheaper prices. She agonized over spending money, worried about her husband's expressed loneliness, and urged him to find in his faith the strength to endure their separation.

Although these 1880 letters do not attain the richness of the court-ship letters written almost a decade earlier, they provide an essential continuity to the saga of this middle-class, middle-American marriage. In his first 1880 letter to Martha, Leroy confessed to tears when his family departed, but he reassured her that he would be able to endure her absence. She meant more to him than life itself, he wrote, and she should get the very most out of her short visit.

Martha found herself barraged by questions about life in Colorado, and she pleaded with Leroy to help her identify all the benefits of living there. He responded by sending a sample of wheat and what he referred to as a "sand cactus." He also underscored the benefits of good roads, cool nights, fresher water from mountain streams, and the abundance of game for hunting. Martha assured him that she and the boys were well, that they were in fact having the time of their lives, and that she had plenty of money to do the things she needed to do. She encouraged Leroy to "grow in grace," to do good works for others, to make sure the tomato plants and strawberries were well cared for, and to encourage the chickens to lay plenty of eggs.

Unfailingly polite, considerate, and self-effacing, Martha and Leroy retained their courtesy, their sense of humor, and the mutual affection developed during courtship that had further matured during eight years of marriage. The teasing, intimacy, and desire for privacy characteristic of their initial correspondence also continued, albeit to a lesser extent, in the 1880 letters. When Martha expressed her restless-ness to get home "to annoy" Leroy after almost two months of visiting, readers may be certain they were both ready for her odyssey to end. How nice it would be, Martha wrote in her last letter, if Leroy would have her house "whitewashed and cleaned," especially the bedroom and kitchen, so she wouldn't have to attend to these duties when she got home. Surely this request made Leroy smile, and as noted in his diary, he at least made an effort to clean up the kitchen before his family returned.[3]

For the next forty-six years of his life, Leroy showed unfailing devotion to his wife and children. What we know about him and Martha comes largely from bits and pieces in newspapers, Leroy's pithy diaries, and unpublished recollections of friends and family.

In 1881 they moved out of the house where their children were born, selling the eighty-acre farm and moving in with Leroy's parents. Agriculture was going through one of its many difficult periods, and Daniel was getting too old to meet the demands of irrigated farming. He soon bought a home in Greeley where he died in 1884 at the age of eighty-eight. With Silas's help, Leroy continued to work his father's eighty acres, raising primarily oats, corn, and wheat. A new mill was producing "Snow Flake Flour," and a grain elevator was under construction. Although some years were better than others for them financially, Martha and Leroy earned a reputation in the community for generosity even during the lean years of the 1890s. They often shared their home with students and others who were temporarily down on their luck. They lived what they believed. The principles to which they had committed in their courtship correspondence seem to have solidified and enriched their partnership.

Leroy remained politically conservative. He was a loyal Republican, opposed to strikes and lockouts, supportive of local government, and eager to endorse officials who embraced law and order. He continued to despise any form of liquor traffic, and he spoke out against prize fighting. He was a kind and generous man, and he believed deeply in sharing his home and his good fortune with others.[4]

The Carpenters' Methodist faith served as a stronghold for each other and for the children. Each day began with a reading from scripture, and Sundays were dedicated exclusively to church, family, and friends. On Saturday nights, the irrigation water was set so it would not have to be changed until Monday. After church they gathered at home with family and friends for feasts of chicken pie, vegetables, fruit from their own orchard, and homemade ice cream. Martha taught Sunday school for twenty-eight years, and through the church she also served as president of the Methodist Foreign Missionary Society.

Martha maintained her strong commitment to temperance and preservation of the history of the Union Colony. She was president of the Women's Christian Temperance Union (organized nationally in 1873) and the [Nathan] Meeker Memorial Society, and she was active in the organization of the Union Colony Pioneers. Her sense of history was communicated to her children, as can be seen in the research strategies used by Delph when he was working on interstate compacts. Martha was also a caregiver. She nursed her mother and mother-in-law through their final illnesses, and when she finally succumbed to double pneumonia in 1930 she was seventy-six and survived by only her sister Lydia in the Bennett family. Leroy had passed away in 1927 at the age of eighty-four.

What had begun in 1870 as a courtship by correspondence blossomed into a functional, mutually supportive marriage that made possible a productive life for Martha Bennett and Leroy Carpenter. One cannot judge their marriage or their family as better or worse than others of the time, but the letters they wrote provide evidence of their honesty, intensity, and clarity of purpose. As they celebrated the euphoria of mutual love in their correspondence, they also proved extraordinarily skillful in tempering these powerful emotions with the realities of what a successful life together would require. Far from assuming that things would just work through love alone, they probed each other's strengths and weaknesses in a respectful and considerate effort to forecast their chances as a married couple. They would not have recognized what social historians of today label as "marital unity," "companionate marriage," or "separate spheres," but in their own search for a feasible and lasting partnership, they did the work that was necessary for a marriage to survive and thrive on the frontier in Victorian America. They continued to be bound to certain family traditions, but they also revealed themselves to be independent thinkers, seeking a practical and ideological balance in regard to life's principal challenges. They were not radical, by any means, but they were wise, and they were impressively sensitive to the breadth and meaning and power of romantic love.

As with others who courted by correspondence, Martha and Leroy's long separation and engagement probably represented a pinnacle of emotional drama. They had looked inwardly to find the best person they could be when they were courting. They created in writing that persona who could only be revealed through the love of their betrothed. But there was no artifice in these exchanges, and one senses that, in addition to feelings of comfort and trust, what was really meant by their declarations of "love" was an appreciation that each had given the other a gift of rebirth and a promise of a life together that would enable this new persona to function productively in a marital union. In sum, the courtship correspondence of Martha and Leroy made possible a kind of "love" that elicited the best individual characteristics of human beings and provided confidence that the trials of married life on the Colorado frontier could be resolved.

These letters were and are by their very nature intensely private. For the descendants of Leroy and Martha, they will continue to be personal and intimate. To expose them in published form is to share delicate sentiments with readers who may not readily appreciate how profoundly the letters personified the physical form and presence of their authors. But Martha and Leroy both stated on separate occasions that they were proud of what they had written, and Leroy even hoped the letters might prove useful to future lovers. Believing that he meant what he said, Betty Henshaw and I have transcribed and edited the story of their courtship in as honest and forthright a manner as possible. Leroy and Martha built their love based on trust. We have no doubt that they would have wanted to trust the ones responsible for undertaking the publication of their courtship correspondence. We have attempted to honor this trust by presenting these letters as an example of thoughtful, considered, and informed communication between two people who knew that, because of the distance that separated them, they could only come to know each other by means of the written word. If this publication makes possible a broader understanding of the very elusive topic of romantic love in the late nineteenth century, Betty and I will feel satisfied, fulfilled, and ultimately trustworthy.

# Family Genealogies

## The Bennett Family

Mary Ann Wood (1819–1889) *m* William H. Bennett (1815–1877)[*]
    Mary (b. 1844) *m* Harry H. Green (Decorah, Iowa)
    Lucy (b. 1847) *m* W. B. "Billie" Milligan (Davenport, Iowa)
    Lydia (b. 1850) *m* Marshall D. Fox (Odebolt, Iowa)
    Martha (b. 1854) *m* Leroy Carpenter (Greeley, Colorado)
    Sylvania (Vanie) *m* Benjamin Kough (Davenport, Iowa)
    William W. (Billings, Montana)

---

[*]William H. Bennett's father died before he was born. His mother remarried to Thomas Stone. William H. Bennett bought land in Iowa in 1849 and brought his family from Brownsville, Pennsylvania, in 1855.

## THE CARPENTER FAMILY

Daniel Carpenter (1796–1888) *m* (1819) (1) **Sally Northway** (1799–1837)

George F. (1820)—married with three children

Emaline (1821) *m* (1846) Silas Scott (Nancy Scott's brother)
—no children

Electa Ann (1823)—married with two children

William Barney (1825)—married with eight children

Samuel Northway (1828)—unmarried

Don Alonzo (1830)—married with one child

Peter Alexander (1833–1871) *m* Mary Pierce Scarborough (1837–1924)

George (1861–1940)

Harry (1865–1940)

Don (1869–1939)

Sarah Elizabeth (1837)—married Revilo Loveland. No children.

*m* (1840) (2) **Nancy Scott** (1809–1886)[*]

James—unmarried. Killed in 1863.

Leroy S. (1843–1927) *m* (1872) Martha Bennett (1854–1930)

Alfred B. (1873–1953)

Delphus E. (1877–1951) *m* (1901) Michaela Hogarty

Fred George (1881–1963)

Silas (1849–1929)—unmarried

Martha (Mattie) (1845–1922)—married with two children

Cyrus (d. at birth)

---

[*]Nancy Scott was the daughter of William Scott (1765–1854) and Elizabeth Coe Scott (1777–1857). Among her ten siblings were two brothers and a sister who were connected to the Carpenters: Dr. James Scott (1800–1881) was born in Pennsylvania and died in Greeley, Colorado. His son Frank was Leroy Carpenter's cousin. A second brother, Silas Scott, was married to Emaline Carpenter. They had no children. Nancy's sister, Martha Scott, was married to Reverend Andrew Coleman. They introduced Leroy Carpenter to Martha Bennett. They had two children, Albert and Howard.

# Notes

## Introduction

1. This feeling of discovery and possessiveness is hard to describe, but it was expressed powerfully by the protagonists Roland and Maud in A. S. Byatt's *Possession* (New York: Random House, 1990). They, too, had discovered love letters that they didn't want to disappear into the hands of another interested party. The dialogue on page 101 goes as follows: "If he gets advised to go to Sotheby's, the letters'll vanish into America or somewhere else, or Blackadder'll get them if we're lucky. I don't know why I think that'd be so bad. I don't know why I feel so *possessive* about the damned things. They're not mine." "It's because we found them. And because—because they're private."

2. Betty Henshaw and I made an effort to locate comparable collections in Iowa, Colorado, and elsewhere. There are plenty of letters from midwestern women to each other describing the exigencies of frontier and family life (see, for example, Elizabeth Hampsten, *Read This Only to Yourself*). But to the best of our knowledge, the Martha-Leroy letters are the only known courtship letters from the post–Civil War Midwest. Surely, there are other collections in attics, trunks, and family archives. Hopefully, this volume will speed the search for such documents. For those readers interested in courtship letters written by well-educated, eastern, urban men and women, the Huntington Library in San Marino, California, is the place to go.

3. Information about the Carpenter and Bennett families comes from many sources, including newspapers, collections in Iowa and Colorado libraries and historical societies, the Greeley Museum, and several family histories and genealogies available in the Carpenter Papers at the Colorado State University Water Resources Archives in Fort Collins. Much of what is written herein about the families has been verified by interviews with Carpenter and Bennett descendants, librarians, archivists, and local historians.

4. Developed by a German physician around 1800, phrenology was a theory claiming that an individual's character, personality, and tendency toward criminality could be determined by evaluating bumps on the head. Although this theory was popular in the nineteenth century, it had been discredited by 1900 as a

pseudoscience. Even so, phrenology is sometimes given credit for contributing to medical science the idea that the brain is the basic organ of the mind and that certain brain areas have certain functions. Some marriage advisors of the nineteenth century recommended phrenologically controlled mate selection. See Karen Lystra, *Searching the Heart*, p. 193.

5. I am indebted to a number of authors whose works have aided me in placing the Martha-Leroy correspondence in context. The following works, cited more fully in the notes and bibliography, were especially useful: Nancy Cott, *Public Vows*; Sara M. Evans, *Born of Liberty*; Lori D. Ginzburg, *Women and the Work of Benevolence*; Sarah Barringer Gordon, *The Mormon Question*; Elizabeth Hampsten, *Read This Only to Yourself*; Hendrik Hartog, *Man and Wife in America*; Joseph M. Hawes and Elizabeth I. Nybakken, eds., *Family and Society in American History*; Anya Jabour, *Marriage in the Early Republic*; Timothy Kenslea, *The Sedgwicks in Love*; Sarah Kortum, "The Well-Mannered Courtship"; Peg A. Lamphier, *Kate Chase and William Sprague*; Karen Lystra, *Searching the Heart*; Ellen K. Rothman, *Hands and Hearts*; Mary P. Ryan, *Cradle of the Middle Class*; and Daniel Vickers, *Farmers and Fishermen*.

6. The doctrine of separate spheres emerged in the nineteenth century to challenge male domination of the workplace and the home, the raising of children, and religious instruction. It was based on the idea that women were more virtuous than men, that because of their fundamentally different nature, they should control the emotional space in the home, influencing husbands and children by their example. Concurrently, the concept of romantic love became the guide for couples when selecting a spouse and cultivating an egalitarian marital arrangement. As with most theoretical models of social behavior, the idea of separate spheres encountered friction, conflict, and controversy as society modernized, industrialized, and urbanized. The idea that women should focus on nurturing their families in a home that was expected to be a "man's Elysium" experienced tension caused by the increasing participation of women in public life. As described in Evans, *Born of Liberty* (p. 142), the contradiction for women was between the lure of "Republicanism," in which she was asked to support suffrage and citizenship, and "Motherhood," which sprang from Victorian ideas of domesticity and a "maternal commonwealth." By the 1870s, women were less likely to emphasize their gender's claim to virtue and more likely to accept the fact that male gender strengths were necessary for society to function legally and systematically. Elizabeth Cady Stanton's appeal to women that "only in the rejection of the ideology of female difference lay the possibilities for the broadest vision of social change and for a true benevolence, based not on sex but on justice," indicated that the doctrine of separate spheres was experiencing a metamorphosis at the time Martha and Leroy were courting. See Ginzburg, *Women and the Work of Benevolence*, pp. 173, 213. Also see Ryan, *Cradle of the Middle Class*, p. 190.

## Letters

1. Emaline M. Scott. She was Leroy's half-sister, the daughter of Daniel Carpenter and Daniel's first wife, Sally Northway. Emaline married Silas Scott, the brother of Daniel Carpenter's second wife, Nancy Scott.

2. Andrew and Martha Scott Coleman were Leroy's uncle and aunt. Martha Coleman was a sister of Nancy Scott. A Methodist minister, Andrew Coleman came to Iowa in 1842 where he was a circuit rider, presiding elder in Cedar County, original pastor of the De Witt Methodist Church, and most probably the first minister of the West Bethel Methodist Church established by Daniel Carpenter. The Colemans were closely connected to Methodist families in Tipton and De Witt and were responsible for introducing Leroy Carpenter to Martha Bennett. Fellows, *Upper Iowa Conference*, pp. 46, 112–14. At one time Fellows was the minister at the Tipton Methodist Church.

3. The West Bethel Church was incorporated in February 1857. Daniel Carpenter was one of seven trustees and the first superintendent of the Sunday school. An acre of land on the southeast corner of Jackson Avenue and Highway F28 (known as Bethel Corners) was purchased and a small frame church was built over the summer and dedicated in November 1857. It is not known how long services were held in the church, but the property was sold at public auction in 1922. The building was dismantled and the lumber purchased by a doctor for use in the construction of a hospital in nearby Tipton. That plan failed, however, and what was left of the old church became the office of Century Burner & Fuel Co. in Tipton. Sandy Harmel of Bennett, Iowa, provided this information from her research in the Tipton *Advertiser*. See also Stout, *Cedar Land*, p. 55.

4. Albert D. Coleman, a cousin to Leroy Carpenter, was the older of Reverend Andrew Coleman's two sons. He served in Company A, 18th Iowa Infantry, became a Methodist minister after the Civil War, and died in 1906 at the age of sixty. See Mahaska County, Iowa, WPA Burial Records.

5. The town of Rockingham, now abandoned, was laid out in 1836 in Rockingham Township, Scott County, Iowa. It was located four miles below the business section of Davenport, Iowa. I am grateful to Robert McCown for this information.

6. The Brushville School was located near the old Pony Express route in rolling hills south of Calamus close to the Wapsipinicon River. For children of farming families in this region, Brushville was a convenient location for schooling. Calamus Station, where Martha mailed her letters, was on the Chicago & North Western Railroad (C&NW) running east and west across Iowa. De Witt, Martha's home, was two stops east of Calamus Station. Tipton, Leroy's home, was connected to the main line by a short spur. The C&NW was the preferred route for connecting to the Union Pacific at the Missouri River.

7. The Order of Good Templars was one of many temperance organizations that focused on eliminating abuse in the manufacture, sale, and consumption of alcoholic beverages. Typical of the benevolent associations that enjoyed their heyday between 1825 and 1845, the Good Templars were focused on improving the quality of family life (see Ryan, *Cradle of the Middle Class*, pp. 108–40). Membership indicated not only a commitment to temperance, but to the articulation of women's rights, because so much alcoholism affected the lives of wives and children at home. Martha joined the International Order of Good Templars (IOGT) on December 29, 1870, at Calamus. Leroy had already been accepted into the Iowa City lodge of the IOGT on January 8, 1866. Fahey's *Temperance and Racism* notes that the IOGT had great appeal to the young, and especially to women, because of the promise of equal rights. See pp. 19, 24–29. Other fraternal societies in the 1870s tended to exclude women and blacks. Because the IOGT welcomed everyone, and because lodge meetings combined ritual, ceremony, and Protestant worship, membership was appealing to rural Iowans who embraced prohibition and looked for ways to express themselves in a socially acceptable group. See also Mattingly, *Well-Tempered Women*, pp. 2, 6, 14–16, 18, 21, 34, 37, 38.

8. John Wesley, one of the early leaders of the Methodist movement, used to hold a watch night service once a month, the exact date depending on a full moon. He argued that early Christian liturgy supported the validity of such services. Other church leaders used the watch night service as a way to combat the tendency of a newly converted Christian to enter an ale house later in the night. By running the night watch, both older and newer Christians could maintain vigil over their covenant with God. It is possible that Martha was referring to a monthly meeting at which parishioners gathered to experience a kind of retreat in order to socialize with fellow Methodists and to reinforce the tenets of their faith. I am indebted to archivist Esther Wonderlich, United Methodist Church of Iowa, for this explanation.

9. The principal years of growth in membership for the IOGT were the years following the Civil War. This growth "occurred in the face of an ever more severe interpretation of the Templar 'obligation,' as the IOGT styled its pledge. For instance, the drinking of sweet cider was banned; moreover, unlike other pledged teetotalers, Templars could not serve alcoholic beverages to guests and customers." Fahey, *Temperance and Racism*, p. 12.

10. Leroy attended the University of Iowa (referred to then as the State University of Iowa) for one year, 1865–1866, as a "preparatory" student. The preparatory program lasted three years and was designed for students whose education in the rural schools of Iowa was inadequate for full admittance to a university department. The university did not preserve academic records of students in the

preparatory program, but according to the "Catalogue of the State University" for the year 1865–1866, first-year students were expected to take intellectual arithmetic, practical arithmetic, English grammar, orthography, descriptive geography, reading, penmanship and drawing, and topical geography.

11. In the 1870s, meetings of the Methodist Church were held every three months. Today such meetings are held once a year and are called the charge, or church conference. At this time reports are made on baptisms, deaths, marriages, membership, budgetary items, and other matters needing a vote. In Leroy's time the quarterly meeting "was of social interest and of spiritual life and fire unknown today." It included sermons "suited to the needs of the community . . . full of unction and the Holy Ghost." Sunday was a feast day. "Testimonies were given with weeping and confession, thanksgiving and praise, followed by the great sermon delivered by the presiding elder." Sunday evening was the time for "victory and the ingathering of souls. No preacher was allowed to speak unless he had ability to stir the people." Fellows, *Upper Iowa Conference*, p. 23. Kathy and Don Hodson, Iowa City, Iowa, assisted me in this research.

12. Templars in the United States reached their peak membership in 1868, although the movement spread successfully overseas after that date. Most who drifted out of the order were young people who migrated west or to better jobs in urban areas. Other defectors joined the National Prohibition Party. As the IOGT became more closely identified with the Prohibition Party, many committed Republicans became alienated. Women, too, found more satisfaction in single-sex societies such as the Women's Temperance Crusade, and the Woman's Christian Temperance Union founded in 1874. The above reasons may not explain Martha's disenchantment with the Templars, but it is clear that both she and Leroy were losing interest at a time when membership was decreasing nationally. Fahey, *Temperance and Racism*, pp. 12–14.

13. By the late 1800s, the Methodist Church was undergoing a transformation from the revivalist form of worship to a more staid and mainstream format. The change was rooted in Methodism's quest for respectability after the Civil War. The church hoped to change from the evangelical style of the holiness movement to something more refined and modest. Hence, the "tableaux," which were religious themes presented silently by parishioners. Esther Wonderlich, archivist of the United Methodist Church of Iowa, provided background on the meaning of tableaux.

14. Martha probably visited Leroy in Tipton in March 1871. It is impossible to know how many times they saw each other before Leroy departed for Colorado, but the tone of their early courtship letters suggests they already felt some attraction for each other, albeit on a very formal level.

15. Leroy is referring here to his aunt and uncle, Andrew and Martha Coleman, and to his half-sister Emaline and her husband, Silas Scott.

16. The date would be Wednesday, April 12, 1871, which was also the one-year anniversary of the locating committee's selection of the Cache la Poudre River site as the future location of the Union Colony of Greeley. The Carpenters were second-wave pioneers.

17. Leroy was mistaken. The Black Hills were 200 miles north of Cheyenne and not visible from Union Pacific Railroad tracks. He was probably looking at the Medicine Bow Range west of Cheyenne. The Carpenters, with their children, Leroy, Silas, Mattie, and Sarah, took the Chicago & North Western Railroad to Omaha. There they boarded the Union Pacific Railroad and traveled along the Platte River through Nebraska and thence due west to Cheyenne, completing their journey from Cheyenne to Greeley on the Denver Pacific Railroad.

18. Aggie (Agnes Murray) was entrusted to the care of Daniel and Nancy Carpenter by her father, an Iowa farmer whose wife had died. Born in Omaha in 1864, Aggie moved with the Carpenters to Colorado and grew up in Greeley. In 1901 she married C. L. Duvall and lived with him in Fort Collins and nearby Stove Prairie. Fifteen years later she suffered a severe attack of measles and died on March 24, 1916, at the age of fifty-two. She was survived by her husband and a son, Homer. Rheba Massey, local history librarian at the Fort Collins Public Library, located her obituary in the Fort Collins *Weekly Courier*.

19. The Bennetts and the Carpenters were both strong advocates of temperance. This social reform movement, with origins in the colonial period, gained strength in the teachings of the Methodist Church, the organization of the American Temperance Union, the writings of Timothy Shay Arthur (*Ten Nights in a Bar-Room and What I Saw There* [Philadelphia: Lippincott, Grambo and Co., 1855]), and the passage of statewide prohibition laws in fourteen states as of 1855. The Union Colony was founded on temperance. Horace Greeley suggested that only temperance men should govern, and the organizers, R. A. Cameron and N. C. Meeker, agreed to this principle, although the actual rules restricting the manufacture and sale of alcoholic beverages were not specified before the first settlers arrived. Consequently, when Leroy came to Greeley in 1871, residents were debating whether or not druggists could sell alcohol as medicine. Miss Emmery found a receptive audience, but she also contributed to the ongoing temperance debate in Greeley that had simmered ever since the first settlers arrived. Local newspapers made no mention of Miss Emmery's talk. The media in general tended "to report in detail only the addresses of the best-known women" who presented themselves as temperance advocates on the lecture circuit. Mattingly, *Well-Tempered Women*, p. 37; Boyd, *A History*, pp. 232–37.

20. The tabernacle was a building brought to Greeley from Cheyenne. Known as the Hotel de Comfort, it was originally used to house people who had no home. Over time it became Colony Hall, a designated general meeting place, and the first location of a Greeley school.

21. Leroy and Martha grew up in Methodist homes. During their courtship, the Methodist Episcopal Church was divided in Iowa into Upper and Lower conferences. The Upper Conference included Clinton (De Witt) and Cedar (Tipton) counties. Andrew Coleman, Leroy's uncle, was presiding elder at Iowa City, headquarters of one of seven districts in the Upper Conference. In general, the church supported abolition and viewed the Civil War as a great moral crusade. It endorsed temperance, opposed gambling and the use of tobacco, embraced the need for educational institutions, and urged farmers to be good stewards of the land. It denied ordination to women but encouraged them to be class leaders and Sunday school teachers, and to bear witness if so inclined. Most appealing to Martha and Leroy was the church's focus on practical Christian living. Their correspondence suggests a strong feeling of compatibility on this subject. For general information on the Methodist Episcopal Church in Iowa, see Nye, *Between the Rivers*, and Fellows, *Upper Iowa Conference*.

22. This was the home of Lyman and Esther Alger. According to several sources of community lore, Esther Alger was the first person murdered in Olive Township, Clinton County. She was found shot and beaten to death in her home on September 25, 1872. Between $1,000 and $1,500 had been taken from a trunk. The grandson, Judson Curtis, who lived with the Algers, was the first to report the murder. Arrests were made, but no one was convicted. Some believed the grandson did the deed. He traveled extensively after the murder. Others speculated that Lyman Alger was aware of his grandson's crime and as a result of his guilt, he built the Free Will Baptist Church with conscience money. None of this is proven, and during her stay with the Algers, Martha felt very safe and welcome.

23. Although the duties of "left hand supporter" at the Lodge are not stated, and the "W. C." is not identified, histories of the period make clear the extent to which women enjoyed various leadership roles in temperance organizations. Martha was attracted to this aspect of the Good Templars, and she believed women should be treated fairly when they held responsible positions. As will be seen in later letters, however, her world view was also traditional, especially in matters of family, home, and religion.

24. It may be that Leroy's comment, to which Martha refers, was intended as a proposal. There is no formal proposal in any of his extant letters to Martha. The formal proposal letter could be lost, but because proposals in the Victorian era were viewed as such a private matter, it might have been destroyed. In the 1863 courtship correspondence between Kate Chase, daughter of Abraham Lincoln's

secretary of the treasury, and Governor William Sprague of Rhode Island, the moment of engagement does not appear in any letter. Lamphier, *Kate Chase and William Sprague*, p. 52. Reading through Leroy and Martha's correspondence, it becomes clear that both assumed early on they would marry, but only if it was "God's will" to do so.

25. In contrast to some Greeley settlers, the Carpenters were full members of the Union Colony. According to articles X and XI of the colony's constitution and by-laws of December 23, 1869, each member in good standing was entitled to a town lot and farming land in return for a membership fee of $155. Town lots varied in price from $25 to $50 according to location. Farm land varied in size and price, depending on distance from town. Once improved by their owners, the lands were to be owned in fee simple. The colony was obligated to provide irrigation water to farmers who were then responsible for assessments relating to maintenance and delivery. Boyd, *A History*, pp. 427–28, and Pabor, *First Annual Report*, pp. 6, 11, 12.

26. Peter A. Carpenter was the seventh child of Daniel Carpenter and Sally Northway. He and sister Sarah were the only children of this marriage to come to Colorado. Peter married Mary Scarborough, whose family came west from New York. They met when Peter was a medical student at the State University of Iowa at Keokuk and married in 1859. At the outbreak of the Civil War, Peter enlisted in the Fifth Iowa Infantry as a surgeon. After two years of relative quiet, he was assigned to General Tecumseh Sherman's forces where he saw duty at Vicksburg, Chattanooga, and Lookout Mountain. While waiting to cross the Tennessee River during a cold rain, he caught cold and later developed what was then referred to as consumption, probably tuberculosis. He was discharged from the army in 1864 and moved with his wife and young child to Mansfield, Ohio, near his brothers and close to where he was born. Although he enjoyed a fine medical practice in Mansfield, his health steadily deteriorated. Along with others who believed the dry western air was a cure for consumption, he traveled to Colorado and experienced such improvement that he took out a homestead along the banks of the Cache la Poudre River, one mile north of Timnath, seven miles east of Fort Collins, and twenty miles northwest of Greeley. When he returned to get his family, he regaled his father, Daniel Carpenter, with the virtues of Colorado. Peter, Mary, and their children left Ohio for Colorado in January 1871. Unfortunately, the climate did not cure him. He died of pneumonia at home on July 28, 1871. In 1906 Mary Scarborough Carpenter wrote "Reminiscences of My Early Life and Later Experiences as a Western Pioneer." This unpublished essay was duplicated in 1908. A copy is in the possession of the author. It is also available at the Fort Collins Public Library.

27. Martha had four sisters and a brother. Lydia was married to Marshall D. Fox. They lived for thirty-one years on a farm in Maquoketa, Iowa, before retiring to Odebolt, Iowa. The other sisters were Mary, who married Reverend Harry H. Green and lived in Decorah, Iowa; Lucy, who married Billie Milligan and lived in Davenport, Iowa; and Sylvania (Vanie), the youngest, who married Benjamin Kough and also lived in Davenport. Martha's only brother, William W. Bennett, lived in Billings, Montana.

28. Martha felt herself engaged to Leroy, but she let him know that there were others who had shown an interest in her. This testing was not unusual in Victorian-era courtship correspondence, and as readers will note, there are several instances in letters from both Leroy and Martha in which other possible suitors are mentioned.

29. Peter Carpenter, Leroy's stepbrother.

30. Both N. C. Meeker and Horace Greeley agreed that irrigation would be necessary for farming in the Union Colony. To that end, three delivery ditches were planned out of the Cache la Poudre River. Number One was never built. Number Three provided the town of Greeley with water for businesses and homes. Number Two, the principal ditch for farmers, was designed to extend twenty-seven miles on the north side of the river. It was the one on which Leroy was working in the spring of 1871. Because so little was known about the proper engineering of irrigation ditches, Number Two proved totally inadequate at first to the farmers' needs, resulting in the loss of most crops and nearly bankrupting the colony when it was revealed how much money would be needed to correct the slope and flow capacity. Many farmers donated their labor in hopes of getting the water they were promised by the colony. In *A History* (p. 64), Boyd states that "[t]he patience, courage and perseverance of the farmers under Number Two saved the dissolution of the colony, and the fruits of their labors were the making of Greeley."

31. Leroy has no doubts about their engagement.

32. Born in 1834, Philip Phillips studied music and taught singing in several New York towns. Raised a Baptist, he converted to Methodism when he married and moved to Cincinnati to open a music store. During the Civil War he sang religious songs around the country and published various song books, some of which sold over a million copies. He traveled the world and came to be known as a celebrated hymn singer. A sketch of his life appears in his *Song Pilgrimage around and throughout the World* (New York: Phillips and Hunt, 1882).

33. Martha's father, William H. Bennett, purchased land a few miles southeast of De Witt, under an Act of Congress dated April 24, 1820. The property, for which

he paid two hundred dollars, was located near a stage road and close to the Wapsipinicon River. Bennett also took out a quarter-section Homestead Claim in 1865 not far from his purchased land. On this claim, noted on an 1865 map of Clinton County, were a "dwelling house" and barn, presumably the home to which Martha refers. It was the location of Leroy and Martha's marriage in 1872. The official record of this claim can be found in Homestead Book I, Clinton County, Iowa.

34. The irrigation system planned for the Union Colony would have sounded very strange to Martha whose farming experience was limited to crop raising controlled by the whims of nature. Leroy had the same background, but he was rapidly learning that his ability to remain in Colorado as a farmer would depend almost entirely on the successful engineering of the colony's ditches. It is not surprising, therefore, that this subject frequently entered their correspondence.

35. Leroy does not mention grasshoppers, but they were problematic during the colony's early years. Between 1873 and 1876, they were especially bothersome, eating corn and onions at will, sparing sorghum and potatoes. With the advent of wetter and cooler spring weather, they disappeared. Boyd, *A History*, p. 160.

36. Most mail from Iowa to Colorado traveled by way of the Chicago and North Western Railroad to Omaha, and then on the Union Pacific Railroad to Cheyenne where it was delivered to the Denver Pacific Railroad. Letters took about a week, but occasionally one would arrive in three days. If Leroy wanted a letter to move quickly to Iowa, he had to post it at the Greeley Post Office by ten o'clock in the morning. Another option was to send mail via the southern route. A letter would leave Greeley no later than four o'clock in the afternoon, traveling to Denver on the Denver Pacific Railroad and connecting with the Kansas Pacific Railroad which had been completed to Denver in 1870. This route was often cheaper and more dependable in the winter.

37. Howard Coleman was Leroy's cousin, the son of Andrew and Martha Coleman. Consumption, ague, and tuberculosis were thought to result from living in damp climates. As stated by Ansel Watrous in his 1911 *History of Larimer County* (p. 64), "The medical profession is rapidly coming to the belief that health depends largely upon the proper assimilation of food. An excess of moisture in the atmosphere has a depressing effect upon the nervous system, governing nutrition, and it is largely because of the absence of moisture in the air of Colorado that digestion is promoted and health preserved." Half a century earlier, N. C. Meeker, who confessed to being bothered by ague when he was a resident in Illinois, promoted the Greeley location as salubrious. Many articles and editorials in his newspaper described the healthy climate of Colorado. Greeley *Tribune*, April 12, May 31, November 15 and 22, 1871.

38. Frank Scott, Leroy's cousin, was the eighth child of Nancy Hammond Scott and Dr. James S. Scott. Dr. Scott was born in Pennsylvania, attended medical school in Cincinnati, resided in Steubenville, Ohio, and came to Colorado in 1870 with the first Union Colony settlers, because he hoped to provide a healthier environment for his son, James C. Scott. Frank Scott was born in Steubenville, Ohio, on October 19, 1847. One of his father's sisters, Nancy Scott, was Leroy's mother. See 1900 United States Census, Heritage Quest Online at http://persi.heritage-questonline.com. and Hazel Johnson, "Dr. Scott First Greeley Physician," Out of Our Past, Greeley Sunday *Journal*, September 25, 1960.

39. Leroy refers to their forthcoming marriage.

40. Construction of the Number Two ditch began in 1870 and was initially completed in the spring of 1871. As Leroy notes, the original Number Two did not function well enough to save the first year's crops. Several very expensive expansions followed. Number Two is now owned by the Cache la Poudre Irrigation Company. Construction of Number Three ditch also began in 1870, with its diversion headgate emerging from the south side of the Cache la Poudre River. The ditch extended eastward about twelve miles into the town of Greeley. The Union Colony was the original owner of this ditch, but by 1882 it was deeded to the City of Greeley and the Greeley Irrigation Company. "Irrigation and Water-Related Structures in the Cache la Poudre River Corridor," prepared for the Poudre Heritage Alliance. A copy is available at the Northern Colorado Water Conservancy District, Berthoud.

41. Leroy was born too early to know that, metaphorically speaking, water may at times run uphill to money.

42. In Victorian America, women exercised more formal control of setting the marriage date. For the most part, men acquiesced. Lystra, *Searching the Heart*, p. 182.

43. By 1871, the women's suffrage movement had been active for more than twenty years. Stanton and Anthony joined forces in 1852 when the United States was engaged in three major reform movements: abolition, temperance, and women's suffrage. After the Civil War, the Republican Party put its energy into passage of the fourteenth and fifteenth amendments to the U.S. Constitution. Proponents of women's suffrage found their voices muted by the national campaign to enfranchise African Americans. In the decade of the 1870s, with both amendments passed by the states, Stanton and Anthony decided to take their message to the people. The trip to Colorado in June of 1871 was part of a grand western tour that ended in the state of Washington. The objective was to raise money for their cause (they charged for each lecture); to give the movement national attention (a splinter movement had resulted in charges that promoters of suffrage were sympathetic to advocates of "free love"); and to spread their message

in the West where the territories of Wyoming and Utah had already accorded women the right to vote. Greeley was just one of many stops in an exhausting trip through the West. Anthony spoke June 24, Stanton June 26.

44. Camp Collins was a military reservation. It was abandoned by the War Department and then bought up by a town company which planned the new city of Fort Collins. Memberships in the Fort Collins Agricultural Colony were sold to persons of good moral character. By 1873 homes and commercial buildings were being constructed, and the town ditch for irrigation was dug that same year. See Ubbelohde, Benson, and Smith, *Colorado History*, pp. 138–39.

45. Nathan Howard Coleman, son of Martha and Andrew Coleman, Oskaloosa, Iowa, died on June 4, 1871, at the age of twenty-four. At the time of his death, he was a member of the senior class of Cornell College (Iowa) where he was studying to become a Methodist minister.

46. Most probably, Martha refers to *The First Annual Report of the Union Colony*, by William E. Pabor. Dated 1871, it examined the organization of the Union Colony in New York City, the establishment of Greeley, and the progress of the colony in agriculture, business, education, religion, and other matters. Officers of the colony were empowered to distribute copies of this report on trains passing through the plains. It was also sold to General William Palmer's Fountain Colony (Pabor was associated with Palmer). Residents of the colony also received a number of copies for their own use. Peggy Ford, research coordinator for the Greeley Museum, assisted the author on this matter.

47. It is not clear why Martha believed she was not of age. She was born April 19, 1854. At the time she wrote this letter she was seventeen. According to the Iowa Code of 1860, marriage between a man of sixteen and a woman of fourteen was considered legal (Title XVII, Chapter 102, Sec. 2516, p. 427). The 1873 Revised Code stated the same age requirements but added that if either individual was a minor, "the consent of the parent or guardian must be filed in the clerk's office after being acknowledged by the said parent or guardian" (Title XV, Chapter 1, Sec. 2191, p. 395). A woman who reached the age of eighteen was no longer considered a minor, and any woman who married automatically achieved majority status if her marriage was legal in the eyes of the law.

48. Martha knew that one of the reasons the Carpenters moved to Colorado was because Mattie's health was poor. Family health concerns formed a large part of Martha and Leroy's courting correspondence.

49. The Denver Pacific Railroad began construction southward from Cheyenne in 1868, reached the site of the future town of Greeley in November 1869, and was completed to Denver by June 1870. The first through train went from Denver to Cheyenne on June 23, 1870, a journey of approximately one hundred miles in

five hours. Greeley was about halfway. The Denver Pacific and Kansas Pacific railroads were merged into the Union Pacific system in 1880. Wilkins, *Colorado Railroads*, pp. 2, 3, 29, and Davis, *The First Five Years*, pp. 17, 49, 70, 88, 106.

50. See note 47.

51. This comment, and others that follow, underscore the fact that Leroy's view of men and women was more representative of a previous time before industry and urbanization brought about changes in the social equation. Although some of the exchanges between Martha and Leroy are intended to be teasing and humorous, they represent a view of sex roles in marriage that applied more to family farms than to industrialized society where men worked away from the home. There is also the possibility that Martha and Leroy were affected to some extent by the national discussion of women's rights and women's participation in the major reform movements of the day. Hawes and Nybakken, *Family and Society*, p. 150; Hartog, *Man and Wife*, pp. 32–33, 100–101, 110, 113; Cott, *Public Vows*, p. 12; Lystra, *Searching the Heart*, pp. 28, 38, 122; Ginzburg, *Women and the Work of Benevolence*, pp. 200, 202; Ryan, *Cradle of the Middle Class*, pp. 187, 190, 191.

52. Of her four female siblings, Martha seems to have been closest to Lucy. At this time, Lucy was unmarried, living with an Uncle John and Aunt Rachel in a suburb of Moline, Illinois. Attempts to determine the surname and relationship of this aunt and uncle to Martha's family were unproductive.

53. Freemasonry, with its roots in the Middle Ages, became in the United States a mysterious brotherhood of laymen with secret rites and an uncertain influence in business and politics. For many rural Iowans whose religion served as the principal guiding force for all behavior, Freemasonry suggested sacrilege. Its reputation for clandestine activities, hidden loyalties, and supposed influence in circles of power made Freemasonry suspect to many who subscribed tenaciously to the tenets of a Protestant faith. In all probability, Peter Carpenter had become a Freemason while serving as a surgeon in the Civil War. In Colorado the first meeting of Masons occurred shortly after the discovery of gold in 1858. In her "Reminiscences," Mary Carpenter notes that "Masonic friends came many miles to watch with and comfort" Peter during the last days of his illness. Had he been well enough, Peter would have belonged to Collins Lodge No. 19, which was formed in 1870. As one of its first recorded acts, the lodge sent a "Resolution of Respect" to Mary Carpenter at the time of Peter's death (*Collins Lodge*, pp. 10, 30). The Masonic seal is on Peter's grave at Grandview Cemetery in Fort Collins. Most Republicans from Iowa were inclined to view Democrats and Freemasons in the same unfavorable light. Ridley, *The Freemasons*, pp. 188–89 and Chapter 21. Also, *100 Years of Masonry in Fort Collins, 1870–1970*; Miller and Fisher, *Timnath*; and Clark, *Our Masonic Heritage*, pp. 48, 61, 65, 68.

54. In great contrast to comments that might be exchanged today between courting correspondents, Leroy's remark about Martha's weight reflected his concern that she might be too thin for survival in Colorado. It was based on his belief that good health and the ability to endure a tough winter would require a woman to be "fleshy."

55. Leroy was probably working for Robert Boyd, who came to Colorado with the Fifty-Niners. When his first crop on the South Platte River was destroyed by Indians, he took up a squatter's claim of 160 acres on the Cache la Poudre River. There he operated a ferry for the Overland Stage. Interested in irrigation, Boyd constructed one of the first ditches in Weld County. Leroy was helping with the grain harvest made possible by irrigation from the Boyd and Freeman Ditch. Peggy Ford, research coordinator for the Greeley Museum, provided this information.

56. The June 7, 1871, issue of the Greeley *Tribune* listed wages as follows: carpenters—$2.25 to $3.50 per day; masons and bricklayers—$4.00 per day; common labor—$2.25 per day. Historically, farm labor has always received lower wages.

57. Because most Greeley farmers owned land under Ditch Number Two, expansion and enlargement of this canal were absolutely necessary if the Union Colony was to survive. The enormous expense required was especially burdensome to the Union Colony because of the unexpected outlay of funds needed to build a cattle-proof fence around the colony. That fence, fifty miles long, cost twenty thousand dollars. But even with the additional and unexpected financial burden of further work on the main ditch, the job had to be done. The Greeley *Tribune* of September 6, 1871, concluded that "Canal No. 2, over the river, must be enlarged before next spring. When we say *must*, we mean positively and without any reservation, that is, if farming is to be done there to any extent." Leroy participated in this endeavor without remuneration.

58. A bellows-driven free-reed instrument, having chords as well as melody notes. It is sometimes referred to as a Vienna accordion.

59. This house, now located in Centennial Village in Greeley, was Leroy and Martha's first home where their three children were born.

60. Leroy probably means that there are a lot of Bennetts in Cedar County.

61. The Union Colony offered a five-hundred-dollar prize for the denomination that built the first church in Greeley. The Baptists won, dedicating their building on September 20, 1871. The Methodists, under Reverend G. H. Adams, after filing articles of incorporation in March 1871, held services in various buildings until their church was completed and dedicated in December 1871.

62. Reeders and Carpenters farmed close to each other in Cedar County and were involved in the Bethel Methodist Church and Sunday school. When Daniel Carpenter left Iowa for Colorado in 1871, the Reeders bought his farm.

63. The last Preemption Act passed by Congress September 4, 1841 (repealed in 1891), authorized settlers who had cultivated land on the public domain to purchase up to 160 acres for $1.25 per acre.

64. Leroy may be referring to a fire at his father's old homestead in Tipton.

65. George R. Strauss, a bachelor, lived near Leroy's brother, Peter Carpenter. Watrous, *History*, p. 277.

66. Mountain fever is not described well enough to determine what it was with certainty. It may have been related to problems with the water supply. Some speculate that it was typhoid fever, while others believe that it was an insect-born disease such as Rocky Mountain spotted fever. The Greeley *Tribune* of November 22, 1871, noted that the mountain fever was an "acclimating disease," and that it had abated with the coming of fall. The best treatment for those affected, noted the *Tribune*, was quinine. Studies of medical treatments after the Civil War make clear that across the country quinine had "replaced calomel in the materia medica as the standard medication in fevers and other acute diseases" (Rothstein, *American Physicians*, pp. 188–89). Residents of the Union Colony were told to continue to be alert for symptoms, while rejoicing in the fact they were living in a most healthy environment. The *Tribune* concluded that "[p]eople who, while in the States, scarcely ever felt well, who frequently had heavy colds, and who were unable to work more than a portion of the time, soon feel exhilarated [in Greeley], and they seldom take cold, and after a time they are able to work all day and every day, while their appetite is good and their sleep profound." Leroy heartily agreed with this assessment.

67. An 1865 map of Clinton County, Iowa, shows that Thomas Hatfield owned two properties about three miles southeast of De Witt, adjacent to the Bennett homestead. The Hatfield School was where Martha was teaching when she first became acquainted with Leroy.

68. A possible source of Leroy's notion is Genesis 29 in which Jacob promises to work for seven years for his Uncle Laban in order to win Laban's younger daughter, Rachel, in marriage. Patty Rettig, Colorado State University Water Resources archivist, provided this information.

69. Reverend Harry H. Green of Decorah, Iowa, married to Martha's oldest sister, Mary.

70. "Rosa Robbins or Life in the Southwest" was a serialized novel that first appeared in the Greeley *Tribune* on August 16, 1871. The *Tribune* hoped to run thirty to

forty segments. The story involved "[a]n intelligent family [that] moves from New England to the South-west, where they are surrounded by ignorant and prejudiced people." Greeley *Tribune*, July 19, 1871.

71. This must be Leroy's answer to one of Martha's questions about an accident. Her letter with the inquiry seems to have been lost.

72. The almost finished house to which Leroy refers is the one he and Martha occupied after they married. Completed in October 1871, it was first inhabited by the entire Daniel Carpenter family. It was conveniently located north of the Cache la Poudre River, a mile and a quarter from the soon-to-be-completed Methodist Church, and high enough above the river's mists and dampness to afford drier and, to Leroy's thinking, healthier living. Visitors to Greeley may view this five-room Union Colony house in Centennial Village at Island Grove Park.

73. This is the school in Low Moor, Iowa, where Martha taught during the fall of 1871 and the spring of 1872.

74. Flattery was frequently discussed in nineteenth-century courtship correspondence. In an 1856 guide to proper courtship, women were advised to "extend no encouraging smile or word" in response to a flatterer. "You may with propriety accept such delicate attentions as polished and refined men are desirous of paying, but never solicit them, or appear to be expecting them" (*The Lady's Guide*, no pagination). Flattery connoted manipulative behavior. An 1871 Clinton, Iowa, newspaper reporter was so upset with the general behavior of males in his community that he wrote, "We have nothing but pity for the young woman who is tied for life to a bi-pedal porcupine, or yoked to a social hippogriff." *The Clinton Daily Herald*, January 13, 1871. In the writer's view, flattery was evil because it masked the barbarian behavior of many men involved in the courting process. Given the nineteenth-century meaning of flattery, it is understandable that both Leroy and Martha declared their aversion to flattery in their writing.

75. Leroy's comment about Catholics and Secessionists makes sense in view of his upbringing. His family members were Methodist Republicans and his brothers fought for the Union. As Sarah Barringer Gordon notes in *The Mormon Question*, for those who supported abolition, polygamy and slavery were viewed as "twin relics of barbarism." Mormon exceptionalism, which included a rejection of the common law, was seen as an attack on civilization and Christianity. Additionally, polygamy confronted the Biblical injunction of "marital unity and the related common-law concept of coverture, which defined married women's legal status" (see pp. 56–57, 60, 74, 80). What Leroy may have felt, as did others, was that tolerance of the Mormons was akin to embracing atheism, and this was a message he would not have wanted to communicate to Martha. Finally, as Nancy Cott notes in *Public Vows* (pp. 107–11, 117), Mormons were compared to

nonwhites, placing polygamists in the category of "savages, or barbarian peoples who had not moved forward in evolutionary progress as the Christian societies." Whatever his reasoning, Leroy wanted Martha to know that he was a monogamist intent on marriage for life.

76. James Chaplin Beecher was the half-brother of Henry Ward Beecher and son of Lyman Beecher and his second wife, Harriet Porter. At the outbreak of the Civil War, James was a Congregationalist missionary in China. He returned to the United States, serving as an officer in the 141st New York Regiment and later as lieutenant colonel of the 35th U.S. Colored Infantry. In 1871, when he might have considered an offer to preach in Greeley, he transferred from a pastorate in Owego, New York, to a church in Poughkeepsie. His health gradually deteriorated from a mental disorder and he committed suicide in 1886. There is no record of his presence in Greeley. The Greeley *Tribune* of September 27, 1871, states that a half-brother of Henry Ward Beecher, who had preached at the Plymouth Church in Brooklyn, New York, would arrive in Greeley "in a few weeks to preach regularly for the Congregationalists." Janis Dunn, archivist for Greeley's Congregational Church, and Greeley historian Louise Johnson researched this matter and found no evidence in church records of any Beecher coming to Greeley. However, the popularity of Henry Ward Beecher was such that the Greeley *Tribune* regularly published his sermons, and Leroy and Martha would have been exposed frequently to his religious and moral philosophy. Additionally, the Beecher family's preaching reputation resulted in many cities offering them employment. In 1870, one of Greeley's founders, General Robert Cameron, had recommended hiring Thomas Beecher (James's brother) to be the Union Colony's nondenominational minister. Horace Greeley was less sanguine about Thomas's moral and intellectual strengths, but the Greeley settlers soon made the matter moot by opting to build their own denominational churches. Forman, *First Congregational Church*, pp. 1–10, 27–33; Boyd, *A History*, pp. 274ff, 276; Rugoff, *The Beechers*, p. 461; and Stowe, *Saints, Sinners and Beechers*, pp. 388–89. Peggy Ford, research coordinator of the Greeley Museum, helped me sort out this riddle.

77. Meanwhile, 150 students, divided into three sections, were attending classes in the Tabernacle building.

78. Martha's sense of humor surfaced more frequently as she gained confidence. In this instance, she is referring to Leroy's previous comment about haying for the Strauss family. By offering Leroy her assistance, as will be seen in other letters, Martha was indicating her comfort level with her view of marriage as a partnership. Given the amount of work demanded of all members of a farming family, it is logical that Martha would make the offer. But her comments are especially noteworthy in this courtship correspondence, because they clearly indicate her comfort with the concept of separate spheres for men and women, as well as her

understanding that successful farm parents would have to share most duties. Hartog, *Man and Wife*, p. 113; Lystra, *Searching the Heart*, pp. 37–38, 122.

79. These tender sentiments reveal Martha's personal commitment to be a good wife. Placed in a broader context, her words coincide with other middle-class, nineteenth-century courtship letters in which lovers demonstrated anxiety over the contrast between courting and marriage. Courting couples tended to speak to each other of bad marriages and the reasons for their failure, thus revealing their own level of concern about marriage as an institution. In the words of Karen Lystra, bad marriage testimonials were a form of "ritualistic incantation" which "functioned to reassure the anxious and compliment the 'good' relationship" (Lystra, *Searching the Heart*, pp. 197–200). Divorce laws were changing in favor of women in the 1870s, but divorce was still a stigma, and women who succeeded in obtaining divorce were rarely awarded child support or alimony. For general information on this subject, see Phillips, *Putting Asunder*, and Riley, *Divorce*.

80. Rats are naturally sociable animals and don't do very well in isolation. While Leroy's comment sounds like midwestern folklore, there is some truth to his statement. Rats prefer to live in large groups with other rats or with a mix of humans and rats. They are also intelligent with a strong survival instinct and an ability to adapt to new circumstances.

81. Leroy's information came from the October 11, 1871, Greeley *Tribune,* which noted that a fire burned all day Sunday and Monday fed by gale-force winds from the southwest. "Thousands of people homeless, naked and without food, filled the streets. Some jumped into the river, so intense was the heat." According to the Chicago Public Library, the fire, started in a cow barn on Chicago's west side on Sunday, October 8, 1871, burned for more than two days, and resulted in three hundred Chicagoans dead, ninety thousand homeless, and property losses in the range of $200 million.

82. Because of the inchoate status of medicine in the 1870s and the paucity of trained doctors, home remedies were the first defense against disease for rural Americans. We don't know whether or not hops were effective in reducing Leroy's pain, but we do know that folk medicine in rural Colorado included the placing of an onion on every windowsill to keep a family healthy; the use of castor oil as a spring tonic; grated potatoes for burns; tobacco juice for stings; black strap molasses and baking soda ingested as a remedy for croup; onion poultices and mustard plasters used for severe colds and coughs, etc. In spite of advances in medical knowledge in the past 130 years, home remedies continue to be popular all over the world. I distinctly remember the insistent offering of tequila by a Mexican lifeguard who swore it was the antidote to a particularly severe bite from a Portuguese man-of-war. I declined the offer, but there is a long precedent in

medicine of using alcohol for injuries and disease. In the last quarter of the nineteenth century, for example, Massachusetts General Hospital administered alcohol as a stimulant to 25 percent of its male patients right up to the 1880s. Warner, *The Therapeutic Perspective*, pp. 144, 145; Cassedy, *Medicine in America*, p. 97; Miller, *Timnath*, p. 311.

83. Narrow-gauge railroads were three feet wide and constructed of lighter rails than standard gauge rails measuring four feet, eight and one-half inches. Most companies that built tracks into the mountains preferred the narrow gauge, because roadbeds could be narrower and less material had to be removed as the tracks wound around narrow canyons. A rail line into the mountains was of great interest to Greeley citizens, because it offered a connection to the mines as well as the possibility of profitable commerce with the miners. As N. C. Meeker noted in his newspaper, the Greeley *Tribune* (May 24, 1871), in addition to the farm produce that would have a nearby market, Greeley citizens could expect to benefit from a booming tourist industry if a railroad were to be built into the mountains. In this, he was most certainly thinking clearly.

84. Low Moor, Iowa, is located about ten miles east of Martha's De Witt home. This was her third teaching assignment (Hatfield, Brushville, Low Moor).

85. The composition of this patent, or proprietary, medicine is unknown. In other letters, Leroy refers to nostrums of the day that claimed to get rid of rats and to cure a bad cough. What is known is that the promotion and sale of patent medicines experienced an exponential increase as a result of the Civil War, and Leroy had his favorites. Crafty merchants and advertising executives knew that the American people craved cures for the many physical, mental, and emotional diseases caused by the war. Some charlatans boasted they could promote and sell the curative powers of dishwater; others claimed they could ensure patient endorsement of any patent medicine, because almost all consisted of one part hope, one part alcohol, and one part opium. As newspapers expanded, they accepted advertisements from just about any proprietor of medicine who would help pay the bills, and some newspapers prepared entire sheets of advertising in advance just to fill space. Such advertising furthered the desire of everyone to be his, or her, own doctor. Young, *Toadstool Millionaires*, chapter 7; William H. Helfand, "Advertising Health to the People," in www.librarycompany.org/doctor/helfand.html.

86. Harry Green, married to Martha's sister Mary.

87. In spite of the "boosterism" of Meeker's Greeley *Tribune*, some colonists experienced disappointment when they arrived in Greeley. David Boyd mentions that ninety people who signed on as colonists wanted their money refunded after they arrived. Some were unhappy with the confusion over who was in charge, the Executive Committee of the Union Colony or the Board of Trustees. Others

felt deceived by the growth figures Meeker had cited, the soil they would have to farm, availability of water, grasshoppers, and a host of other complaints. Nevertheless, the colony leadership adapted and the vast majority of settlers stayed. Boyd, *A History*, pp. 52–53, 55, 58–59. Peggy Ford, research coordinator for the Greeley Museum, provided assistance.

88. Leroy could have been referring to one of the (William H.) McGuffey Readers. These books, published between 1836 and 1857, were a series of six, each one progressively more difficult. *The Eclectic First Reader for Young Children with Pictures* (Cincinnati: Truman and Smith, 1836) was the first. They served as the basis for teaching literacy and basic values. Tens of millions of copies were sold in the nineteenth century, serving as the standard schoolbooks in thirty-seven states after the Civil War where they rode the wave of immigration into the West. Havighurst, *The Miami Years*, chapter 5.

89. Leroy was referring to a publication authored by Harriet and her sister Catherine E. Beecher. It was a revision of Catherine's 1841 work entitled *Treatise on Domestic Economy*. The new publication, which appeared in 1869, was called *The American Woman's Home; or, Principles of Domestic Science: Being a Guide to the Formation and Maintenance of Economical, Healthful, Beautiful, and Christian Homes* (New York: J. B. Ford, and Boston: H. A. Brown, 1869). Catherine Beecher believed that women's place was in the home, but that they should also enter the teaching profession "so that they could influence ever larger numbers of children." See Evans, *Born for Liberty*, pp. 81–82, 105. Leroy equivocates somewhat regarding the Beechers, because he probably knew of their opposition to participation by women in the suffrage movement, and he would not inquire of Martha how she felt about this subject for several months.

90. Mt. Vernon College, founded by Methodists in 1853, became Cornell College, Mount Vernon, Iowa. Mattie's interest in this institution might have been related to the fact that Mt. Vernon was the first college west of the Mississippi River to offer men and women equal rights and privileges, and it was the first college in Iowa to confer a baccalaureate on a woman in 1858.

91. Leroy may have meant to write the word "property."

92. By the 1870s, cattle were being driven north from Texas to railheads in Kansas, Nebraska, Colorado, Wyoming, and Montana. Herds had multiplied exponentially during the Civil War when eastern markets were cut off by the conflict. Because buffalo and grama grasses on the public domain were free to owners of these large herds, and the railroads were pushing west to connect beef herds with feeders in Chicago, the open range livestock industry enjoyed a decade of prosperity. Frequently, however, the needs and interests of agricultural communities clashed with the open range mentality of cattlemen on the Plains. Disputes over fencing, cropped lands, and irrigation ditches often

resulted in damage to farms. The fifty-mile fence built by the Union Colony around its settlement infuriated outsiders, but one of the oldest western customs requires property owners to fence out the intruding livestock. Boyd, *A History*, p. 64; Shwayder, *Weld County Old and New*, p. 37A; Greeley *Tribune*, May 4, 1871.

93. Leroy likes to speak in terms that relate to farming cycles. In this metaphorical language, being "ready for market" means being fit, healthy, and available to an interested suitor.

94. In her 1870–1871 letters from Greeley, Lucy Billings wrote, "We are obliged to burn coal and I don't like it. Wood is very scarce and can be used for kindling only." Williams, *A Pioneer Woman's Life*, p. 3. Coal was dirty, but it was more available than wood.

95. Lyceums, or "Literaries" as they were sometimes called, were places where essays, readings, recitations, and debates were featured. They were attended by men and women, the programs generally reported in the Greeley *Tribune*. In addition to being a principal center for social activity, lyceums represented an aspect of frontier democracy. Everyone was encouraged to participate in discussions. Some topics selected dealt with the pressing issues of the day, such as women's suffrage, temperance, or the suffering of Negroes and Indians. But other subjects were designed to involve everyone: "The Greatness of Little Things," "The Meaning of Glory," or "Is the Dishrag More Beneficial than the Broom?" The only criticism of the lyceums came from some church groups who feared the lyceums were planting doubts about religious principles. Miller, *Timnath*, p. 320; Boyd, *A History*, pp. 263–64.

96. The decade of the 1870s proved calamitous for herds of bison and antelope on the Great Plains. Estimated to comprise thirty million animals at one time, the bison were almost hunted to extinction as the railroads provided easy access to their grazing areas. With the invention of the Sharps rifle, accurate and lethal at six hundred yards, and a general desire to remove wild game as a way of forcing Plains Indians onto reservations, the slaughter of animals by Americans, foreigners, and some Native Americans continued into the 1880s.

97. This might seem to be a covert proposal from Mr. Curtis, but it was not unusual, as seen in the example of Agnes Murray, for a family to take on a child whose mother had died before her daughter was prepared to become an adult.

98. Another letter may be missing here. If this was, in fact, Leroy's suggestion, Martha's reply is most diplomatic.

99. This may be a reference to the trip taken by Delphus Howard to Illinois mentioned in Leroy's December 4, 1871, letter to Martha, but it also may be Martha's response to a question in the missing letter.

100. Paddie, or Paddy, is a corruption of Patrick. As with other ethnic slurs (Nigger, Kraut, Mick, etc.), it carried a pejorative meaning that reflected prejudice. Martha's use of this slang is not meant to be cruel, but it does reflect the general feeling of middle-class Protestant Americans in the 1870s who viewed the Irish as pugnacious, impoverished Roman Catholics whose migration to the United States before the Civil War was polluting the essence of true Americans. Nativism in American history has a deep taproot.

101. Undoubtedly, Leroy had kissing on his mind. He was a healthy, betrothed, twenty-eight-year-old male. But for Victorian-era Americans, kissing had a defined role in courtship. Just as romantic love was seen as a quid pro quo for a serious relationship, kissing was viewed as the holy expression of this love. Some etiquette gurus advised women not to allow a kiss until the couple had agreed to marry. Others urged women to avoid kissing until after the knot was tied. In Martha's case, prayers and kisses were most likely a form of worship that would make sacred her union with Leroy. Lystra, *Searching the Heart*, pp. 63, 76, 249; Kortum, "The Well Mannered Courtship," p. 112.

102. It is worth noting two points here. First, physicians who believed that disease should be stimulated and not depleted (as in leeching or purging) had settled on whiskey, wine, and brandy as the medication of choice. "In the 1850s and 1860s, it was not unusual for a patient with pneumonia or typhoid fever to be given between 8 and 12 ounces of spirits a day and for this treatment to be continued for several days" (Warner, *The Therapeutic Perspective*, pp. 98–99, 145). Secondly, although Union Colony Resolutions called for the prohibition of the sale or manufacture of intoxicating liquor, there was no specific plan to effect that prohibition. Eventually, municipal regulations forbade commerce in alcohol, but the vague wording allowed for violation of the spirit of the laws (Boyd, *A History*, pp. 48–49, 234, 243). It is not surprising, therefore, that the temperance-minded settlers of the Union Colony were conflicted over the sale and distribution of intoxicating liquor.

103. The universal doctrine, or universalism, was a form of moral absolutism in which it was argued that all people would eventually be saved and go to Heaven, even though God might punish his sons and daughters temporarily for their transgressions. In the extreme, proponents of universalism rejected the concept of Hell. They also eschewed public and family prayer in favor of "moments of privacy and meditation," and they opposed revivalism and evangelical reform societies. See Ryan, *Cradle of the Middle Class*, pp. 110–12, 123, 142. In rejecting universalism, Leroy indicated his belief that those who transgressed in this life would be condemned to eternal punishment.

104. Martha may have been a Democrat, although as a woman, she couldn't vote. The Methodist Church in Iowa supported temperance, the Republican Party

in that state advocated prohibition, and Martha was outspokenly opposed to the use of alcohol in any form. Nationally, the Republican Party was also identified with abolition, enfranchisement of Negroes, and women's suffrage, issues with which Martha seems to have had at least a passing interest. That said, however, leaders of the women's rights movement became frustrated by the Republican Party's reluctance to endorse suffrage for both Negroes and women at the same time. It is possible, therefore, that this issue turned Martha away from the Republican Party. Elizabeth Cady Stanton frequently lashed out at the Republican Party for failing to support equal rights for women. In Colorado, much to Martha's approval, the Democrats favored women's suffrage while the Republicans opposed it. Martha's broad interest in equal rights for women, as stated in these courtship letters, might have turned her against the dominant Republican Party of Iowa, but we can only surmise. Noun, *Strong-Minded Women*, pp. 37, 44; Ward, *Not for Ourselves Alone*, p. 112; Stanton, Anthony, and Gage, *History of Woman Suffrage*, p. 714.

105. Citing the text of Matthew 10:5–8 provides a better understanding of Martha's strong commitment to doing good works and her wish to proselytize for the church. "These twelve Jesus sent out, charging them, 'Go nowhere among the Gentiles, and enter no town of the Samaritans, but go rather to the lost sheep of the house of Israel. And preach as you go, saying, heal the sick, raise the dead, cleanse lepers, cast out demons. You received without paying, give without pay'" (Holy Bible, Revised Standard Version).

106. Oysters were taken west in tin canisters as early as the 1830s, along with lobster, mackerel, and some meats and vegetables. By the 1870s, Gail Borden had been granted a patent on canned condensed milk, and users of canned foods were using key openers to get at a large variety of canned foods.

107. The acclimatizing, to which Leroy refers, required getting used to the altitude (4,600 feet). It also meant adjustment to dry winds, unpredictable temperatures and precipitation, the hard clay soil, irrigation, and shortage of wood. Leroy wrote on April 15, 1871, that there were 1,200 settlers in Greeley when the Carpenters arrived. According to the 1870 Census, Weld County had a population of 1,636. Ten years later the census showed a 41 percent increase. These figures would suggest that the few disgruntled members who asked for a refund were replaced by a wave of pioneers who recognized the potential for success on the Cache la Poudre River. Peggy Ford, research coordinator for the Greeley Museum, provided assistance in gathering this information.

108. Leroy and others in Greeley looked to the cutting of timber in the mountains as a way to make money before spring planting and crop cultivation required their attention. With talk of a narrow-gauge railroad coming through Greeley, there was hope that a contract could be let for ties. But additionally, as noted in the

Greeley *Tribune* (January 3, 1872), the town of Greeley needed timber for many purposes. It was suggested that men go into the mountains with a special hammer that had the owner's individual mark, so when the logs were delivered by the spring flood, each person would be able to claim what was his. The *Tribune* estimated that ten-foot logs could be delivered down the Cache La Poudre River for less than one dollar a cord.

109. In 1798 Dr. Edward Jenner privately published a paper in which he concluded that people vaccinated (a word derived from the Latin *vaccinia*, meaning cowpox virus) with the cow pox would be immune to the dreaded smallpox virus. By 1801, more than one hundred thousand people had been vaccinated in Great Britain. The following year the British Parliament voted Jenner a ten-thousand-pound reward. Although the technique was evolving, vaccination didn't always work. The cowpox virus was (and is) fairly fragile. It frequently died before it could be given to patients. Nevertheless, in the 1870s the American medical profession was comfortable with vaccination as a preventative procedure. As Leroy's example indicates, however, the techniques of inoculation were evolving. For a delightful read, and a fascinating study of early struggles in Great Britain and America to accept inoculation against smallpox before Jenner's work, see Jennifer Lee Carrell, *The Speckled Monster: A Historical Tale of Battling Smallpox* (London: A Plume Book, 2004).

110. Perhaps this was a dangerous question for Leroy to ask, but it reveals his confidence in the relationship and a genuine interest in knowing how his future bride would respond to social reform movements of the 1870s. The principal women's rights issue on which he might have expected Martha's response was suffrage and the concept of citizenship for women. Placing his question in historical context, it should be noted that the Territory of Wyoming had enfranchised women in 1869, and the Territory of Utah followed suit in 1870. The National Woman Suffrage Association of Elizabeth Cady Stanton and Susan B. Anthony and the American Woman Suffrage Association of Lucy Stone were both organized in 1869, the former attempting to achieve the right to vote for women through an amendment to the United States Constitution, the latter working for the same goal through the state legislatures. The fourteenth and fifteenth amendments to the Constitution, guaranteeing voting rights for all persons born in the United States, had been ratified respectively in 1868 and 1870. Martha and Leroy knew that times were changing, but both seem to have felt nervous about pushing too hard against the limits of tradition. See Lamphier, *Kate Chase*, p. 8; Bredbenner, *A Nationality of Her Own*, p. 19; Cott, *Public Vows*, p. 67; Lystra, *Searching the Heart*, pp. 140, 147, 250; Hawes and Nybakken, *Family and Society*, pp. 146, 150, 157–58; Hartog, *Man and Wife*, p. 110.

111. Considering the distance between Greeley and Low Moor, the possibility of severe winter weather on the Plains, and the limitations of rural post offices, the arrival of letters in three to eight days is understandable. What is noteworthy is the anxiety level that developed in both Leroy and Martha if delays occurred. In today's courtship by correspondence, especially e-mail, many of the same questions are asked, but they can be addressed and answered electronically or by telephone in an instant. Martha and Leroy had to endure inconsistent mail service at a time when serious accidents and disease took lives unexpectedly.

112. This remark is in reference to Leroy's comment in his January 9, 1872, letter in which he mentioned that N. C. Meeker's son had stood up in a meeting to identify the man who was selling liquor in Greeley. Martha had strong views on temperance.

113. Leroy and Martha were both musical. Daniel Carpenter trained Leroy as a public speaker, and Leroy, who tended to be shy in public, used his resonant voice to sing bass in the Methodist Church choir. In addition to her interest in playing the melodeon, Martha sang alto. Her third son, Fred George Carpenter, remembered that her voice was clear until her last days. "Of the family of Martha," he wrote, "her sisters Mary Green, Lucy Milligan, and Sylvania Kough were all very musical. Their father sang a perfect tenor at the morning worship, singing the old Christian songs, as the five sisters and the brother, William, joined in the singing. Especially attractive and harmonizing was the group singing of the family of Reverend Harry Green and wife Mary, with their two daughters and three sons, one of whom was Marion, the noted baritone, who was honored especially when called to England to fill a difficult role, and he was the first American singer to be so honored" (typescript by Fred George Carpenter, dated August 27, 1960, located in the Carpenter Papers, Water Resources Archive, Colorado State University).

114. How very wise of Martha to urge her husband-to-be to share with her his most private and personal feelings! Not only is this request consistent with exchanges between other courting individuals in this age of romantic love, but it is Martha's way of encouraging both of them to work at bridging the gender gap between male and female natures and roles.

115. A rod is 5.5 yards.

116. Reflecting on the winter of 1871–1872, Leroy's brother Silas recalled that it was the only time snow conditions made possible one hundred days of sleighing. The first storms arrived in the middle of November and three feet of snow stayed on level ground until a thaw commenced the middle of February. Range cattle not owned by Greeley settlers had to be driven outside the colony fence because of the shortage of feed, and fuel for heating and cooking was expensive and hard to come by. "How glad we were to see a break," Silas wrote. The Carpenters picked

the worst Colorado winter in memory to begin life in the Union Colony. See Leroy Carpenter diaries, 1922–1928, Carpenter Papers, Water Resources Archive, Colorado State University.

117. Leroy was probably helping to shovel out the Denver Pacific Railroad track between Cheyenne and Greeley. But quite a few westbound Union Pacific trains had also been stopped by heavy snows in January 1871, prompting the Greeley *Tribune* to scold the railroad for having chosen a transcontinental route that departed the Platte River at Julesburg, Colorado, in order to follow a more direct route up steep grades to Cheyenne. With hyperbole reflecting the finest western boosterism, editor Meeker wrote, "[I]nasmuch as this is the only line from ocean to ocean, and as no other one is likely to be built for several years, it would seem that the commercial interests, not only of America, but of Asia, can not well be subject to the losses and great expense connected with the present route." He lamented the fact that Union Pacific leaders disregarded the original survey up the Platte River in favor of a route that required trains to summit Sherman Hill in Wyoming at 8,242 feet. Leroy would have agreed, although he was probably only interested in getting Martha's letters in a timely manner.

118. Leroy was trying to say that he was not someone who took pleasure in making fun of someone else's foibles. This is a character trait he passed on to his son Delphus, who learned early on that sensitive negotiations to achieve compromise in interstate water compacts would require utmost respect for every view, regardless how extreme, troublesome, or irritating.

119. In his 1865 diary, Leroy noted that he had visited "Susie dear," and that on one occasion, he "fell sick on account of sitting all night with my beloved Susie and catching severe cold." When Leroy remarked in a February 15, 1872, letter to Martha that Susan C. never interested him, he was conforming to timeless courtship rules by assuring Martha that she was the only one to win his heart. See Leroy diaries, Carpenter Papers, Water Resources Archive, Colorado State University.

120. Grand Duke Alexis, the third son of Russian Emperor Alexander II, toured the United States in 1871–1872. After brief stops in New York, Washington, Boston, Philadelphia, Chicago, Milwaukee, and St. Louis, he came to Denver by way of Cheyenne, passing through Greeley on the Denver Pacific Railroad. After being feted in Denver, the twenty-two-year-old duke headed east on the Kansas Pacific Railroad accompanied by General George Armstrong Custer, General Philip H. Sheridan, and Buffalo Bill Cody. Somewhere near Kit Carson, Colorado, the grand duke experienced the high point of his trip, killing a cow buffalo with his pistol. In his excitement, he hugged and kissed General Custer and shortly thereafter telegraphed his father that he had killed the first wild horned monster that had met his eye in America. Davis, *The First Five Years*, pp. 172–73;

"Buffalo Hunt in Nebraska by the Grand Duke Alexis of Russia in 1872," *Your Guide Book to the Pacific Railroad, 1879,* http://www.americahurrah.com/PRR/ GrandDukeAlexis.htm.

121. Leroy's letter is positioned chronologically in this volume toward the end of January with a date of "January 2nd [24th], 1871," so as to accurately reflect when he actually wrote that particular letter to Martha. Based on information contained therein, this positioning is accurate.

122. When I first encountered the courtship letters in the Carpenter Papers, they were stuffed into a small wooden box. I do not know if this is the same box to which Martha refers, but hiding letters in boxes for posterity was not uncommon in the Victorian era, possibly because the authors wanted to preserve for later viewing what each revealed so personally about their private feelings during courtship. Lystra, *Searching the Heart,* p. 27.

123. Martha's comments show that she was quite aware of the women's rights movement as it developed in Iowa in the late 1860s and early 1870s. The first Iowa Suffrage Association convention was held in Mt. Pleasant, 85 miles south of Martha's De Witt home, in the spring of 1870. Suffrage speakers came to Iowa, urging women to support an amendment to the Constitution, but the women's suffrage movement became tainted by criticism that some of its proponents were loose women, free love advocates, supporters of abortion, divorce, sexual promiscuity, and abandonment of the Bible as a guide to life. When the Iowa Woman Suffrage Association met in the fall of 1871, these accusations were the dominant theme of the meeting. Martha's reference to female "modesty," and her opinion that the right to vote might not change much, except in the liquor question, shows that she was also rooted in traditional values. Having worked away from home for two years, however, she was eager to see women achieve equal pay for equal work. When Iowa revised its Code in 1873, women's rights in marriage were substantially improved. Noun, *Strong-Minded Women,* pp. 116, 121, 135, 158, 160, 182, 186, 189, 222.

124. *Watchword* was most probably a temperance publication of the Good Templars, but it might also have been an Edinburgh, Scotland, publication subtitled, "A Magazine for the Defense of Bible Truth and the Advocacy of Free Church Principle," published between 1866 and 1873. *Country Gentleman* was an agricultural journal. In 1920 it published an article recognizing Leroy's son Delphus, which aimed at educating readers about the importance of water in the West (*Country Gentleman* 85, no. 41 [October 9, 1920]: 6, 7, 26). The *Clinton Bee* circulated between 1871 and 1873 when it became the *Clinton Weekly Herald.*

125. One wonders if Leroy wrote this to tease Martha. He surely expected a reaction.

126. This may not be what Martha wanted to hear, but when combined with Leroy's mature thoughts about the gravity of entering into marriage, she probably appreciated his sincerity and wisdom. Additionally, readers will appreciate the fact that Leroy fully recognized the adversities facing both of them on the Colorado frontier. Hard work would challenge them constantly as they struggled to make a living and raise a family. To this extent, his comment was realistic, if not altogether romantic.

127. Hardly! This is exactly what Martha needed to hear. Leroy is, in effect, sealing the deal with these remarks. And, quite incredibly, he is articulating the frustration inherent in Victorian courtship. On the one hand, revelation of the self through expressions of romantic love was essential if two people were going to form a relationship leading to marriage. At the same time, both needed to understand that the individualism encouraged by such personal exposure would encounter potential conflict in the marriage institution because of the ongoing cultural expectation of separate spheres for each gender. Leroy knew that the bloom would come off the rose fairly soon if he and Martha failed to face the reality of what marriage would mean for both of them. His perceptive comments in this letter suggest he realized that while marriage for him would have little impact on his status as a male, for Martha it presented a dramatic break in what she had known, because what defined marriage for her was, in fact, "the transformation of the single woman into wife." See Hartog, *Man and Wife*, pp. 101–2; see also Lystra, *Searching the Heart*, Introduction, pp. 31, 192, 197, 226.

128. James Cook Higley opened a coal mine ten miles north of Greeley. Because of the three railroads in the vicinity, coal was always in short supply for home heating and cooking. Most of what came into Greeley households originated in outlying communities. The Greeley *Tribune* urged its readers to support Higley, because the purchase of his coal at $6.50 per ton would cause the money spent to recirculate and the local economy to improve. See *Tribune* articles dated November 8 and December 6, 1871.

129. Davenport and St. Paul Railroad. Construction that began in July 1870 resulted in Davenport being connected to the Chicago North Western Railroad at De Witt in October. The De Witt *Observer*, July 15 and October 14, 1870.

130. This thoughtful and passionate response to Leroy's remarks about the nature of love and marriage is as profound a revelation of Martha's feelings as anything she writes in these letters. While Victorian Americans were gradually shifting their views from a God-centered to a person-centered world, Martha remained firmly committed to traditional views of the Protestant ethic in which Heaven and Hell played dominant roles. With the secularization of life after the Civil War, marital conflict sometimes resulted from clashes between love of God and love of another person. What is remarkable about this aspect of the

correspondence between Leroy and Martha is their ability to reach harmonious agreement on an issue that could have torn their marriage apart had their perspectives not been defined, thought out, and articulated. Lystra, *Searching the Heart*, pp. 25, 132–36, 237, 250.

131. It is likely that Leroy and Martha's second son, Delphus Emory Carpenter, was named after Leroy's friend, the late Delphus Howard. Their first son was probably named after another Iowa friend, Alfred Reeder.

132. Leroy refers to an article in the February 21, 1871, Greeley *Tribune* that stated: "Mr. [Daniel] Carpenter will build a nice house in the spring on his farm immediately north of town and about two miles distant. The situation is sightly. He will plant forest trees and fruit of all kinds and make a nice home. His son will live in the house he now occupies which is nearby."

133. Martha is probably referring to meningococcal meningitis (also known as cerebrospinal fever, spotted fever, and cerebrospinal meningitis). In a letter to the author, Jennifer Carrell (*The Speckled Monster*) noted that Londoners used to refer to typhus and typhoid fever as spotted fever. Meningitis was caused by many different viruses and bacteria, or by diseases that caused inflammation of tissues of the body without infection. A red rash, or brownish pinprick spots, caused by blood under the skin could develop into purple-colored bruises and blood blisters. High fever, persistent headache, stiff neck, sensitivity to light, and nausea accompanied this disease. See "Old Medical Terms and Diseases" at www.linkquestusa.com/disease.htm and www.patienthealthinternational.com/article/501636.aspx.

134. H. T. West was one of five trustees of the town of Greeley in 1872. He later founded and became president of the Union Colony Pioneer Society, an organization of which Martha Bennett Carpenter was president in 1912, the year of West's death. West's arguments with Meeker over the liquor question resulted from two problems: (1) West was a druggist, and as such was suspected of providing alcohol-based drugs to clients; and (2) Meeker was very rigid and suspicious in his outlook on temperance, and he frequently accused West of "slackness and favoritism" in administering the Union Colony's ordinances on the subject. H. T. West, family file (1824–1921), Greeley Museum. This information provided to me by Peggy Ford, research coordinator for the Greeley Museum.

135. William Barney Carpenter, son of Daniel Carpenter and Sally Northway, Leroy's stepbrother. William operated a large tannery in Ohio near where he was born.

136. The most important part of Martha's trousseau was her wedding dress. She sent a sample of this dark colored material with a white trim to Leroy, but unfortunately the swatch has been lost. Very few brides wore white in the 1870s. One can only guess at the items she prepared for her hope chest, but generally speaking, a bride

would provide linens, a sewing basket, weaving supplies, seeds, recipes, bedding, dresser scarves, doilies, flannel towels, braided rugs, a wash basin, mirror, chamber pot, kitchen items, baskets, oil lamps, dried medicinal herbs, and a Bible. Traditionally, the bride's mother, family, and friends helped sew the linens and quilts. The bride was instructed in needlework, housework, and cooking. Because Martha would travel to Colorado soon after marriage, space was a consideration in what she chose to assemble. Wilson, *The Hope Chest*, pp. 36–42; Truer, "Hope Chests and Honeymoons," pp. 12–24.

137. The Kansas Pacific Railroad would have taken Leroy across eastern Colorado and Kansas to the Missouri River at Kansas City. From there he would have had to take another line to St. Louis and then travel by boat up the Mississippi River to Clinton, Iowa. As he surmised, this trip would have taken longer than the one he eventually chose on the Union Pacific to Omaha, connecting with the Chicago and North Western Railroad to Tipton and De Witt, Iowa.

138. Donald Alonzo Carpenter, Leroy's stepbrother, was married to Mary Aldrich of Jones County, Iowa. They had one child, Jeanette Carpenter, who became a teacher of Latin, German, and English at what was then called the Teacher's College, Cedar Falls, Iowa. Donald served in the Mexican War and again in the Civil War. He was engaged in the battle of Pea Ridge and at the first assault on Vicksburg. He died of consumption while on furlough in 1864, a major in the Ninth Iowa Infantry. See Amos B. Carpenter, *In Re Daniel Carpenter, Genealogical History of the Rehobeth Branch of the Carpenter Family in America*, No. 950, 1898 edition, p. 575.

139. Erysipelas is an acute infection of the skin and underlying fat tissues, usually caused by the streptococcus bacteria. It is most common in old people, children, and those with immune system deficiencies. It was especially dangerous to pregnant women. See Hampsten, *Read This Only to Yourself*, p. 101, and www.netdoctor.co.uk/disease/facts/erysipelas.htm.

140. See note 133.

141. Martha's insight into the quintessential nature of a good relationship, and her ability to communicate her essence to Leroy, are noteworthy.

142. Since Iowa Territory was formed in 1838, several legislatures had succeeded in passing laws modifying the common-law rules that had left a wife civilly dead when she entered marriage. In contrast to the rules of coverture that required a wife to give all her service and labor to her husband, and prevented her from entering into lawsuits or contracts, or owning assets without her husband's collaboration, post–Civil War Iowa recognized a woman's right to own property, engage in trade, and keep the profits arising from her endeavors. The law provided, however, that the wife had to obtain her husband's consent in writing.

The Iowa Code of 1873, which represented laws passed in earlier years, finally recognized a woman's right to own and manage her own property without the husband's interference. Some argued that the legislature's enlightenment on this subject was necessary to appease women who were disappointed by the state's failure to approve their right to vote. But taken in context, the liberalization of women's property rights in Iowa was part of a national trend that had begun to develop during Reconstruction. See Bredbenner, *A Nationality of Her Own*, p. 19; Cott, *Public Vows*, pp. 11, 12; Hartog, *Man and Wife*, pp. 99–101; Noun, *Strong-Minded Women*, pp. 54–58; Wilson, *Legal Status of Women*, pp. 82–83; *Code of Iowa, 1873*, chapter 2.

143. Lyons, Iowa, a suburb of Clinton, on the Mississippi River, about seventeen miles east of De Witt.

144. Although it may appear to present-day readers that Leroy was trying to compare Martha to a prize heifer, he just wanted her to know that he was most relieved that she had been well cared for and that she was healthy.

## Postscript

1. Oakdale Cemetery, Davenport, Iowa, microfilm of Sexton Records, No. 1503405, notes burial location number 1723 as that of William H. Bennett, age sixty-one, who died September 22, 1877. The *Davenport Democrat* of that same date states that W. H. Bennett died at his residence on the northwest corner of 17th and Rock Island streets. In plots next to him were later buried his wife, Mary Ann Wood Bennett (who died in Greeley in 1889 and was transported back to Davenport for interment), daughter Lucy Milligan, and her husband, William Milligan.

2. Except for William Wood Bennett, who lived in Montana, all of Martha's siblings were married and living in Iowa. See note 27 in the letters.

3. Leroy's diary entry for July 7, 1880, states: "I also worked at cleaning the kitchen stove (oven). Jaques [hired hand] and I put it in condition tonight." His entry for July 8 states: "I went after Martha and the boys, they . . . having just returned from their visit to Iowa." Laconically, he added, "All well." Two weeks later, July 26, Leroy's diary contains an entry stating that he and Martha had just whitewashed the kitchen and bedroom. See Leroy Carpenter diaries, Carpenter Papers, Water Resources Archives, Colorado State University.

4. A loose page found in the back of Leroy's diaries, probably composed toward the end of his life, states the following: "The bonds of true friendship are welded in one unbroken chain. Time may go by, changes of life may come over us, but those united links of truth and honesty will still retain their original firmness

of the once unbroken seal of kind words. Men may pass away, but kind words can never die. Cherished in the friends, they will be handed down to others in grateful remembrance of those kind words once *spoken*, and growing in strength in the course of time, they will still live in hearts of their posterity." See Leroy Carpenter, diaries, 1922–1928, Carpenter Papers, Water Resources Archive, Colorado State University.

# Bibliography

Adler, Robert E. *Medical Firsts: From Hippocrates to the Human Genome.* Hoboken, N.J.: Wiley and Sons, 2004.

Allen, George W. "The 1871 Historical Sketch of Clinton, County, Iowa. Embracing a Full Description of Its Thriving Cities and Towns. Past History, Present Conditions and Future Prospects." Originally published as an insert in the *Clinton Daily Herald.*

Allen, Lucius P. *History of Clinton County.* Chicago: Western History Company, 1879.

Anderson, Lee. *Iowa Pharmacy, 1880–1905: An Experiment in Professionalism.* Iowa City: University of Iowa Press, 1989.

Boyd, David. *A History: Greeley and the Union Colony of Colorado.* Greeley: The Greeley *Tribune* Press, 1890.

Bredbenner, Candice Lewis. *A Nationality of Her Own: Women, Marriage, and the Law of Citizenship.* Berkeley: University of California Press, 1998.

Bynum, W. F. *Science and the Practice of Medicine in the Nineteenth Century.* Cambridge: Cambridge University Press, 1994.

Carpenter, Harold George, comp. *Some of Our Carpenter Family History.* Alamosa, Colo.: Ye Olde Print Shop, 1960.

Cassedy, James H. *Medicine in America: A Short History.* Baltimore: Johns Hopkins University Press, 1991.

Clark, Dan Elbert. "The History of Liquor Legislation in Iowa, 1861–1878." *Iowa Journal of History and Politics* 6, no. 3 (July 1908): 1–14.

Clark, George B. *Our Masonic Heritage: A Glimpse of the Historical Background of Freemasonry.* Denver: Great Western Publishing Company, 1936.

Clinton County Historical Society. *History of Clinton County, Iowa.* Clinton, Iowa: Clinton County American Revolution Bicentennial Commission, 1976.

Cott, Nancy C. *Public Vows: A History of Marriage and the Nation*. Cambridge: Harvard University Press, 2000.

Davis, E. O. *The First Five Years of the Railroad Era in Colorado*. Golden, Colo.: Sage Books, 1948.

Dubois, Ellen Carol. *Feminism and Suffrage: The Emergence of an Independent Women's Movement in America, 1848–1869*. Ithaca, N.Y.: Cornell University Press, 1978.

Dunbar, Robert G. "Water Conflicts and Controls in Colorado." *Agricultural History* 22 (July 1948): 180–86.

Ellis, Franklin, ed. *History of Fayette County, Pennsylvania, with Biographical Sketches of Many of Its Pioneers and Prominent Men*. 2 vols. Philadelphia: L. H. Leverts, 1882.

Evans, Sara M. *Born for Liberty: A History of Women in America*. New York: Free Press, 1989.

Forman, Dorothy S., ed. *First Congregational Church: 100 Years of Service, 1870–1970*. Greeley, Colo.: First Congregational Church, 1970.

Fahey, David M. *Temperance and Racism: John Bull, Johnny Reb, and the Good Templars*. Lexington: University of Kentucky Press, 1996.

Fellows, Stephen Norris. *History of the Upper Iowa Conference of the Methodist Episcopal Church, 1856–1906*. Cedar Rapids, Iowa: Laurance Press, 1907.

*First Congregational Church: 100 Years of Service, 1870–1970*. Greeley, Colo.: First Congregational Church, 1970.

Freemasons, Collins Lodge No. 19. *100 Years of Masonry in Fort Collins, 1870–1970*. Fort Collins, Colo.: Robinson-Warfield Company, 1970.

Ginzburg, Lori D. *Women and the Work of Benevolence: Morality, Politics, and Class in the Nineteenth-Century United States*. New Haven: Yale University Press, 1990.

Gordon, Sarah Barringer. *The Mormon Question: Polygamy and Constitutional Conflict in Nineteenth-Century America*. Chapel Hill: University of North Carolina Press, 2002.

Grant, Roger H. M., ed. *Iowa Railroads: The Essays of Frank P. Donovan, Jr*. Iowa City: University of Iowa Press, 2000.

Hampsten, Elizabeth. *Read This Only to Yourself: The Private Writings of Midwestern Women, 1880–1910*. Bloomington: Indiana University Press, 1982.

Hartog, Hendrik. *Man and Wife in America: A History*. Cambridge: Harvard University Press, 2000.

Havighurst, Walter. *The Miami Years, 1809–1894*. New York: G. P. Putnam's Sons, 1984.

Hawes, Joseph M., and Elizabeth I. Nybakken, eds. *Family and Society in American History*. Urbana: University of Illinois Press, 2001.

*History of Clinton County, Iowa, Containing a History of the County, Its Cities, Towns, Etc*. Chicago: Western Historical Company, 1879.

Hodder, Harbour Fraser. "The Future of Marriage: Changing Demographics, Economics, and Laws Alter the Meaning of Matrimony in America." *Harvard Magazine* 107, no. 2 (November–December 2004): 37–46, 97–99.

Holland, Patricia G., and Ann D. Gordon, eds. *The Papers of Elizabeth Cady Stanton and Susan B. Anthony*. Guide and Index to the Microfilm Edition. Wilmington, Del.: Scholarly Resources, Inc., 1991.

Jabour, Anya. *Marriage in the Early Republic: Elizabeth and William Wirt and the Companionate Ideal*. Baltimore: Johns Hopkins University Press, 1998.

Kenslea, Timothy. *The Sedgwicks in Love: Courtship and Marriage in the Early Republic*. Boston: Northeastern University Press, 2006.

Kortum, Sarah. "The Well-Mannered Courtship." *Victoria* 10, no. 2 (February 1996): 112.

Lamphier, Peg A. *Kate Chase and William Sprague: Politics and Gender in a Civil War Marriage*. Lincoln: University of Nebraska Press, 2003.

Lystra, Karen. *Searching the Heart: Women, Men, and Romantic Love in Nineteenth Century America*. New York: Oxford University Press, 1989.

Mattingly, Carol. *Well-Tempered Women: Nineteenth Century Temperance Rhetoric*. Carbondale: Southern Illinois University Press, 1998.

Miller, Del, and Elsie Fisher. *Timnath*. Fort Collins, Colo.: Columbine Club of Timnath, 1996.

Morse-Kahn, Deborah, and Joe Trnka. *Clinton, Iowa: Railroad Town*. Minneapolis: Bolger, Concept to Print, 2003.

Noun, Louise R. *Strong-Minded Women: The Emergence of the Woman-Suffrage Movement in Iowa*. Ames: Iowa State University Press, 1969.

Null, Gary, and Barbara Seaman. *For Women Only: Your Guide to Health Empowerment*. New York: Seven Stories Press, 1999.

Nye, John A. *Between the Rivers: A History of Iowa United Methodism*. Des Moines: Commission on Archives and History, Iowa Annual Conference of the United Methodist Church, 1986.

Pabor, William. *First Annual Report of the Union Colony of Colorado, Including a History of the Town of Greeley from Its Date of Settlement to the Present Time*. New York: George W. Southwick, 1871.

Peirce, Newton. *The History of the Independent Order of Good Templars*. Philadelphia: Daughaday & Becker, n.d.

Phillips, Roderick. *Putting Asunder: A History of Divorce in Western Society*. Cambridge: Cambridge University Press, 1988.

*Portrait and Biographical Album: Clinton County, 1886*. Book 2. Chicago: Chapman Bros., n.d.

Pratt, LeRoy G. *The Counties and Courthouses of Iowa*. Mason City, Iowa: Klipto Printing and Office Supply Co., 1977.

Ridley, Jasper. *The Freemasons: A History of the World's Most Powerful Secret Society*. New York: Arcade Publishing, 1999.

Riley, Glenda. *Divorce: An American Tradition*. New York: Oxford University Press, 1991.

*Ritual of the Independent Order of Good Templars for Subordinate Lodges under the Jurisdiction of the Right Worthy Grand Lodge of North America*. Adopted at Cleveland Session, May 24, 1864. Cleveland: Right Worthy Grand Lodge, 1869.

Rothman, Ellen K. *Hands and Hearts: A History of Courtship in America*. New York: Basic Books, 1984.

Rothstein, William G. *American Physicians in the Nineteenth Century: From Sects to Science*. Baltimore: Johns Hopkins University Press, 1972.

Rugoff, Milton. *The Beechers: An American Family in the Nineteenth Century*. New York: Harper and Row, 1981.

Ryan, Mary P. *Cradle of the Middle Class: The Family in Oneida County, New York, 1790–1865*. Cambridge: Cambridge University Press, 1981.

Shwayder, Carol Rein. *Weld County Old and New*. Greeley, Colo.: Unicorn Ventures, 1992.

Stanton, Elizabeth Cady, Susan B. Anthony, and Matilda Joslyn Gage, eds. *History of Woman Suffrage*. 2nd ed. Vol. 1, 1848–1861. Rochester, N.Y.: Source Book Press, 1889.

Stout, Donald. *A City Called Tipton, 1840–1890*. Tipton, Iowa: C & S Enterprises, 1990.

Stout, Donald Franklin, and Dorothy Jean Miller Stout. *Cedar Land: A History of Living, 1836–1980*. Vol. 1. Burlington, Iowa: Craftsman Press, 1981.

Stephen, Barbara Carpenter. *Dearest Grandchildren: A Grandmother's Account of the Beginnings and Growth of Horace Greeley's Union Colony*. Greeley, Colo.: Barbara Carpenter Stephen, 1987.

Stowe, Lyman Beecher. *Saints, Sinners and Beechers*. Indianapolis: Bobbs-Merrill Company, 1934.

Swierenga, Robert P. "The Iowa Land Records Collection: Periscope to the Past." *Books at Iowa* 13 (November 1970).

Thornwell, Emily. *The Lady's Guide to Perfect Gentility*. Two chapters reproduced in facsimile from the copy in the Huntington Library. New York, 1856; San Marino, Calif.: Huntington Library, 2003.

Truer, Tamara. "Hope Chests and Honeymoons—Marriages in America Still Wedded to Tradition." *Ramsey County History* 27, no. 2 (summer 1992): 12–24.

Ubbelohde, Carl, Maxine Benson, and Duane Smith. *A Colorado History*. 6th edition. Boulder, Colo.: Pruett Publishing Company, 1988.

Vickers, Daniel. *Farmers and Fishermen: Two Centuries of Work in Essex County, Massachusetts, 1630–1850*. Chapel Hill: University of North Carolina Press, 1994.

Ward, Geoffrey C. *Not For Ourselves Alone: The Story of Elizabeth Cady Stanton and Susan B. Anthony*. New York: Alfred A. Knopf, 1999. Based on a documentary film by Ken Burns and Paul Barnes.

Warner, John Harley. *The Therapeutic Perspective: Medical Practice, Knowledge, and Identity in America, 1820–1885*. Cambridge: Harvard University Press, 1986.

Watrous, Ansel. *History of Larimer County*. Fort Collins: Courier Printing Company, 1911; Fort Collins: Old Army Press, 1972.

Wilkins, Tivis E. *Colorado Railroads: Chronological Development*. Boulder, Colo.: Pruett Press, 1974.

Williams, Alice B., ed. *A Pioneer Woman's Life in Greeley, Colorado, 1870–1871*, as told in the letters of Lucy M. Billings. Typescript located at Greeley Museum, Greeley, Colo.

Wilson, Jennie L., comp. *Legal Status of Women in Iowa*. Des Moines: Iowa Printing Company, 1894.

Wilson, Rebecca. *The Hope Chest: A Legacy of Love*. Littlerock, Calif.: Hope Chest Legacy, 2003.

Young, James Harvey. *The Toadstool Millionaires: A Social History of Patent Medicines in America before Federal Regulation*. Princeton, N.J.: Princeton University Press, 1961.

# Index

Page numbers in **bold type** indicate photos.